The Metropolitan Midwest

The
Metropolitan
Midwest

POLICY PROBLEMS AND
PROSPECTS FOR CHANGE

Edited by
Barry Checkoway and Carl V. Patton

UNIVERSITY OF ILLINOIS PRESS

Urbana and Chicago

© 1985 by the Board of Trustees of the University of Illinois.
Manufactured in the United States of America.

This book is printed on acid-free paper.

Library of Congress Cataloging in Publication Data

Main entry under title:

The Metropolitan Midwest.

   Includes bibliographies.
    1. Cities and towns—Middle West—Economic conditions.
2. Cities and towns—Middle West—Social conditions.
3. Urban policy—Middle West.   4. City planning—Middle
West.   5. Urban renewal—Middle West.   6. Metropolitan
areas—Middle West.   I. Checkoway, Barry.   II. Patton,
Carl V.
HT123.5.A14M47   1984   307.7'64'0977   83-18213
ISBN 0-252-01114-7 (alk. paper)

Preface

It is common to view the Midwest as an area of rural farmlands and small towns distant from urban centers where policy and planning decisions are made. Yet the Midwest is a region of major cities and metropolitan areas inextricably related to the decisions and institutions of the nation. Today the metropolitan Midwest is undergoing changes that have important implications for policy and planning in both region and nation. These changes and their consequences are the subject of this book.

This book on the metropolitan Midwest examines the leading policy problems, planning issues, and prospects for change. The focus is on the Midwest, but the aim is to use the Midwest as a basis to address broader problems and prospects and to define issues in terms of their wider significance. The book thus seeks to provide understanding of the factors affecting a particular region at the same time as it sheds light on urban policy problems and prospects elsewhere. It developed out of an interdisciplinary faculty seminar on urban problems at the University of Illinois at Urbana-Champaign. The seminar involved scholars and practitioners from several units on the campus and across the nation, and it served as a major vehicle for authors and others to share ideas, learn from one another, and provide a basis for collaboration.

It is a pleasure to acknowledge some of those at Illinois who contributed to this book. The Center for Advanced Study was a source of assistance throughout the work. Daniel Alpert, director of the center, provided intitial support for faculty members to begin the discussions that gave this project its start. The Office of Interdisciplinary Planning gave an award that helped develop the urban problems seminar and sharpen the Midwest focus. The Graduate College Research Board provided financial assistance to support some of the research reported here.

The Bureau of Urban and Regional Planning Research was a principal sponsor of the project. The bureau, as part of the Department of Urban and Regional Planning, provides a vehicle for faculty and student involvement in research projects, community public service activities, and continuing education programs. It was highly fortunate that Michael Romanos, then director of the bureau, viewed this book as consistent with its mission and provided support needed to complete the project.

Several individuals provided needed and appreciated assistance to help make this book a reality. Erna Olafson Hellerstein provided editorial assistance and support during the final days of manuscript preparation. Among others who deserve special mention are Kathleen Ard, Karen Chinn, Samuel Gove, Barbara Hartman, Lynn Hethke, Judith Lieberman, Anna Merritt, Keith Mitchell, and Jane Terry. We sadly note the death of Milton Rakove in the time since the completion of the manuscript.

Our families—Margie, Amy, and Laura Checkoway, and Gretchen, Jane, and John Patton—gave patience, understanding, and love while this book was being written. Together we recognize many of the changes and problems discussed in this book at the same time that we find the Midwest a good place to live and work.

Contents

III PLANNING AND POLITICS

The Metropolitan Midwest

1
The Metropolitan Midwest in Perspective

BARRY CHECKOWAY and CARL V. PATTON

In recent years there have been important changes in midwestern central cities and metropolitan areas. Although the Midwest has long been known as America's urban heartland, its cities are now slowing, even declining, in population, employment, and other measures of urban activity. These changes are creating consequences and causing problems in land use, housing, neighborhood development, social and human services, transportation, and other areas. New policy initiatives are needed to respond to these changes.

What are the leading problems and issues that face the cities of the Midwest? What are the underlying causes of these problems? What are the policy alternatives? What are the prospects for change? Although the urban affairs of the Midwest are closely related to the rest of the nation, very few studies address these questions and the issues they raise. Few would doubt the importance of the Midwest, but relatively little scholarly work has been published about its cities, their problems and their prospects.

A great deal has been written about regional activity in America. There are many studies of New England, the Middle Atlantic, the West, and the South, but not so many about the Midwest. Historical studies of the midwestern region and its cities do exist, but few works document recent changes and future prospects. Chicago has been the focus of much social science scrutiny, but less attention has been given to St. Louis, Cleveland, Detroit, Minneapolis, and other urban areas of the region. The Midwest has been included with the Northeast in studies of the frostbelt-to-sunbelt movement, but these studies are not about the consequences of change or about citywide and neighborhood responses to change.[1]

This book is about the metropolitan Midwest, its policy problems and prospects for change. It focuses on changes in the Midwest, but it also considers selected changes elsewhere, including the so-called sunbelt of the South and West, because the "rivalry" and the "shifting" of population and power among regions bear directly on the future of the Midwest. For convenience the authors use the census definition of the North Central region as a general definition of the Midwest—Illinois, Indiana, Iowa, Kansas, Michigan, Minnesota, Missouri, Nebraska, North Dakota, Ohio, South Dakota, and Wisconsin—although they also recognize that regions are often difficult to define, that they may operate more as states of mind and heuristic devices for analysis and explanation than as distinct geographical areas, and that they may lose their meaning when subjected to close, systematic scrutiny (Browning and Gesler, 1979; Rice, 1981). We thus consider the Midwest as a useful entity for the study of urban problems and policy while recognizing that the Midwest is not a distinct and homogeneous region, that it shows rich internal variation and differentiation, and that it has characteristics that overlap with other regions in the nation.

Population Change

Population in the Midwest region is growing more slowly than in the nation as a whole. Midwestern cities and Standard Metropolitan Statistical Areas (SMSAs) are declining relative to cities and SMSAs in the South and West, and population is redistributing from central cities to suburban and nonmetropolitan areas.[2]

Overall population growth in the Midwest lags behind both the national average and that in many other regions. These differentials reflect the movement from frostbelt to sunbelt, a shift that is not recent, for the South and West have been growing faster than the Midwest since at least 1930 (Perry and Watkins, 1977; Russell and Robey, 1981). However, the 1980 census confirmed a dramatic increase in the size of the shift of population from the Midwest and Northeast to the South and West and showed that for the first time in history, the South and West together constitute the most populous area in the nation, with 52 percent of the nation's population.[3] Between 1970 and 1980 the Midwest population grew by 4.0 percent and the Northeast declined by 0.2 percent, while the South grew by 20.0 percent and the West by 23.9 percent. In the same period Illinois, Indiana, Iowa, Kansas, Michigan, Minnesota, Missouri, Nebraska, North Dakota, South Dakota, and Wisconsin all grew more slowly than the national average, while some southern, western, and mountain states grew far faster than the national average, including Florida, up 43.4 percent; Arizona, up 53.1 percent; Texas, up 27.1 percent; and California, up 18.5 percent. Except for Florida and

Texas, the top ten states in rate of growth during the decade were western (U.S. Bureau of the Census, 1981a).

Major Midwest cities are also slowing, even declining, in relation to cities elsewhere. Decline of central city population in the United States has been the pattern for years. What is new, however, is the quickening pace of decline in midwestern cities relative to cities in other parts of the country. Between 1970 and 1980 all but one of the larger central cities in the Midwest lost population. The biggest losers were St. Louis, down 27.2 percent; Cleveland, down 23.6 percent; Detroit, down 20.5 percent; Dayton, down 16.2 percent; Cincinnati, down 15.0 percent; Minneapolis–St. Paul, down 13.9 percent; Kansas City, down 11.7 percent; Milwaukee, down 11.3 percent; and Chicago, down 10.8 percent. Only the central city of Columbus, Ohio, grew, but its 4.6 percent growth was a result of the annexation of suburban areas. Urban decline went beyond central cities to entire metropolitan areas, including Cleveland, down 8.0 percent; Dayton, down 2.6 percent; St. Louis, down 2.3 percent; and Detroit, down 1.9 percent. Some smaller midwestern metropolitan areas did grow, but this was not typical of the region, and the growth was small nonetheless (U.S. Bureau of the Census, 1981b).

While Midwest cities declined, some sunbelt cities grew by impressive proportions, including San Jose, up 38.4 percent; Phoenix, up 35.2 percent; Houston, up 29.2 percent; and San Antonio, up 20.1 percent. Many sunbelt cities grew in part because of annexation. Others that did not annex territory posted only small population increases, and some declined: Atlanta, down 14.1 percent; New Orleans, down 6.1 percent; and San Francisco–Oakland, down 5.5 percent. But the image of sunbelt city growth pervades. Sunbelt metropolitan areas also advanced, including Ft. Lauderdale–Hollywood, up 63.5 percent; Phoenix, up 55.3 percent; Houston, up 45.3 percent; Dallas–Fort Worth, up 25.1 percent; and San Diego, up 37.1 percent (U.S. Bureau of the Census, 1981b). The shift of urban population caused the former mayor of Houston to conclude: "[Houston] is the new Detroit, the new New York. This is where the action is" (Sterba, 1976, p. 24).

Within midwestern metropolitan areas population is redistributing from central cities to suburban and nonmetropolitan areas. This outward movement dates from the nineteenth-century growth of suburbs and exurbs outside such cities as Chicago, Cincinnati, Cleveland, St. Louis, St. Paul, and Kansas City. The pattern continues today and involves more midwestern cities and metropolitan areas than in the past. As examples, between 1970 and 1980 the central city of Chicago declined 10.8 percent while its suburbs increased 13.6 percent; St. Louis was down 27.2 percent, its suburbs up 6.3 percent; Detroit was down 20.5 percent, its suburbs up

7.8 percent; and Minneapolis–St. Paul was down 13.9 percent, its suburbs up 20.6 percent. Suburbanization also characterizes cities of the
South and West, with the suburbs of Houston up 71.2 percent, those of
Dallas–Fort Worth up 47.9 percent, and Phoenix suburbs up 85.6 percent in the decade. Despite popular images of "back to the city," the
larger metropolitan movement, in both frostbelt and sunbelt, is toward
the suburbs and beyond (U.S. Bureau of the Census, 1981b).

In this volume Arthur Getis examines changing population patterns
in the Chicago metropolitan area and finds that, despite increased
energy costs, movement to the suburbs continues. Earlier Chicago
migrants moved to the edges of the central city and inner suburbs.
Today, however, these inner suburbs have joined the central city as an
origin area of outmigration, as Chicago urban and suburban migrants
move to outer suburbs and other regions of the country. Getis envisions
an emerging metropolis with a small central city and increasingly large
suburban areas that are focused around new centers such as O'Hare
Airport and surrounded by shopping centers, industrial and office concentrations, apartment houses, and other residential uses. Such suburbanization already characterizes many midwestern metropolitan areas.

The redistribution of population from central cities and metropolitan
areas to nonmetropolitan areas is not new. The so-called "nonmetropolitan renaissance" is often overlooked in population studies.
Curtis Roseman analyzes this renaissance as well as several other types of
population redistribution. He shows that many types of population
change characterize the Midwest. While large central cities are slowing
or declining, their surrounding suburban counties and many smaller
urban areas are growing. A number of amenity, recreation, or retirement
areas in the Midwest are expanding rapidly. Some counties, after decades
of decline, are "turning around" and increasing in population. These
findings caution against painting too gloomy a picture of the Midwest,
for decline is not pervasive, and although some large urban areas have
declined, other small places have actually grown. Nonetheless, the
region as a whole is changing and declining.

Economic Change

Many factors have contributed to this change and decline in the
metropolitan Midwest, including shifts in national economic activity,
government policies, and consumer preferences. In the past natural
resources, agricultural and industrial structures, and favorable locations
produced regional economic growth by attracting population, materials, and capital and by providing high living standards. During earlier

decades the region experienced relatively high productivity and employment. In recent years, however, economic activity in the Midwest has declined, in part as a result of shifts in the composition of demand from heavy industry and manufacturing to other forms of industry and to services, and in part as a result of a deceleration in national growth rates (Kosobud and Resek, 1981; Perloff et al., 1960).

A recent study of the Great Lakes industrial area reveals some of the factors that have impacted regional economic growth. Heavy manufacturing is dispersing out of the region's central cities to other parts of the country and to other nations. In fact, heavy manufacturing, which has been the dominant force in the region, is growing slowly nationally and not at all in the Great Lakes area. Sluggish employment growth in the region has made it difficult for new and displaced workers to be absorbed into the labor force, while the stagnant national economy has caused a lowered demand for goods produced in the region. Furthermore, non-manufacturing jobs in the area are not growing fast enough to employ the labor force, and the job growth that is taking place is occurring in the suburbs and nonmetropolitan areas. The larger cities and the older industrial towns are experiencing the most severe problems (Academy for Contemporary Problems, 1977).

The Northeast and Midwest have been hurt by the shift of capital to the South and West. Capital disinvestment, the running down or liquidation of the net productive capacity of a business, has been widespread and has taken many forms. Capital might be moved by owners who allow older facilities to deteriorate and use the savings for investments elsewhere, by the actual closing of older facilities, by the shifting of the bulk of production to newer facilities while older facilities continue at a reduced level, and by the reallocation of profits to new product development. Because much of this disinvestment is difficult to measure, the amount of capital shifting taking place is probably underestimated (Bluestone and Harrison, 1980).

Job losses in midwestern manufacturing have been large, and these losses have occurred in the metropolitan areas. Five of the eight metropolitan areas in the Great Lakes states with more than one million population lost manufacturing jobs between 1966 and 1973, and 85 percent of the manufacturing job gains were in nonmetropolitan areas (Widner, Rainey, and Moore, 1979). Between 1973 and 1976 almost half of the nation's job losses were in the industrial Midwest (Widner and Buxbaum, 1981).

Differences between growth rates in the frostbelt and the sunbelt are dramatic. Even during the 1960s most central cities in the sunbelt gained jobs at an increasing rate while industrial cities in the frostbelt lost them.

The 1970s saw jobs increase by 25 percent in the South and West while they declined in the Midwest, and real incomes grew more than twice as fast in the sunbelt as in the frostbelt. Moreover, during the 1970s capital spending grew two and one-half times faster in the South and West than in the Midwest.

Sunbelt gains were evident in every sector of the economy. Frostbelt declines took place primarily in manufacturing, while slight gains were experienced in certain services and in local government. Declines in the frostbelt were merely slowed by national economic booms; the booms did not seem to produce frostbelt employment gains (Watkins, 1980a). On the whole, households of most large sunbelt cities now have higher median incomes than their counterparts in the frostbelt. In addition, taxes are lower on the average in the sunbelt than in the Midwest, because southern cities provide a smaller range of social and public welfare programs (Katzman and Sommer, 1980).

Employment data for the period 1958-72 highlight the differences between frostbelt and sunbelt. By 1972 frostbelt cities had lost an average of 14-18 percent of their 1958 employment in manufacturing, retailing, and wholesaling; sunbelt cities were up 60-100 percent. Even in growing components of frostbelt economies, the rate was below that of sunbelt cities. The one sector in which frostbelt cities grew faster than sunbelt cities was the local government sector, where growth helped to offset losses in the private sector. Local government contributed little to employment gains in the sunbelt (Watkins, 1980a).

The growth of jobs in the Midwest is simply not keeping pace with the number of job seekers. Existing businesses are not being expanded nor are new businesses being created quickly enough to offset the death rate of industries in the region (Academy for Contemporary Problems, 1977; Bendick and Ledebur, 1982). Continued recession and a slow population growth rate have deterred new firm formation in both traditional and younger industries. Improved transportation, new technology, and worker mobility mean that firm location is less tied to particular sites than in the past. Thus new firm formations are taking place in amenity and population growth areas and in places that offer cheap labor (Shaul, 1979). Even efforts to retain firms and attract new ones through tax incentives have had little effect in the Midwest, except to create competition between midwestern locales (Kosobud and Resek, 1981). When taxes have been effective in attracting industry, they have caused movements from one state to another in the region or between cities within the same state, not from one region to another (Giertz, 1981).

Labor conditions, and the readiness of state and local governments in the sunbelt to make those conditions attractive to industry, also affect the regional shift of jobs. During the 1970s most of the country's job growth took place in the least unionized parts of the country (Goodman, 1979). New jobs have been created where there is a "good business climate," that is, where there is little union militancy, a low wage scale, and a political environment that views most taxation, corporate regulations, and social services as unnecessary burdens on the rights of private property (Watkins, 1980b). These less unionized areas are largely located outside the Northeast and Midwest.

Alfred Watkins (1980a) uses shift-share analysis to examine national growth, industrial mix, and competitive advantage as factors in economic decline in the frostbelt. He finds that the national growth component has not principally contributed to the economic decline in the frostbelt. If every industry in the frostbelt had grown at the average rate of the U.S. economy, then there would have been a 26.9 percent gain between 1958 and 1972. He also finds that the decline cannot be traced to a disadvantageous industrial mix; the industrial mix of the frostbelt should have allowed for the addition of jobs. He finally concludes that the principal factor seems to be the frostbelt's competitive disadvantage in manufacturing, retailing, and wholesaling, which is caused by a disparity between national and local growth rates in particular industries. Those industries in the frostbelt that have expanded have done so too slowly to offset declines in other industries in the region. Frostbelt cities have been losing their traditional economic dominance and at the same time have been failing to attract new economic activities.

Results of this shift and decline are apparent in plant closings and job losses across the Midwest. The impacts are especially visible in states like Michigan, where in early 1982 unemployment reached 16 percent, with 677,000 persons unemployed and 20,000 workers running out of unemployment benefits each month. When the *Detroit Free Press* let unemployed job seekers run a free classified ad offering their skills, nearly 5,000 people responded (Kelly, 1982). Although jobs were once plentiful in the automobile industry, between 1979 and 1981 in Michigan, to give one example, more than half a million automobile-related jobs were lost and many unemployed workers moved out of the state. Michigan has been hit exceptionally hard, but Ohio and Indiana entered 1982 with unemployment rates of 11.8 and 12.4 percent respectively, and more than one-third of the 38 metropolitan areas with unemployment rates above 10 percent were in the Midwest (Kelly, 1982). In Detroit local bookstores report competition over the "help wanted" sections of the new bestsellers—the Sunday *Houston Chronicle*, the *Dallas Morning News*, and the *San Antonio Light*.

Economic experts believe that more change is on the way. They hold that marginally profitable plants in the North are closing permanently and not relocating in the South. Different jobs are appearing there, jobs caused by expansion in the export bases of sunbelt urban areas, and jobs in new fast-growing industries that are seeking attractive tax rates and lower energy and labor costs (Academy for Contemporary Problems, 1977; Beyers, 1979; *Business Week*, 1981; *Industrial Distribution*, 1981). Competition for new jobs comes not only from the South but from foreign countries as well. Severe job shortages in the Midwest are projected, unless substantial outmigration occurs (Academy for Contemporary Problems, 1977).

Some analysts argue that the Midwest is now paying the price for its past successes, and that the current decline of the region reflects a long-term trend toward equalization of incomes among regions of the nation (Giertz, 1981). These analysts view the population and economic changes in the Midwest, South, and West as part of regional life cycles, with a shift now taking place from an old cycle dominated by the growth and decline of the manufacturing belt to a new cycle in which the South and West act as seed-beds for technological innovation (Rees, 1979). Researchers question whether the shift to the sunbelt is a long-term or short-term phenomenon. One interpretation is that the decline is part of a national ebb and flow of population and economic activity, that the region's role in the economy is changing, and that by the year 2000 the economic pendulum may swing back toward the Midwest (Widner and Buxbaum, 1981). Yet others argue that the regions are not converging, but that the sunbelt is catching up and is beginning to show signs of pulling ahead of the frostbelt. The latter may indeed be the case, since the rate of industrial growth in the South has not slowed as income and wage increases have occurred (Rees, 1979).

There are exceptions to the pattern of midwestern economic decline and some states in the Midwest have exceeded national growth averages. For example, the upper midwestern states of Iowa, Nebraska, Montana, North Dakota, South Dakota, Minnesota, and Wisconsin posted a 26.2 percent increase in nonfarm jobs between 1970 and 1978, compared with a 19.9 percent average national increase. These states led the national averages in growth in six of eight major classifications, the exceptions being mining and government employment (Upper Midwest Council, 1979).

This anomaly notwithstanding, the economy of the Midwest will probably continue to grow more slowly than the economy of the nation as a whole, in part owing to the anticipated sluggishness in manufacturing. Analysts at the Bureau of Economic and Business Research at the University of Illinois forecast a long-range Midwest industrial production growth rate of 3.63 to 3.77 percent, compared to a national rate of 3.88 to 3.9 percent, and a Midwest employment growth rate of 0.62 percent, compared to a national rate of 0.6 percent. These analysts examine the component parts of the region and project slower growth for Plains than for Great Lakes states (Resek, Junkus, and Panerali, 1981). By 1985 the South is expected to surpass the North Central region in total employment in manufacturing (Widner and Buxbaum, 1981).

Government Policies

Government policies also contribute to change in the metropolitan Midwest. Since the Midwest as a whole is an area of neither high growth nor low incomes, it receives a relatively low proportion of federal program funds. Defense expenditures tend to go to the South and West, price supports for crops such as tobacco and peanuts benefit agriculture in other regions, while embargoes on foreign sales of soybeans and grains hurt the midwestern economy (Kosobud and Resek, 1981). Furthermore, the Midwest sends more money to Washington than it receives in return. For example, between 1975 and 1979 the Midwest had a negative "balance of payments" with the federal government of $110 billion, while the South and West received over $100 billion more than they sent to Washington (Flint, 1981).

Several studies have shown that the Midwest is at the lower end of the scale when the ratio of federal funds received to taxes paid is computed (Pack, 1982). For fiscal year 1979 the ratio was .82 for the Midwest, 1.21 for the South, and 1.07 for the West. The Great Lakes portion of the Midwest had a ratio of .74 and the Plains states portion had a ratio of 1.02 (Schoeplein, 1981). The West and South are above the national mean and are moving even higher, while the North Central and Northeast regions are below the national mean and are continuing to decline (Anton, Cawley, and Kramer, 1980). Analysis at the county level shows that the slow-growing, frostbelt counties have received less than the national average (U.S. Congress, 1977).

There is debate over the usefulness of the "balance of payments" concept, especially when such regional comparisons imply that a region should receive its "fair share" of payments back from Washington in proportion to taxes paid (Markusen and Fastrup, 1978; Oakland and Chall, 1979; Pack, 1982). Such programs as rural electrification and social security would be ineffective if they had to be distributed proportionately to all states. Although federal allocation decisions should consider type of expenditure as well as regional source, analysts conclude that no one knows where federal dollars are spent (Anton, Cawley, and Kramer, 1980). As a consequence, consistent, generally acceptable principles for expenditure reallocation are almost impossible to devise (Pack, 1982). Analysts are able to show that the West and South lead the nation in per capita receipts, the West benefits from federal formula grants, and the North Central region benefits most from direct and indirect loans. Agency, functional, and program spending change greatly from year to year in terms of distribution by state, indicating federal responsiveness to changing conditions and political forces. Nevertheless, there is great stability across time in terms of state of regional rankings, because of the link of most types of domestic federal spending to individuals. This means that when federal dollars are distributed, counties and cities with large populations receive more federal funds (Anton, Cawley, and Kramer, 1980).

Federal favoritism toward the South and West may contribute to urban problems. For example, federal policies regarding capital investments, procurement, tax structure, and regulation have encouraged jobs to move from the Northeast to the South or West, and from central cities to suburbs and nonmetropolitan areas, because such policies explicitly or implicitly favor new development over rehabilitation. Capital investment in the interstate highway system has opened up new areas of the South and West. Tax policy has favored new construction, and capital gains policies have encouraged firms to purchase large tracts in areas where land prices are rising. FHA and VA mortgage guarantees have encouraged the development of new suburban housing. Local government expenditures have also been influenced by the cost-sharing requirements of federal grant programs and by the requirements of federal regulatory programs (Vaughan, Pascal, and Vaiana, 1980).

Federal increases in defense and decreases in community development spending may contribute to further decline in the metropolitan Midwest. Increases in Defense Department procurements will most likely create jobs in regions other than the Midwest, while cuts in net domestic outlays would approximate national per capita averages. The South would gain from increases in defense spending, but this would be offset by reductions in net domestic outlays. The West as a region would gain in all categories. Cities, counties, and metropolitan areas across the nation may be the bigger losers, and the harder-pressed lower-growth areas will have the most difficulty because they will have to assume a greater portion of governmental expenses (Schoeplein, 1981). The biggest losers may be the no-growth middle-sized cities that do not fall within the requirements for large federal grants (Kosobud and Resek, 1981).

Quality of Life

The shifting preferences of consumers also contribute to change in the metropolitan Midwest. The customary view contends that many consumers leave the region to escape from decaying cities, a declining economy, and harsh winters, often migrating to sunbelt cities, which are believed to offer more jobs, better amenities, and a superior quality of life. Sunbelt cities are portrayed as offering new opportunities away from the problems left behind.

However, the new migrants do not always find what they seek. Some move with jobs already lined up, but others find that the transition is difficult, that their training and skills are not in demand, and that the shift from the unionized Midwest and Northeast to the non-unionized South and West can mean cuts in pay and benefits. As 1982 began, unemployment rates in many sunbelt states were below the national average but they were on the rise, with Georgia at 6.8 percent, Arkansas at 10.4 percent, and Florida at 7.7 percent in the South, and California at 8.6 percent, Oregon at 11.4 percent, and Washington at 11.1 percent in the West.

Life in the high-growth urban areas of the sunbelt has its costs. Houston and Atlanta have traffic problems caused by the influx of new residents. The cost of living is increasing faster in the sunbelt than in the rest of the nation. Increases in the consumer price index for 1981 were 9.8 percent for the South, 9.6 percent for the West, and 7.0 percent for the Midwest, compared with a national average of 8.7 percent (U.S. Department of Labor, 1982). High taxes, crime, pollution, inner city decay, suburban flight, dwindling natural resources, and serious environmental problems have caused experts on conditions in the South to suggest that "the bloom is off the rose" and that the South's growing pains spell a possibly troubled future. Residents of many southern cities have banded together to reject downtown revitalization plans, to turn away new industries, and to defeat bond issues that would finance the expansion of municipal services, because they fear that the South will soon have the same problems as the North, problems many of the northern migrants thought they had left behind (Peterson, 1981).

The very things that have made the South attractive may also undo it. Within the next 20 years Texas expects to double in population, an increase that translates into the need for 170,000 more jobs per year if the state is to avoid serious unemployment. Some observers believe that by the end of the 1980s the South will no longer have the advantage of lower labor costs, inexpensive housing, and lower living costs (Peterson, 1981). Other analysts predict problems for sunbelt cities as economic strength shifts to sunbelt suburbs, as sunbelt cities run out of suburbs to annex, and as lower-income, low-skilled, and improperly skilled people continue to migrate to sunbelt cities (Abbott, 1981; Johnson, 1981; Wallis, 1981).

The decline of recent years may overshadow the positive aspects of life in the Midwest and may cause the benefits of the South to be overstated. One recent study compared regions of the country on a hardship scale that included measures of unemployment, limited education, crowded housing, and poverty (adjusted for cost-of-living differences) in central cities of 54 large metropolitan areas. Many sunbelt cities did not fare well. Seven of the 19 sunbelt cities had higher hardship ratings than New York City. New Orleans was worse off then Cleveland or Detroit. Atlanta and Sacramento were worse off than Chicago (Johnson, 1981).

In another study U.S. cities were rated on such factors as climate and terrain, housing, health and environment, crime, transportation, education, recreation, the arts, and economics (taxes and job availability). The top-ranked city was Atlanta, a sunbelt city, but a number of frostbelt cities outranked sunbelt cities. Cleveland was tied at 14 with San Francisco–Oakland. Cincinnati at 17 outranked Miami. Chicago, at 21, was rated superior to San Diego. Minneapolis–St. Paul at 23, St. Louis at 24, and Kansas City at 26 were rated above Tucson and San Jose. Madison, Wisconsin, at 34 and Indianapolis at 35 were rated above Houston. Milwaukee at 39 was rated above Albuquerque. Fort Wayne, Indiana, at 42 and Detroit at 43 were rated above Phoenix, and Evansville, Indiana, at 46 was rated above Los Angeles and San Antonio (Boyer and Savageau, 1981). Midwestern cities rate well because of their more reasonable housing costs, comparatively low crime rates, and cultural and educational facilities, whereas southern cities are handicapped in the ratings by high housing costs and high crime rates. Although such ratings do not change the fact that the Midwest is in decline, they do illustrate that the Midwest still has much to offer and has a good base upon which to rebuild in the future.

Even as sunbelt cities begin to acquire the problems of the frostbelt, however, the problems of the Midwest and Northeast remain severe, and the unemployed and others continue to leave these areas in substantial numbers.

Changes in the Midwest have produced a lively policy debate among scholars and practitioners. As Alfred Watkins shows in this volume, some policy analysts believe that the decline of the Midwest is inevitable and that the United States would be served by accelerating and facilitating the exodus. He cites the President's Commission for a National Agenda for the Eighties, which concludes that the national shift is inevitable and desirable, that municipal and state efforts to lure manufacturing industries back to older midwestern central cities must fail, and that government should facilitate adjustment to redistribution trends in this postindustrial period. Other analysts, Watkins continues, argue that the pattern is neither inevitable nor desirable but has been created by the investment decisions of large corporations. Business executives and other corporate actors, following orthodox market investment criteria, threaten local economies and choose nonmidwestern locations. He cites the cases of Cleveland, where a consortium of six banks withheld credit and plunged the city into bankruptcy when the mayor took an anticorporate stance, and of Youngstown, Ohio, where corporate executives closed plants and put workers out of jobs because they believed they could earn higher profits elsewhere.

Whatever the explanation and resolution of the debate, there is no doubt that the Midwest is slowing, even declining, in relative growth. Some observers worry that when the national economic slump has ended, the Midwest will still be suffering and that many of the jobs in the Midwest's key industries—autos, steel, and metalworking trades—will have largely disappeared (Flint, 1981).

Despite change and decline, rich and varied images of the large cities of the Midwest still remain. In this volume John Jakle takes us on tour of Chicago, Detroit, St. Louis, Cleveland, Minneapolis and St. Paul, Milwaukee, Cincinnati, Kansas City, Indianapolis, and Columbus. He examines their skylines, landmarks, open spaces, enclosures, streetscapes, and special districts. He finds that the centers of these cities share common images and a prevailing urban fabric that includes a business district on a river or lakefront, a transportation hub, industrial plants surrounded by housing, major thoroughfares lined with businesses, and "the new city" growing at the edge. Although these cities share common images, Jakle also finds variety, because each place has sought to promote a distinctive image for itself. And, amidst change, he encourages citizens and officials to go beyond their central districts to consider distinctive images in the total fabric of landscape. "Future metropolitan promotion in the Middle West should reach out to the neighborhoods to plumb the positive aspects of ethnic diversity and to emphasize the quality of life," he concludes. "Middlewestern cities should be made to stand for what is best in the American way of life."

Policy Problems

Change and decline in the metropolitan Midwest have had consequences and created problems for those who still live there. In this volume Robert Mendelson and Michael Quinn analyze St. Louis as a case where change and decline have worsened housing conditions and intensified racial segregation. Once the largest city in the region and set on a solid economic base, St. Louis today is known as "the nation's most distressed big city." Mendelson and Quinn describe a pattern in which powerful economic institutions have disinvested from the central city in favor of other, more "advantaged" locations. Population has decreased nearly 50 percent, the largest percentage decrease of any major U.S. city between 1950 and 1980. Viable neighborhoods have declined into abandonment, the infrastructure has badly deteriorated, public services are severely inadequate, and people and institutions have withdrawn. Those who remain face poor housing, health care, and education and a worsening quality of life.

Declining conditions in St. Louis also have class and racial implications. Low-income blacks are increasingly located in and identified with the most decayed and deteriorated parts of the city. In the past, as poor nonwhites migrated to St. Louis seeking inexpensive housing, central city ghettos were established that grew and spread. These segregated the city into broad divided racial areas with an inequitable distribution of resources and opportunities among them. St. Louis today has grown from a compact central city on a firm economic base to a large metropolitan area that offers limited resources and opportunities for mobility and has a peripheral zone of suburban and nonmetropolitan communities for those who can pay the price. By 1980 St. Louis had become the most segregated of all midwestern cities, followed closely by Chicago, Cleveland, and Indianapolis.

Other authors document the worsening housing and social conditions of urban neighborhoods left behind. Barry Checkoway describes conditions in a predominantly black, low-income area on the north side of St. Louis within 12 blocks of the central business district. Between 1970 and 1980 this area lost consistently higher proportions of its residents than white south-side neighborhoods, in a process of "class skimming" in which some neighborhoods have been left with a core of elderly, young unemployed, and other poor people dependent on government aid. Housing in many such neighborhoods is badly overcrowded, poorly maintained, or abandoned.

Those left behind also face employment problems. David Berry and Stephanie Wilson discuss barriers to employment which they argue are deeply woven into the fabric of the midwestern economy. The industrial cities of the Midwest have been relatively more dependent on heavy manufacturing industry than has the nation as a whole at a time when the manufacturing sector in American society is weakening. Plant closings and job loss have had serious effects on workers and their families, including income loss, underemployment, and physical and mental health problems. Many of those left behind in central cities are low-income minorities who have limited skills, education, experience, or familiarity with the labor market. In addition, these minorities do not have access to suburban jobs, and many of them experience discrimination. The central cities and metropolitan areas of the Midwest thus have a disproportionate share of discouraged workers (those unemployed workers who have given up looking for work and are often not counted in unemployment surveys), displaced homemakers, unemployed and underutilized workers, and occupationally segregated minorities and women.

The problems of housing and employment are exacerbated by urban transportation practice in the metropolitan Midwest. Norman Krumholz and Janice Cogger in their chapter analyze Cleveland as an example of the barriers to mobility that many people in the central cities of the Midwest confront. Although the automobile has become the dominant mode of urban transportation, and most of the population has enjoyed a dramatic increase in automobile utilization and mobility, a substantial segment of the population in large midwestern cities has not shared in this expanded mobility. The authors show that one-third of all Cleveland households—primarily the households of the poor, the elderly, and the disabled—do not own automobiles. These "transit-dependent" people, who cannot afford to own an automobile or are unable to drive, have failed to share in the expanded mobility of the majority. They are victimized by transportation policies that emphasize reliance upon automobiles, so that their housing and employment problems are exacerbated. Current urban transportation policies further narrow the range of choices for those who have few, if any, choices at best. This problem afflicts not only Cleveland but many midwestern metropolitan areas.

Change and decline reach beyond the most deteriorated neighborhoods of the Midwest. Indeed, Carl Patton shows that declining populations, lowered densities, shrinking budgets, and reduced federal aid all combine to worsen the entire capital infrastructure of many midwestern cities. Drawing on a study of cities throughout the Midwest, Patton shows that the streets, highways, bridges, and the very nuts and bolts that hold midwestern cities together and make them viable are in disrepair. He cites cases such as Cleveland, where rusty pipes have cut water supply and interrupted service, where bridges are rated unsatisfactory or unsafe, and where the streets need to be resurfaced; East St. Louis, where schools do not meet state health and life safety codes; Milwaukee, where untreated sewage violates water quality standards and endangers health; Lansing, where major streets and bridges are in dismal shape; Indianapolis, where many bridges should be closed to traffic and repaired immediately; St. Paul, where insufficient sewers back up in homes, businesses, and streets; and smaller cities and rural areas that experience infrastructure deterioration as well.

Those left behind also face problems of governance and planning. Milton Rakove, a political scientist with experience in the precincts, analyzes Chicago as a case of a midwestern city where community changes have influenced politics and government. Chicago has experienced economic decline, a population that is decreasing in number and changing in racial composition, and the replacement of ethnic neighborhoods by racial areas. Race has replaced ethnicity as the dominant cultural factor in the city. These community changes—and the death of Richard J. Daley—have weakened the control once held by an entrenched, ethnic-based, Democratic machine over the city's political and governmental systems. The result is a city council forced to respond to the pressures of the deepening racial fragmentation of the city; aldermanic representatives cast adrift from their constituencies by deterioration of the ward system organizations in their neighborhoods; a bureaucracy that no longer functions to make the city work and assure the quality of life for its citizenry; and a mayoralty that finds it ever more difficult to close the deepening racial gaps, satisfy the most intransigent elements of divided constituencies, and resolve the city's deepening social problems. As poor blacks and Hispanics continue to migrate into Chicago and white middle-class people continue to flee to the suburbs, the political system is increasingly incapable of dealing with the social and economic problems that result.

Efforts at Change

Among the consequences of change and decline in the metropolitan Midwest have been planning efforts to address the resultant problems. But previous planning at various levels has yielded mixed results. Authors in this volume describe federal efforts to solve housing and community development problems of midwestern cities. Mendelson and Quinn note that some federal housing programs intended to ameliorate local problems have exacerbated conditions or have confronted strong local resistance. They cite the Federal Housing Administration, which in the past rejected projects that failed to conform to its *Underwriting Manual* guidelines against "inharmonious racial groups" and thus acted in concert with local real estate boards that directed their members not to sell to blacks. They also cite more recent federal programs for subsidized housing that have effectively restricted public housing for blacks to ghetto areas and rental assistance to units located in low-income areas. However, when federal policies have aimed to improve housing conditions and reduce racial segregation, they have met with strong local opposition. Mendelson and Quinn describe the resistance of local officials and suburban municipalities to federal proposals to construct subsidized housing outside "impacted" areas as well as to regional planning agency attempts to mobilize federal resources for programs designed to increase housing mobility of low-income residents. They acknowledge that results in the past have been mixed, but they reassert the need for new public initiatives to increase subsidies for housing the poor and to foster public support for fair housing measures. They are not, however, sanguine about the prospects. On the contrary, they expect little from national officials who are now opposed to expansion of federal programs or from local officials who are opposed to the location of subsidized housing in their neighborhoods. They conclude that while effective federal housing programs are needed, the prospects for achieving them are dim.

Roger Montgomery draws similar conclusions in a chapter on Pruitt-Igoe, the public housing project in St. Louis that has become a symbol of American public housing failure. First occupied in 1954, Pruitt-Igoe housed 13,000 people in 2,700 apartments in 33 11-story slab-shaped buildings. Although many early residents were satisfied with their apartments, conditions declined by the early 1960s, resulting in physical deterioration, high crime rates, skyrocketing vacancies, tenant anxieties, and a "tangle of pathologies." In a dramatic display federal officials dynamited Pruitt-Igoe. Montgomery reviews previous research and analysis; goes beyond those who have viewed Pruitt-Igoe as a failure of social architecture, public housing, or social welfare; and questions the very possibility of effective public housing and social policy in a society that has a de facto commitment to maintain poverty and racism. He wonders if the failures of public policy are not accidental at all but, rather, more basically related to the racial and class contradictions that afflict American urban society.

Heywood Sanders also analyzes the impact of federal programs on urban conditions in the Midwest. Under the Housing and Community Development Act of 1974, Congress aimed to develop viable urban communities with decent housing, good living environments, and expanded economic opportunities for low- and moderate-income persons. The new legislation offered relatively flexible block grants that secured the participation of most eligible midwestern communities. Sanders analyzes the block-grant practice of 20 midwestern communities, ranging from older "urban crisis" cities like Chicago, Detroit, Cleveland, and St. Louis, to cities that had received no previous aid including older suburbs such as Cleveland Heights, Evanston, and Oak Park, to smaller central cities such as Muncie, Kalamazoo, and Kenosha, and to twentieth-century suburbs such as Skokie, Illinois, and South-field, Michigan. He finds that community development has assumed a variety of meanings. Local governments have emphasized public works, including street improvements and physical repairs; housing rehabilita-tion, including loans to homeowners, grants for rehabilitation, and purchase and renovation of buildings; and urban renewal activities, including land acquisition, clearance, and relocation. Although in some selected cases this program was used to provide housing, physical improvements, and social services to eliminate slums and respond to urban needs, in other cases it was used to build a gazebo in the shopping district of a St. Louis suburb, rehabilitate municipal offices in Evans-ville, Indiana, and remove snow in Chicago. The reader of this chapter will find that the program has shown no sustained concern for those in the poorest neighborhoods of the central cities of the Midwest.

Federal efforts to remove employment barriers in the metropolitan Midwest have also yielded mixed results. Berry and Wilson find that the Minnesota Work Equity Project, a federal demonstration employment and training program in St. Paul and several Minnesota counties, oper-ated to remove some human capital and behavioral barriers through provision of labor market experience and job training for low-income persons. They find that the Civil Rights Act of 1964 has been effective in promoting employment opportunities for minorities, especially black males, and in reducing the effects of discrimination in midwestern metropolitan labor markets. However, they find that, except in some important instances, affirmative action has been less successful in enhancing employment opportunities than the Civil Rights Act has been in overcoming discrimination. They conclude that while federal programs can help remove employment barriers in some cases, they have little influence on structural barriers.

Berry and Wilson are not sanguine about prospects for strengthening federal employment programs, for they recognize that the current ad-ministration seeks to reduce federal programs and shift away from "demonstration projects" to "forced work" approaches. They also note that the commitment of the American people toward enforcement of anti-discrimination programs is uncertain and suggest that no solution to the problems of the hard-core unemployed seems imminent. They conclude that the metropolitan Midwest suffers from serious structural problems that are currently solved by outmigration, and that continued industrial decline will create even more obstacles to employment in the Midwest. As a consequence of structural barriers, outmigration of workers will continue, and if this process proves selective, it may leave an increased concentration of hard-core unemployed in midwestern cities.

Other authors in this volume describe citywide efforts to wrestle with problems of change and decline. Patton, for example, examines local government efforts to solve capital infrastructure problems. Although deterioration in midwestern cities is widespread, some cities are working to overcome the forces of capital infrastructure decline. He analyzes the cases of Joliet, Milwaukee, Lansing, Kansas City, Indianapolis, St. Paul, and Dayton as cities that have sought to solve the problem of capital infrastructure decline. These cities have all developed a procedure for capital improvement planning and programming. They have devised a variety of models—technical, fiscal, political, or citizen review—that have enabled them to produce concrete results and show tangible accomplishments.

Patton is not, however, confident about the prospects for solving the problem of capital infrastructure deterioration in the metropolitan Midwest. He finds that the case cities have experienced problems in mounting an effort, that staff support remains limited, that local and state resources are insufficient, and that federal assistance has not kept up with the need. Most seriously of all, citizens and their representatives tend to ignore the widespread evidence of urban infrastructure decay and often do not support efforts to repair the damages. And while these organized municipalities face limits and obstacles, they have at least tried to cope with the problem; most midwestern cities appear virtually unorganized in their attack on the capital infrastructure deterioration problem. The need is so great that the cities of the Midwest may never catch up. In the absence of concerted action, many capital facilities will have to be abandoned while midwesterners learn to live with deterioration. Patton concludes that midwestern cities face a formidable task in rebuilding their urban plants, and that declining populations, lowered densities, shrinking budgets, and reduced federal aid may make this task even more difficult.

City planners concerned about equity also face obstacles. Krumholz and Cogger describe their efforts to use urban transportation as a means to promote a wider range of choices for the "transit-dependent" of Cleveland. Previous transportation policies had emphasized automobiles, worsened conditions for those who lacked access, and contributed to the decline of the public mass transit systems on which these people depended. The planners chronicle their efforts to advocate the interests of transit-dependent persons and alleviate transit deprivation through the county transit study and plan, the establishment of the regional transit authority, and the transfer of the Cleveland transit system to the authority. Cleveland planners were able to win guarantees of strong service for the city, reduced fares for the elderly, and the creation of service to expand access to the handicapped and elderly. The planners ultimately declared victory, but their efforts had been seriously challenged by county commissioners, suburban politicians, and downtown business interests who supported fixed-rail systems as a means to stimulate growth and raise property values.

Robert Einsweiler describes planning changes in the Minneapolis–St. Paul metropolitan area. Previous population growth and redistribution had resulted in fragmentation among a large number of local governmental units and had created the need for planning and coordination at the metropolitan regional level. The Metropolitan Council was established in 1967 to satisfy this need and has produced an impressive record of accomplishments. Einsweiler, a veteran participant-observer of Twin Cities planning, goes beyond earlier accounts of the council to draw lessons for representation, legislation, and decision making. He presents this as a case in which planners and citizens were able to overcome some, but not all, of the obstacles to metropolitan regional planning, while problems of fragmentation and coordination continue to challenge both planners and citizens throughout the Midwest.

Other authors analyze grass-roots neighborhood activity that has produced results and created change. Barry Checkoway analyzes the case of Jeff-Vander-Lou, a neighborhood organization located in a low-income-area in St. Louis. Formed in response to community crises, JVL has grown into a successful organization with an impressive record of concrete results. Working in a neighborhood that many had considered beyond revitalization, JVL has built and rehabilitated housing, generated capital development, operated social services, attracted new industry and jobs, and formulated plans to boost the local economy. The organization has also increased awareness of neighborhood problems and issues and has undertaken neighborhood planning and participation with fervor. JVL represents a case of individuals helping themselves to improve their neighborhood and might be used as a model of local initiative.

Some readers may warm to the promise of local initiative to address the problems of the metropolitan Midwest, and such ideas are echoed in national political circles today. But Checkoway warns that these may be false promises and may fail on a larger scale. Despite the magnitude of the JVL accomplishment, the surrounding areas and the city of St. Louis as a whole remain in decline. Local initiative is an important means to neighborhood revitalization, but it should not be used to retreat from official government action. As Checkoway concludes, neighborhood problems result from a decision process and institutional context that operate largely outside the neighborhood, and both the consequences and the policy problems flow from the nature of that process. To alter the consequences, it is first necessary to alter the process. At its worst, local initiative as national policy runs the danger of diverting attention from national obligations and may fail to recognize that change and decline in the neighborhoods of the metropolitan Midwest operate in a larger, national context. The problems that face the metropolitan Midwest, in the final analysis, are not local.

Citizens and planners are working at various levels to stem decline in the metropolitan Midwest. Innovative neighborhood, city, metropolitan, and regional efforts have been set in motion. As significant as these efforts are, however, it is clear that prospects for the Midwest are tied to prospects for the nation. Regional decline must be viewed as a national problem, and efforts to solve regional problems must be placed in a national and even international context (Miernyk, 1979; Sternlieb and Hughes, 1978). National policies cannot treat regions as if they were independent and separable from the future of the nation as a whole.

Focus of the Book

This book on the metropolitan Midwest examines leading policy problems, planning issues, and prospects for change. It assesses the state of knowledge, identifies unanswered questions, and clarifies the future policy and action agenda. Individual chapters analyze such topics as population redistribution, metropolitan change, economic development, housing patterns, residential segregation, neighborhood revitalization, employment training and jobs, federal programs, urban transportation, political change, citizen participation, and innovations in planning. These are not the only topics or issues that face the metropolitan Midwest, which is a region as large and diverse as many nations, but they are among the most important. The problems of the Midwest may foretell problems to come in other regions.[4]

The contributors include leading scholars and practitioners in the urban policy and planning fields. Among them are policy analysts and academics, agency administrators and planning professionals. Each author has worked in one way or another to influence or understand the problems and issues facing the region. Together they share a commitment to apply policy analysis and planning skills to the major problems and issues that confront the cities and metropolitan areas of the region. They represent a remarkable range of individuals, each highly experienced, deeply committed, and eager to communicate.

Notes

1. General works on regional development and problems include *Regional development experiences and prospects in the United States of America* (Cumberland, 1971), *Metropolis and region* (Duncan et al., 1960), *Metropolis and region in transition* (Duncan and Lieberson, 1970), *Regional development and planning: A reader* (Friedmann and Alonso, 1964), *Regional policy: Readings in theory and applications* (Friedmann and Alonso, 1975), *Territory and function: The evolution of regional planning* (Friedmann and Weaver, 1979), *Rural poverty and the urban crisis: A strategy for regional development* (Hansen, 1971), *Regions of the United States* (Hart, 1972), *American regionalism* (Odum and Moore, 1938), *Regions, resources and economic growth* (Perloff et al., 1960), and *Regional growth and decline in the United States: The rise of the sunbelt and the decline of the Northeast* (Weinstein and Firestine, 1978).

Sunbelt studies include *The new urban America: Growth and politics in sunbelt cities* (Abbott, 1981), *Urban growth dynamics in a regional cluster of cities* (Chapin and Weiss, 1962), *The South* (Hart, 1976), *Southern regions of the United States* (Odum, 1936), and *The rise of the sunbelt cities* (Perry and Watkins, 1977).

Frostbelt studies include *The North Central United States* (Akin, 1968), *National growth and economic change in the upper Midwest* (Henderson and Krueger, 1965), *Population redistribution in the Midwest* (Roseman et al., 1981), *Revitalizing the Northeast* (Sternlieb and Hughes, 1978), and *Regional economic development in the Plains region: 1870–1960* (Waxmonsky, 1972).

Studies of individual cities include *The twin cities of St. Paul and Minneapolis* (Abler, 1976), *Contemporary metropolitan America* (Adams, 1976), *Chicago: Transformations of an urban system* (Berry et al., 1976), *Cities of the prairie: The metropolitan frontier and American politics* (Elazar, 1970), and *Chicago: Growth of a metropolis* (Mayer and Wade, 1969).

A single-volume reference guide is *A bibliographical guide to midwestern literature* (Nemanic, 1981).

2. An area qualifies as a Standard Metropolitin Statistical Area (SMSA) if it has a central city of at least 50,000 persons or an urbanized area of one or more towns of at least 50,000 persons located in a county or counties with a total population of at least 100,000. SMSA boundaries coincide with county boundaries. Contiguous counties are included when they are linked by economic and social relationships to the central city. Metropolitan areas are defined as counties in Standard Metropolitan Statistical Areas. The larger cities in the Midwest region are central cities in metropolitan areas. In most cases the terms "SMSA" and "metropolitan area" are synonymous. The term "nonmetropolitan" refers

to all counties that are not in Standard Metropolitan Statistical Areas. Non-metropolitan areas include rural areas, many small towns, and some medium-sized cities.

3. Population change was also reflected in Congress. Reapportionment based on the 1980 census resulted in a loss of two House seats for both Illinois and Ohio. Indiana, Michigan, Missouri, and South Dakota each lost one seat (*Congressional Quarterly*, 1981).

4. The time lapse between completion of the manuscript and publication affects the currentness of some statistics. We updated critical figures as the book was going to press, but, of course, we have to rely to a great extent on 1980 census data. We believe that the problems, trends, prospects, and conclusions are affected little by recent statistical fluctuations.

References

Abbott, C. 1981. *The new urban America: Growth and politics in sunbelt cities.* Chapel Hill: University of North Carolina Press.

Abler, R. F. 1976. *The twin cities of St. Paul and Minneapolis.* Cambridge: Ballinger.

Academy for Contemporary Problems. 1977. *Stimulating the economy of the Great Lakes states.* Columbus, Ohio.

Adams, J. S., ed. 1976. *Contemporary metropolitan America.* Cambridge: Ballinger.

Akin, W. E. 1968. *The North Central United States.* Princeton, N.J.: Van Nostrand.

Anton, T. J., J. P. Cawley, and K. L. Kramer. 1980. *Moving money.* Cambridge: Oelgeschlager, Gunn & Haun.

Bendick, M., Jr., and L. C. Ledebur. 1982. National industrial policy and economically distressed communities. *Policy Studies Journal* 10 (Dec.):220–35.

Berry, B. J. L., et al. 1976. *Chicago: Transformation of an urban system.* Cambridge: Ballinger.

Beyers, W. B. 1979. Contemporary trends in the regional economic development of the United States. *Professional Geographer* 3 (Feb.):34–44.

Bluestone, B., and B. Harrison. 1980. *Capital and communities: The causes and consequences of private disinvestment.* Washington, D.C.: Progressive Alliance.

Boyer, R., and D. Savageau. 1981. *Places rated almanac.* Chicago: Rand McNally.

Browning, C. E., and W. Gesler. 1979. The sun belt–snow belt: A case of sloppy regionalizing. *Professional Geographer* 31 (Feb.):66–74.

Business Week. 1981. Dislocations that may deepen. 1 June, pp. 62, 64.

Chapin, F. S., and S. F. Weiss, eds. 1962. *Urban growth dynamics in a regional cluster of cities.* New York: John Wiley.

Congressional Quarterly. 1981. *Congressional quarterly weekly report* 39 (10 Jan.):49–120.

Cumberland, J. H. 1971. *Regional development experiences and prospects in the United States of America.* Paris: Mouton.

Duncan, O. D., and S. Lieberson. 1970. *Metropolis and region in transition.* Beverly Hills, Calif.: Sage Publications.

Duncan, O. D., et al. 1960. *Metropolis and region.* Baltimore: Johns Hopkins University Press.

Elazar, D. J. 1970. *Cities of the prairie: The metropolitan frontier and American politics.* New York: Basic Books.

Flint, J. 1981. Trouble in the heartland. *Forbes,* 16 Mar., pp. 120–26.

Friedmann, J., and W. Alonso, eds. 1964. *Regional development and planning: A reader.* Cambridge: MIT Press.

———. 1975. *Regional policy: Readings in theory and applications.* Cambridge: MIT Press.

Friedmann, J., and C. Weaver. 1979. *Territory and function: The evolution of regional planning.* Berkeley: University of California Press.

Giertz, J. F. 1981. Taxes and economic activity in the midwestern states. Working paper in R. F. Kosobud and R. W. Resek, eds., *The Midwest economy issues & policy.* Urbana: University of Illinois, Bureau of Economic and Business Research.

Goodman, R. 1979. *The last entrepreneurs: America's regional wars for jobs and dollars.* New York: Simon and Schuster.

Hansen, N. M. 1971. *Rural poverty and the urban crisis: A strategy for regional development.* Bloomington: Indiana University Press.

Hart, J. F., ed. 1972. *Regions of the United States.* New York: Harper & Row.

———. 1976. *The South.* 2d ed. New York: Van Nostrand.

Henderson, J. M., and A. O. Krueger. 1965. *National growth and economic change in the upper Midwest.* Minneapolis: University of Minnesota Press.

Industrial Distribution. 1981. The sunbelt—shape of things to come. 71 (Jan.):49–53.

Johnson, J. A. 1981. The sunbelt and the frostbelt. *New York Times,* 29 Dec., p. 25.

Katzman, M. T., and J. W. Sommer. 1980. The fiscal health of large sunbelt and frostbelt cities. *Texas Business Review* 54 (Mar.–Apr.):61–67.

Kelly, J. 1982. Unemployment on the rise. *Time,* 8 Feb., pp. 22–28.

Kosobud, R. F., and R. W. Resek. 1981. Overview of the Midwest economy present and future. Working paper in R. F. Kosobud and R. W. Resek, eds., *The Midwest economy issues & policy.* Urbana: University of Illinois, Bureau of Economic and Business Research.

Markusen, A. R., and J. Fastrup. 1978. The regional war for federal aid. *Public Interest* 53 (Fall):87–99.

Mayer, H. M., and R. C. Wade. 1969. *Chicago: Growth of a metropolis.* Chicago: University of Chicago Press.

Miernyk, W. 1979. Resource constraints and regional development policy.

Atlantic Economic Journal 7 (Sept.):16-24.

Nemanic, G. 1981. *A bibliographical guide to midwestern literature.* Iowa City: University of Iowa Press.

Oakland, W. H., and D. E. Chall. 1979. *Measuring the economic impact of federal expenditures: A technical paper.* Columbus, Ohio: Academy for Contemporary Problems.

Odum, H. W. 1936. *Southern regions of the United States.* Chapel Hill: University of North Carolina Press.

Odum, H. W., and H. E. Moore. 1938. *American regionalism.* New York: Henry Holt.

Pack, J. R. 1982. The states' scramble for federal funds: Who wins, who loses? *Journal of Policy Analysis and Management* 1 (Winter):175-95.

Perloff, H. W., et al. 1960. *Regions, resources and economic growth.* Lincoln: University of Nebraska Press.

Perry, D. C., and A. J. Watkins, eds. 1977. *The rise of the sunbelt cities.* Beverly Hills, Calif.: Sage Publications.

Peterson, S. A. 1981. Worries on the rise of the sunbelt, too. *U.S. News and World Report,* 15 June, pp. 30-31.

Rees, J. 1979. Technological change and regional shifts in American manufacturing. *Professional Geographer* 31 (Feb.):45-54.

Resek, R. W., J. Junkus, and R. Panerali. 1981. Composition and future prospects of the Midwest. Working paper in R. F. Kosobud and R. W. Resek, eds., *The Midwest economy issues & policy.* Urbana: University of Illinois, Bureau of Economic and Business Research.

Rice, B. R. 1981. Searching for the sunbelt. *American Demographics* 3 (Mar.):22-23.

Roseman, C. C., A. J. Sofranko, and J. D. Williams. 1981. *Population redistribution in the Midwest.* Ames: Iowa State University, North Central Regional Center for Rural Development.

Russell, C., and B. Robey. 1981. Follow the sun: Census shifts explained. *American Demographics* 3 (Mar.):18-21.

Schoeplein, R. N. 1981. The federal balance of payments within Midwest states. Working paper in R. F. Kosobud and R. W. Resek, eds., *The Midwest economy issues & policy.* Urbana: University of Illinois, Bureau of Economic and Business Research.

Shaul, M. 1979. *Capital for investment in the industrial Midwest.* Columbus, Ohio: Academy for Contemporary Problems.

Sterba, J. 1976. Houston as energy capital sets pace in sun belt boom. *New York Times,* 9 Feb., p. 1.

Sternlieb, G., J. W. Hughes, eds. 1978. *Revitalizing the Northeast.* New Brunswick, N.J.: Rutgers University, Center for Urban Policy Research.

U.S. Bureau of the Census. 1981a. *1980 census of population and housing: U.S. summary—Final population and housing unit counts.* Washington, D.C.: U.S. Government Printing Office.

——. 1981b. Standard metropolitan statistical areas and consolidated statistical

areas. *Census of population*. Washington, D.C.: U.S. Government Printing Office. Supplementary Report PC80-51-5.

U.S. Congress. Congressional Budget Office. 1977. *Troubled local economies and the distribution of federal dollars*. Washington, D.C.: U.S. Government Printing Office.

U.S. Department of Labor. Bureau of Labor Statistics. 1982. *News*, 22 Jan., Table 6.

Upper Midwest Council. 1979. *Upper Midwest employment trends*. Minneapolis: Upper Midwest Council.

Vaughan, R. J., A. H. Pascal, and M. E. Vaiana. 1980. Federal urban policies: The harmful helping hand. *Taxing & Spending* 3 (Fall):27–39.

Wallis, C. 1981. Southward ho for jobs. *Time*, 11 May, p. 23.

Watkins, A. J. 1980a. Employment changes in frostbelt and sunbelt cities. *Texas Business Review* 54 (Mar.–Apr.):68–73.

———. 1980b. Good business climates. *Dissent* (Fall), pp. 476–85.

Waxmonsky, R. W. 1972. *Regional economic development in the Plains region: 1870–1960*. Urbana: University of Illinois, Department of Geography.

Weinstein, B. L., and R. E. Firestine. 1978. *Regional growth and decline in the United States: The rise of the sunbelt and the decline of the Northeast*. New York: Praeger.

Widner, R. R., and R. W. Buxbaum. 1981. The implications of population change for public policy in the Midwest. In Roseman, Sofranko, and Williams (1981).

Widner, R. R., K. D. Rainey, and J. L. Moore. 1979. *Strategies for urban transition in the industrial Midwest*. Columbus, Ohio: Academy for Contemporary Problems.

I

People and Places

2
The Population of the Midwest: Changing Composition and Distribution

CURTIS C. ROSEMAN

In the United States during the 1970s several trends in population composition and distribution became prominent and dramatically affected a variety of regions within the nation. Among these trends were: a gradual aging of the population; changes in household composition and associated decreases in household size; an increase in the number of legal and illegal immigrants; an accelerated movement of population toward the sunbelt states; and a metropolitan-to-nonmetropolitan migration stream that was larger, for the first time in memory, than its opposite.

This chapter analyzes population changes in the Midwest from 1960 to 1980 and emphasizes population redistribution patterns and the migration processes that formed these patterns. Migration, residential movement across county boundaries, is emphasized here because it is the major process that affects both the overall growth of the Midwest relative to the nation and the growth or decline of specific areas within the midwestern region. The analyses suggest that although the Midwest will experience considerably slower growth rates in the next two decades than the nation as a whole, many areas within the region will have to cope with rapid growth; other midwestern areas will face declining numbers or changing population composition.

In order to place the discussion of midwestern population trends in context, this chapter begins with a summary of important national population growth and composition trends in the 1970s. Second, national population redistribution patterns are discussed briefly. Third, patterns of change in midwestern populations are examined as they relate to interregional migration throughout the nation. Fourth, population redistribution within the Midwest during the 1960s and 1970s is examined and interpreted. The concluding section makes projections about population changes in the Midwest during the 1980s.

Population Composition Trends in the United States

Population Growth and Immigration

After a 15-year period of rapid increases in birth rates during the postwar baby boom that lasted from 1945 to 1960, birth rates steadily declined into the 1970s and may now be leveling at the lowest rates in the history of the country. In the last half of the 1970s the number of births did increase, but this was because the baby boom generation came into its fertile years. It was not the result of an increase in the birth rate. The postwar increase in the birth rate, and its more recent decline, are reflected in the overall growth rate for the nation. Between 1955 and 1965 the nation's population increased by an average of 1.6 percent per year; thereafter the rate declined gradually to the present level of 0.8 percent (Morrison, 1981).

Given the low birth rates, the nation would clearly be approaching zero population growth were it not for the net influx of international migrants. In the early 1970s approximately 20 percent of the U.S. population growth was due to net immigration. Today, after an abrupt increase in immigration during a period of lowered birth rates in the late 1970s, net immigration accounts for perhaps as much as 50 percent of U.S. population growth. This increase was caused by rises in all three major immigration categories: legal immigrants, refugees, and illegal immigrants.

In the 1970s the flow of legal immigrants rose to the highest levels since the early 1920s, but both source areas and settlement patterns for these new immigrants differed from earlier patterns. Because of changes in immigration policy in the 1960s, new sources for immigrants emerged; Asia and the West Indies replaced Europe as the dominant source regions, and countries on several continents sent substantial numbers of migrants to the United States. Legal immigrants entering this country settled in various geographical regions depending on country of origin. Asians, for example, tended to congregate on the West Coast, Europeans in large eastern cities, Mexicans in the Southwest and the Chicago area, and West Indians in Miami and New York (INS, 1970–79; Carlson, 1973).

The 1970s was also an important decade for a second type of immigrant—the refugee. The United States received large numbers of refugees from Southeast Asia and Cuba during this decade. Southeast Asian refugees initially settled throughout the nation as American communities of all sizes welcomed and hosted small numbers of them. Recently, however, a secondary migration has created concentrations of Southeast Asians in Texas (particularly Houston) and in southern California. Cubans, on the other hand, migrated in huge numbers to Florida; their impact on the Miami area is well known.

The third group, illegal or "undocumented" immigrants, is, for obvious reasons, the most difficult one to study. It seems probable that the largest segment of illegal immigrants comes from Mexico, often on a temporary basis, to the Southwest and to the Chicago area. In addition, unknown numbers of undocumented immigrants from a variety of countries live in large U.S. cities, notably New York City. A large number—but an unknown proportion—of illegal immigrants were counted in the 1980 census.

Illinois offers a striking example of the impact of immigration upon a given locality. Between 1970 and 1980 Illinois grew by about 320,000 people (U.S. Bureau of the Census, 1981b). During that decade the state received about 230,000 legal immigrants (INS, 1970–79), plus an unknown (but apparently large) number of illegal immigrants, minus an unknown (but considerably smaller) number of emigrants. It is therefore a distinct possibility that virtually the entire population growth of Illinois in the 1970s can be accounted for by immigrants from abroad! Furthermore, perhaps 70 percent of Illinois's immigrants settled in the city of Chicago and as many as 90 percent live in the Chicago metropolitan area (INS, 1970–79). In Illinois, then, as in the nation as a whole, the contribution of immigration to population growth can be significant, and, on a finer geographic scale, effects of immigration on particular places, such as Chicago, can be very substantial.

Changing Age Structure

The median age of the U.S. population has risen from 27.9 in 1970 to over 30 in 1981 (DeAre and Long, 1981). Meanwhile, the age structure of the population has been changing through the 1960s and 1970s: (1) because of the lower birth rate, relatively few children are now being added to the population; (2) the population aged 20 to 40 has increased greatly as the baby boom set matures; and (3) the elderly population has increased steadily.

There are many consequences of the declining number of children in the population, most notably in the school systems. In the United States between 1970 and 1977, the population aged 5 to 13 declined by 13 percent (Morrison, 1981). In Illinois the grade school population peaked in 1970, followed by a peak in the high school population in 1976. Both have declined considerably since those peak years, creating excess capacity and fiscal problems for many Illinois schools. Indeed, school closings are a key issue in many communities in the Midwest, especially in inner city and inner suburban areas where the population is aging ahead of the state or nation as a whole. While school-age population has declined, the U.S. population 25 to 34 years of age (a group composed of prospective homeowners) increased by 32 percent between 1970 and 1977 (Morrison, 1981).

Two demographic trends have caused the increase in the elderly population: the long-term gradual increase in life expectancy, and the aging of more and more people into the elderly category. The growing elderly population is not evenly distributed geographically. Concentrations of the elderly are found in the Phoenix, Arizona, and Tampa, Florida, areas, in other parts of Florida, and in scattered locales through the sunbelt. Within metropolitan areas, including those in the Midwest, concentrations of elderly persons are found in retirement communities or in certain neighborhoods where they constitute a residual population. In addition, large parts of the rural Great Plains, Midwest, and South are inhabited by aging populations as young people migrate steadily out. Such communities are said to be "aging in place" (Wiseman, 1978). Because of the uneven geographic distribution of the elderly, their impact on social systems such as the health care delivery system is expected to vary widely from place to place within the United States during the 1980s and 1990s.

Changing Household Size and Composition

While the population of the United States increased by some 11.4 percent during the 1970s, the number of housing units increased by 28.4 percent (Table 1). In the Midwest all states had considerable housing growth compared to population growth, although the percentage increases in both categories were uniformly lower than the national rates.

Several factors contribute to the large increase in the demand for housing units. First, lowered birth rates have meant smaller families; the average household size in the United States is now 2.7 persons, down from 4.0 in 1930 and 3.0 in 1973; it is projected to be approximately 2.3 in 1995 (DeAre and Long, 1981). Second, there have been dramatic increases in divorce, separation, and unmarried motherhood. Moreover, single young persons are delaying marriage and parenthood, affecting both the birth rate and household size and composition. Finally, increased numbers of the elderly, particularly widows, now live in individual households. For these and other reasons the number of non-

Table 1. Population and Housing Changes, 1970–80, North
Central Census Region

State	1980 Population	Percent Population Change. 1970–80	1980 Housing (Incl. Vacant)	Percent Housing Change. 1970–80
Illinois	11,418,461	2.8	4,298,088	16.1
Indiana	5,490,179	5.7	2,084,242	20.4
Iowa	2,913,387	3.1	1,129,256	17.1
Kansas	2,363,208	5.1	952,842	20.7
Michigan	9,258,344	4.3	3,584,653	21.2
Minnesota	4,077,148	7.1	1,610,097	26.1
Missouri	4,917,444	5.1	1,982,424	18.4
Nebraska	1,570,006	5.7	621,846	20.6
North Dakota	652,695	5.6	258,479	26.6
Ohio	10,797,419	1.3	4,094,526	18.1
South Dakota	690,178	3.6	276,287	22.6
Wisconsin	4,705,335	6.5	1,857,957	26.2
U.S. Total	226,504,825	11.4	88,190,034	28.4

Source: U.S. Bureau of the Census (1981a).

family households (those maintained by a man or woman living alone
or with unrelated individuals) increased by 73.1 percent from 1970 to
1978 (U.S. Bureau of the Census, 1981b).

Other related trends include the following: whereas the vast majority
of households with children under 18 years of age still have two parents
present (five out of six), the number of households with children headed
by one parent has increased. Households headed by females are up 44
percent since 1970 to over 6 million and the labor force participation rate
for women increased from 43 to 52 percent between 1970 and 1980 (U.S.
Bureau of the Census, 1981b).

Population Redistribution

The national pattern of geographic redistribution of population
experienced in the 1970s is intimately connected with many of the factors
discussed above, and it is also of fundamental importance to the understanding of Midwest population changes. Migration is the principal
mechanism by which the population is redistributed within the United

States. Because so many Americans move between communities, internal migration is even more important than immigration in determining the differential growth of American localities and regions.

During the nineteenth and well into the twentieth century the dominant migration pattern was rural to urban, farm to factory, as employment opportunities in the manufacturing sector replaced those in the agricultural sector. Migration from the rural South to the urban Midwest was a significant part of this movement, particularly after World War I, and it contributed to the rapid twentieth-century growth of a good number of midwestern cities. Before World War I many urban jobs were taken by European immigrants, but when immigration was severely restricted in the 1920s, both blacks and whites from the rural South replaced immigrants in city jobs. Concomitant with the rural-to-urban trend was a westward movement and, after World War II, the emergence of fast-growing "amenity" areas like southern California, Arizona, and Florida. Furthermore, federal defense spending and other government expenditures in the South and West have encouraged people to move to these areas in search of employment.

Two important changes in these long-standing patterns occurred in the 1970s (Morrison and Wheeler, 1976; Roseman, 1977). First, growth in the sunbelt expanded spatially. Whereas migration tended to focus on Florida and southern California from the 1940s through the 1960s, today there is widespread migration-caused growth in broader areas of the South and West, including the entire West Coast, much of the interior West, most of east Texas, the Missouri and Arkansas Ozarks, and large portions of the Appalachian region.

The second change was more dramatic and not unrelated to the sunbelt movement. Since about 1970, and for the first time in our history, more people have been moving toward nonmetropolitan areas than toward metropolitan areas. This "rural renaissance" has created unprecedented growth in many rural areas in the Midwest and Northeast, such as northern Wisconsin and Michigan and northern New England, in addition to rural locales in the sunbelt. Added to this is the growth of nonmetropolitan areas near the fringes of metropolitan areas all over the country. In general, nonmetropolitan areas with climatic, scenic, or recreational amenities are growing most rapidly, whether or not they are in the sunbelt. On the other side of the coin, many metropolitan areas, including some of the larger ones, are losing population. In fact, many were losing population through migration in the 1960s, a trend that was obscured by high birth rates until the 1970s, when these cities began to experience an overall loss of population. Between 1970 and 1980, 8 of the 20 largest Standard Metropolitan Statistical Areas in the United States lost population (including Detroit, St. Louis, and Cleveland in the Midwest) and an additional 5, including Chicago, grew by less than 5 percent (*Numbers News*, 1981).

It is important to note that neither of these trends, the sunbelt migration or the nonmetropolitan migration, is a one-way stream. For every ten persons moving to the sunbelt in the southern and western United States, five are moving to the frostbelt in the Midwest and Northeast. For every ten persons relocating in nonmetropolitan areas, eight are moving toward metropolitan areas (U.S. Bureau of the Census, 1981c). Thus, although the net shifts are clear, individual migrants are moving against each trend in fairly large numbers.

Underlying Reasons

Reasons for the two population redistribution trends of the 1970s are interrelated.[1] First there has been a dispersal of jobs toward the sunbelt. This is largely due to more new jobs being created in the sunbelt than in the frostbelt rather than to the migration of existing jobs from the frostbelt to the sunbelt. Relatively more jobs are also available in nonmetropolitan America. In the Midwest, for example, 20 percent of the manufacturing jobs were in nonmetropolitan areas in 1947, but the figure is now approaching 30 percent (Lonsdale, 1981). Not only are jobs dispersing geographically in particular sectors such as manufacturing, but the overall structure of employment is changing. Whereas the primary sector (agriculture and mining) and secondary sector (manufacturing) are declining relatively, the tertiary sector (sales and services) is expanding rapidly. So too are the government and quaternary sectors, which, like the tertiary sector, tend to be geographically dispersed throughout the country. Thus gradual changes in the structure of employment have contributed to the dispersal of the population, both toward the sunbelt and toward nonmetropolitan areas.

Another major factor pertains to people—their availability to move and their residential location preferences. There are more Americans today who are free to move from one locale to another than there were a generation ago. The proportion of our population supported by non-earnings income, including welfare, social security, rent, and dividends, has risen from 18 percent in 1950 to over 30 percent today (Beyers, 1979). This category, of course, includes the increasing numbers of elderly, and in general it comprises a set of people who are not tied to a particular work location and therefore can potentially live where they choose.

Personal tastes and preferences also affect migration patterns. The general results of residential preference studies show that the middle-

and upper-middle-class white population prefers to live in the country, in small towns, or in the sunbelt (Fuguitt and Zuiches, 1975). There are apparently both repulsions and attractions underlying these preferences. Many citizens perceive metropolitan areas, including suburbs, as beset with fiscal, crime, and quality-of-life problems, whereas they see small towns and rural areas as insulated from those problems. In the 1970s more and more people were able to convert their desires into actual residential moves.

The preference surveys also show that the majority of those who prefer to live in small towns or rural areas would also like to be near, but not in, a metropolitan area. As a result, a high percentage—perhaps over 60 percent—of the nonmetropolitan growth is occurring in places that are near, and often within commuting distance of, the fringes of metropolitan areas. Growth of these "exurban" places has been made possible in part by the suburbanization of jobs to the metropolitan fringe during the 1960s and 1970s (Fuguitt and Zuiches, 1975).

In addition to the dispersal of jobs, the increased freedom to move, and changing preferences during the 1970s, this period was also one during which a geographic phenomenon tied together people in metropolitan areas with places in nonmetropolitan America, and connected people in the frostbelt with places in the sunbelt (Roseman and Williams, 1980). These place ties have been built up through a variety of geographic behaviors. Many people have roots in nonmetropolitan or sunbelt places, such as, for example, blacks in Chicago who grew up (or whose parents grew up) in Mississippi and whites in Chicago who grew up in midwestern rural areas. Other people have become tied to rural or sunbelt places because of repeated vacation visits. Still others have become attached to places because they were in the military or college there, have visited friends or relatives who live there, or have traveled to these places for business or other reasons.

Thus, to many people residing in any midwestern metropolitan area, the "sunbelt" or the "country" is not a distant or mysterious place; it refers to familiar communities in which social, psychological, or even economic (such as property ownership) attachments have already been solidified. The existence of such ties explains the growth of many particular areas. For instance, the recent growth of northern Wisconsin is apparently caused in large part by people who migrate (sometimes upon retirement) from Chicago or Milwaukee to the only rural setting they know about—the place where they have ties through family roots or through repeated vacation stays.

Going against this trend is the smaller flow of people back to the city. There are large areas within Chicago, New York, Philadelphia, and other cities in which "gentrification," or revitalization, is taking place. Those who move to such areas often come from the suburbs. In relation to the movement outward toward the suburbs, however, this flow is still small, and there are important qualitative differences between the two migrations. The outward movement tends to be made up of families, whereas the movement inward includes many young single persons and professional-class couples. The result is that central cities are still declining in population, although not as rapidly as in the late 1960s, but the composition of population in central cities is becoming more diverse.

The Midwest and National Population Redistribution

During the 1970s both the West North Central (that part of the Midwest which is west of the Mississippi River) and the East North Central census divisions grew in population at rates considerably less than the nation as a whole (Table 2). This pattern is clearly related to the sunbelt/frostbelt differential in population growth: each census division in the West and South grew at rates greater than the national level, and each of those in the North Central and Northeast grew at lesser rates. At the extreme, the Middle-Atlantic division, which encompasses many very large metropolitan areas, lost population in the 1970s.

Table 2. Population Growth by Census Regions and Divisions, 1970–80

Region/Division	1980 Population	Absolute Change, 1970–80	Percent Change, 1970–80
West	43,165,199	8,326,956	23.9
Mountain	11,368,330	3,078,429	37.1
Pacific	31,796,869	5,248,527	19.8
South	75,349,155	12,536,175	20.0
South Atlantic	36,943,139	6,264,313	20.4
East South Central	14,662,882	1,854,805	14.5
West South Central	23,743,134	4,417,057	22.9
North Central	58,853,804	2,263,510	4.0
East North Central	41,669,738	1,406,991	3.5
West North Central	17,184,066	856,519	5.2
Northeast	49,136,667	76,153	0.2
New England	12,348,493	501,248	4.2
Middle Atlantic	36,788,174	−425,095	−1.1
U.S. Total	226,504,825	23,202,794	11.4

Source: U.S. Bureau of the Census (1981a).

The continued sunbelt growth results largely from migration trends that have been gradually evolving for several decades rather than from changes that suddenly began in the 1970s. The following section will examine the flows of migrants to and from the Midwest during the late 1970s and will trace some of the changes in these flows from the two previous decades.

Regional Interchanges: Net Migration and Efficiency

Migration between the Midwest (the North Central census division) and the other three census divisions has been measured for various periods by the Census Bureau. For this study three time periods have been chosen: migration for 1955–60 and 1965–70 from the respective decennial censuses (U.S. Bureau of the Census, 1963, 1973), and migration for 1975–80 from the March 1980 Current Population Survey (U.S. Bureau of the Census, 1981c).

Over the last three decades the North Central region has gradually shifted in its net exchange with other regions. Net migration figures (Table 3) indicate that the region has been receiving an increasing volume of migrants from the Northeast during the study period, although in relatively modest numbers. The North Central region has lost much greater numbers to the West and South (the sunbelt). The largest net loss was to the West in the 1955–60 period, but the smaller net losses to that region in 1965–70 and 1975–80 corresponded with steady increases in the losses to the South. This is one indication that the sunbelt movement is no longer focused dominantly on a few places, such as southern California and Florida, as it was in the 1950s.

Table 3. Net Migration and Efficiency of Migration between the Midwest and Three Other Regions, 1955–60, 1965–70, and 1975–80

| Period | Net Migration in Thousands (Efficiency) | | |
	Northeast	South	West
1955–60	+40 (6.0)	−123 (−6.0)	−760 (−49.9)
1965–70	+53 (6.3)	−275 (−12.0)	−406 (−26.0)
1975–80	+144 (21.2)	−738 (−28.0)	−579 (−31.5)

Source: Calculated by author; data from U.S. Bureau of the Census (1963, 1973, 1981c).

Net migration data, however, provide insufficient information for the adequate examination of interregional population shifts. Any net migration figure is the product of two gross migration streams passing each other in opposite directions. When the individual streams are considerably larger than the net difference, the total amount of migratory activity vastly overshadows the net result. To assess the relative importance of gross versus net interregional streams affecting the Midwest, an efficiency measure is utilized.[2] A high efficiency value indicates that the flow in one direction is much higher than in the other, so that the migration exchange between two places is characterized by a near one-way flow. This is an unusual occurrence in migration streams, because there are many forces (communication linkages, family and friendship ties, potential return migrants) that reciprocate between pairs of places and therefore tend to stimulate migration in both directions. In an inefficient situation the two gross flows are relatively close in size, meaning that many migrants move each way with little net effect.[3]

Efficiencies of streams to and from the Midwest (Table 3) are highly varied. With respect to the Northeast, the values are low but increasing, showing that the Midwest is gradually gaining a larger share of the gross migration that links these two regions. Linkages with the South started in the 1950s at low efficiency levels as considerable rural-to-urban migration of both blacks and whites was directed northward, while large migrations to Florida and the growing southern cities balanced the equation. The efficiency has increased substantially since then, so that the southward movement is now beginning to dominate the system. By far the highest efficiencies occur in the migration streams to and from the West. In the 1950s this linkage was dominated by a westward movement, but in the later decades this domination waned somewhat as the migration system matured into one characterized more by two-way movement.

Gross Migration Flows

An examination of gross flows yields more information about the major interregional distribution trends (Table 4). With respect to the Northeast, gross flows in both directions in the recent period are considerably lower than in the 1960s, indicating a lessening of migration potential between the two regions as the migration potential of both regions with the sunbelt increases. Nonetheless, the net gain of the Midwest from the Northeast has increased (Table 3).

The dramatic increase in net migration and efficiency with respect to the South was largely the product of increases in migration *from* the Midwest (from 1,089,000 in 1955–60 to 1,688,000 in 1975–80) (Table 4), rather than from any significant change in migration from the South to

Table 4. Outmigration from the Midwest, 1955–60, 1965–70, and 1975–80

| Period | Migrants in Thousands (Percentage) from the Midwest to: | | | |
	Northeast	South	West	Total
1955–60	314 (12.3)	1,089 (42.8)	1,142 (44.9)	2,545 (100.0)
1965–70	395 (14.9)	1,282 (48.2)	932 (36.9)	2,661 (100.0)
1975–80	268 (8.5)	1,688 (53.3)	1,210 (38.2)	3,166 (100.0)

Source: Calculated by author; data from U.S. Bureau of the Census (1963, 1973, 1981c).

Table 5. Inmigration to the Midwest, 1955–60, 1965–70, and 1975–80

| Period | Migrants in Thousands (Percentage) to the Midwest from: | | | |
	Northeast	South	West	Total
1955–60	354 (20.8)	966 (56.8)	382 (22.4)	1,702 (100.0)
1965–70	450 (22.1)	1,007 (49.5)	576 (28.3)	2,033 (100.0)
1975–80	412 (20.6)	950 (47.7)	631 (31.7)	1,993 (100.0)

Source: Calculated by author; data from U.S. Bureau of the Census (1963, 1973, 1981c).

the North Central region (Table 5). Whereas there were significant decreases in particular segments of the south-to-north streams, such as the interregional rural-to-urban movement of blacks, there was an over-all stability in the northward stream. Much of the South-to-Midwest migration is now inter-urban in nature. Increases in Midwest-to-South migration have been much more varied, both demographically, as the black, white, and elderly streams have increased, and geographically, as midwesterners have moved both to southern cities and to nonmetropoli-tan amenity areas such as the Arkansas Ozarks, parts of Appalachia, east Texas, and Florida.

Movement from the Midwest to the West has been relatively stable (Table 4), although gradually increasing. In the last two decades, how-ever, the migration stream *from* the West to the Midwest was larger than in the 1955–60 period, apparently for two reasons: (1) the West has ma-tured economically as a region since the surge of westward migration in the 1950s, promoting migration exchange in both directions; and (2) many people who were part of the massive westward movement of the 1950s either returned in later decades or established kinship and com-munications networks between the two regions upon which later migrants depended in moving to the Midwest. As in the case of the movement to the South, the stream to the West is quite diversified, and a wide variety of western localities are drawing midwestern migrants, including rural amenity areas, major cities, retirement communities, and the many western areas in which energy sources are being developed.

In summary, the most dynamic stream of interregional migration between the Midwest and other regions has been the one from the Midwest to the South, as indicated by the distribution of outmigration among the regions (Table 4). Reorientation of outward migration toward the South is the major factor in the changing migration linkages between the Midwest and the remainder of the country. This reorientation is part of the sunbelt movement in general, a movement that has resulted in considerable urban and rural growth in a variety of localities throughout the South in the 1970s.

Population Redistribution within the Midwest

Intraregional migration is an important phenomenon in the Midwest; approximately 10 million people moved from one county to another between 1975 and 1980 (U.S. Bureau of the Census, 1981c). Again, migration is more important than differential natural population change in determining the variation in growth from place to place within the region. For this reason, the examination of county-level population changes in this section will rely largely upon interpretations rooted in intraregional migration patterns.

Absolute Population Changes, 1970–80

Just as the sunbelt migration movement affects regional population growth differentials, so do the suburban, exurban, and metropolitan-to-nonmetropolitan movements determine redistribution within the Midwest. When the raw numbers of population change between 1970 and 1980 are examined by county (Figure 1), the suburban and, to some extent, exurban trends are isolated. The big losers were the counties containing the larger cities, for example, Chicago, Detroit, Cleveland, Cincinnati, St. Louis, and Milwaukee. Beyond the big cities, few counties suffered large numerical losses. Conversely, the large gainers were the "collar" counties forming bands around such cities as Chicago, Detroit, Cleveland, and Minneapolis–St. Paul. Thus the largest population gains and the largest losses within the Midwest tend to occur in areas that are close together.

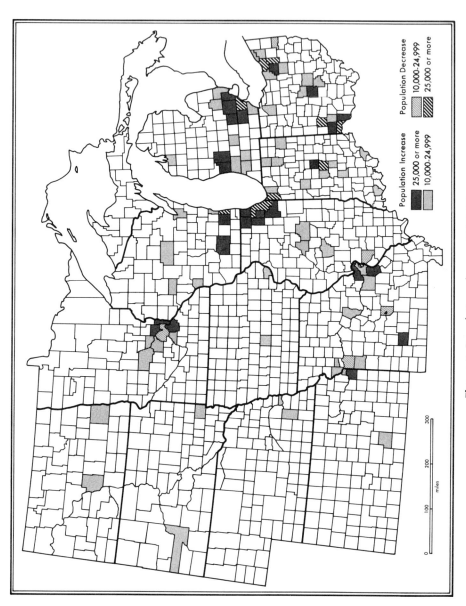

Figure 1. Population change, 1970–80.

Population Increase
- 25,000 or more
- 10,000-24,999

Population Decrease
- 10,000-24,999
- 25,000 or more

miles
0   100   200   300

Counties containing small and medium-sized metropolitan areas, such as Sioux Falls, Wichita, Lincoln, Des Moines, Springfield, Illinois, Fort Wayne, Madison, and Lansing also gained population, although at a lesser rate than the "collar" counties. This is partly explained by the fact that at this smaller urban scale, suburban growth is contained within one county, counterbalancing inner city population declines. Nonetheless, many of these medium-sized metropolitan centers are growing in jobs and population partly at the expense of large ones. Some of these cities are also seats of major universities or state capitals; they exemplify the importance of nonlocal government activities as a stimulant to growth in the 1970s (Roseman, Ives, and Shelley, 1980).

Relative Population Changes, 1960–70 and 1970–80

Redistribution trends affecting counties with smaller populations are better analyzed by considering relative rather than absolute population change. Comparison of counties losing more than 10 percent of their population between 1960 and 1970 (Figure 2) and between 1970 and 1980 (Figure 3) reveals a distinct shrinkage in the area of major population loss in the 1970s. In the earlier decade (Figure 2) substantial loss of population was experienced in a wedge-shaped sector including most of Iowa, the Dakotas, Nebraska, and Kansas, plus northern Missouri and southwestern Minnesota. In this sector rural-to-urban migration of the young was still the rule and populations were aging in place as a result. In fact, parts of this region lost population during the 1960s not because of outmigration but through natural processes, that is, more deaths than births, because the long history of rural outmigration before the 1960s had left a fairly old residual population. Other areas of substantial loss include parts of "Ozarkian" southern Illinois, the Mississippi Delta extension into the boot heel of Missouri, and parts of the upper peninsula of Michigan—all places that had experienced significant net outmigration from mining or agricultural economies for decades.

By the 1970s (Figure 3) the area of greater than 10 percent population loss constricted considerably. In that decade it was limited for the most part to a number of counties in the Great Plains, especially those along the humid/arid border through the central parts of the Dakotas, Nebraska, and Kansas. In general, these counties are heavily dependent upon agriculture and have very high percentages of rural farm population (Rogers et al., 1974). In addition, by the 1970s some counties containing large cities—Wayne County (Detroit) and Cuyahoga County (Cleveland)—had passed the 10 percent loss threshold, and the more

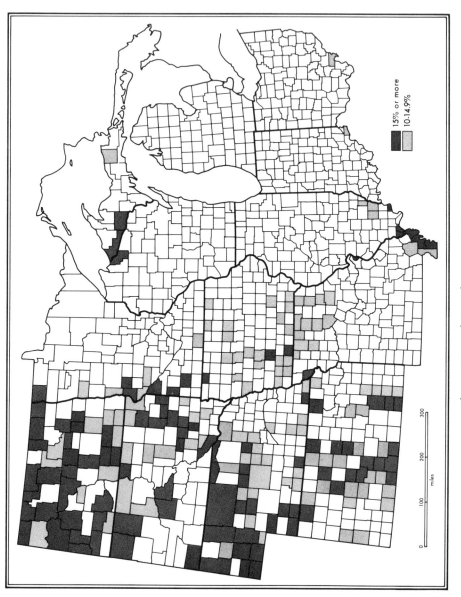

Figure 2. Population decrease, 1960–70.

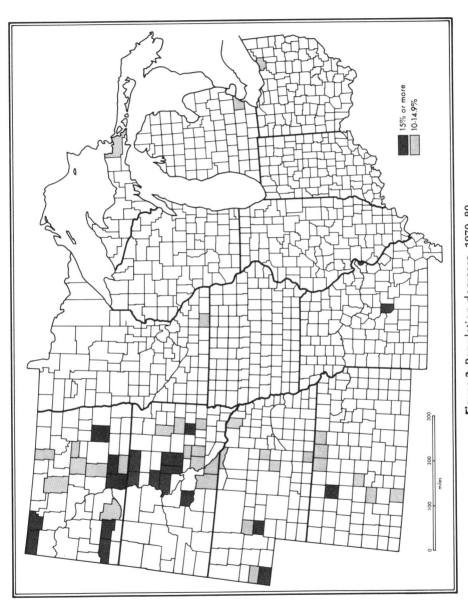

Figure 3. Population decrease, 1970–80.

spatially restricted independent city of St. Louis had reached a loss of 27.7 percent.

As expected, important relative population increases (Figures 4 and 5) show an expanding pattern from the 1960s through the 1970s. In the earlier decade large relative increases occurred in suburban and exurban counties around large cities such as Minneapolis–St. Paul, Kansas City, St. Louis, Milwaukee–Chicago, Indianapolis, Detroit, Cincinnati–Dayton, and Cleveland. Other clusters include vacation/amenity areas in the northern part of lower Michigan and some counties in central Wisconsin and the Missouri Ozarks. For the most part, however, growth of suburban counties dominated the population redistribution pattern during the 1960s.

A notable spread of significant relative growth into recreation/amenity areas is evident in the 1970s (Figure 5). This is consistent with Beale and Fuguitt's (1981) observation that within the Midwest (and in the nation as a whole), a slowing overall population growth has been accompanied by population increase in a greater number of counties.

Major recreation/amenity areas have expanded to encompass most of the northern half of lower Michigan and a broad area of northern Wisconsin and Minnesota, including, in the latter case, some exurban growth near Minneapolis–St. Paul. Sources of migrants to these areas reflect the individual decisions that underlie much of the migration to these and other developing amenity areas (Roseman and Williams, 1980). The flow to the Michigan area was predominantly from Detroit in the 1970s, and much of the flow to the Minnesota/Wisconsin area was from Chicago, Milwaukee, and Minneapolis–St. Paul. In many cases previous ties to these amenity areas, mostly through vacation experiences, were found to be influential in the choices of the migrants from those cities, indicating that the population growth of these areas is at least partly affected by the large number of people who had vacationed there in the past. In general, vacation ties today are helping to shape future American migration patterns. However, in both Michigan and Wisconsin/Minnesota a few return migrants also contributed to the recent growth (Roseman and Williams, 1980).

The case of the Missouri Ozarks, another major recreation/amenity area, is similar in process to the Michigan and Minnesota/Wisconsin cases but somewhat different in terms of source areas. Migrants come from a wider variety of places, including Kansas City, St. Louis, Chicago, and many locales. Many of these migrants may have vacationed previously in the Ozarks. Moreover, some people had previously lived in Missouri, most of whom migrated from as far as the West Coast. As an amenity area, then, the Missouri Ozarks region has a broad appeal,

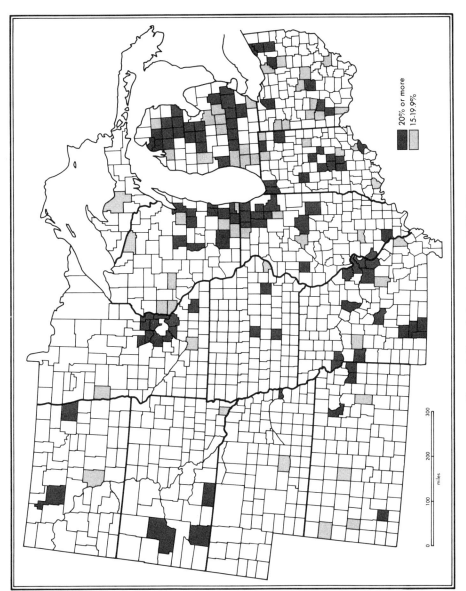

Figure 4. Population increase, 1960–70.

20% or more

15-19.9%

0   100   200   300

miles

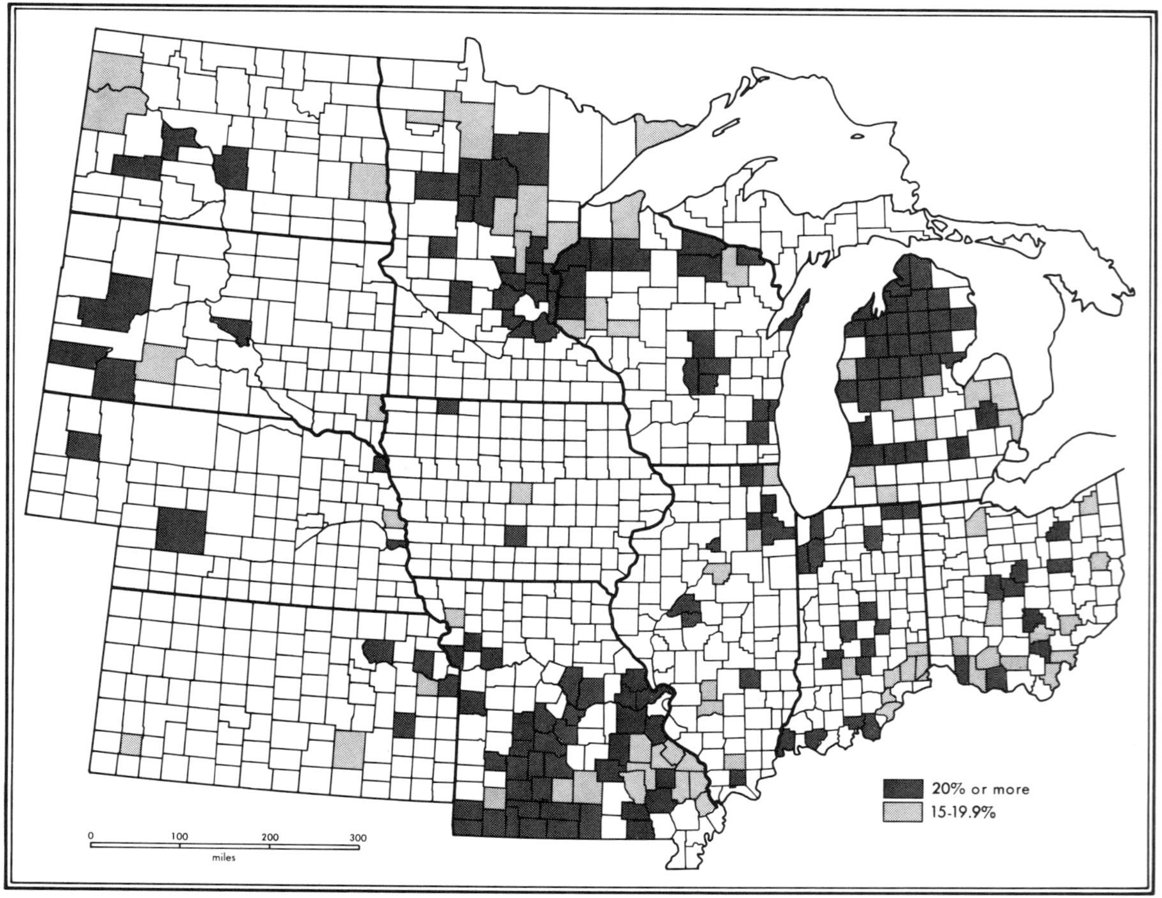

Figure 5. Population increase, 1970–80.

20% or more

15-19.9%

0   100   200   300
miles

owing partly to its central and accessible location within the nation and partly to a previous history of outmigration to a variety of locations including the West Coast (Roseman and Williams, 1980).

Smaller, environmentally similar areas experienced surges of migration in the 1970s as well, including southern Indiana and Ohio (Figure 5). Beyond that, only scattered nonmetropolitan areas grew significantly within the Midwest. Migration to the suburbs and exurbs showed a pattern similar to that seen in the 1960s, although some of the older (in both demographic and urban settlement senses) suburban counties, such as Oakland County, Michigan, Lake County, Illinois, and St. Louis County, Missouri, did not grow as rapidly as they did in the 1960s.

Growth/Decline Shifts: 1960–70 to 1970–80

A comprehensive picture of the recent dynamics of population distribution within the Midwest requires direct comparison of the population change pattern of the 1960s with that of the 1970s. For that purpose this analysis utilizes a four-way classification of counties based upon whether they grew or declined in each of the two decades.

First, a large number of counties within the region gained population in both decades (Figure 6). They are found in a broad band within the American "manufacturing belt" (bounded roughly by Flint, Milwaukee, Cedar Rapids, St. Louis, Columbus, and Wheeling, West Virginia). The emerging amenity areas of the northern part of lower Michigan, northern Wisconsin/Minnesota, and southern Missouri also grew in both decades. Most of the remaining counties that experienced growth in the 1960s and 1970s are in or near metropolitan areas, including many in the western part of the region, such as Kansas City, Omaha, Des Moines, and Minneapolis–St. Paul.

Second, counties that turned the "wrong way"—from gain to loss (Figure 6)—included a few in the Great Plains, where the population numbers were often very small. More significant were the losses suffered by the central counties of major metropolitan areas, particularly in the eastern half of the region, such as Milwaukee and Cook (Chicago), Wayne (Detroit), and Hamilton (Cincinnati). Third, counties with losses in both decades (Figure 7) are largely confined to the wedge-shaped areas of agriculturally dominated counties in the Great Plains and Iowa. Finally, positive "turnaround" counties (Figure 7) are those that have been of particular interest to social scientists in the 1970s as evidence of a "rural renaissance" (Morrison and Wheeler, 1976). In the Midwest, from 1960 to 1980, many more counties went from loss to gain

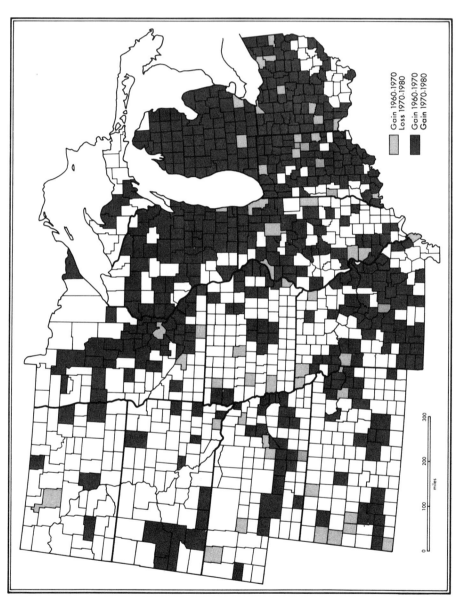

Figure 6. Population changes, 1960–70 and 1970–80—(gain/loss-gain/gain).

Gain 1960-1970
Loss 1970-1980

Gain 1960-1970
Gain 1970-1980

0   100   200   300
miles

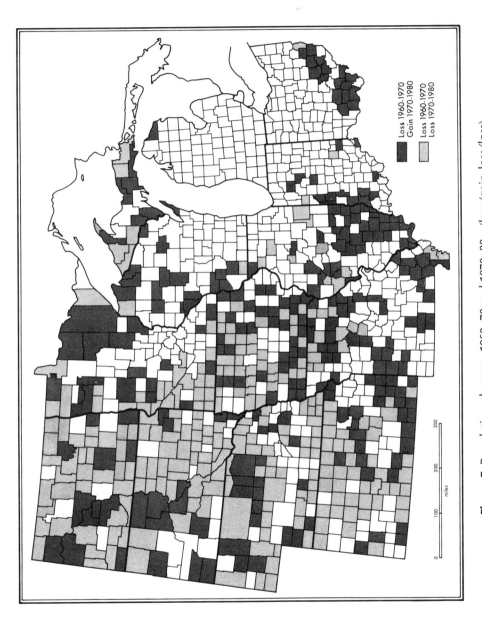

Figure 7. Population changes, 1960–70 and 1970–80—(loss/gain-loss/loss).

than from gain to loss. They tended to be located on the margins of the wedge of agriculturally dominated counties in the western part of the region and on the margins of the spatially expanding amenity areas in Michigan, Wisconsin, Minnesota, Missouri, southern Ohio, and southern Illinois.

Conclusion

Although projections of growth rates for the Midwest through the year 2000 vary depending upon assumptions about interstate migration (Morrison, 1981), it is clear that continued slowing of growth will characterize the population of the region as well as of the nation as a whole. In the 1980s the population growth of the Midwest will lag behind that of the nation, a reflection of the general interregional shifts of both economic activities and people toward the sunbelt, a trend that is not likely to reverse itself in the foreseeable future.

Apart from the lower rates of overall population growth, however, the trends in midwestern population composition and distribution generally reflect those of the nation. The region has experienced a reduction in the average size of households but an increase in the number of households and a gradual aging of its population. The impacts of these trends are as visible in the Midwest as in other regions, and include increased housing demand because of the increase in number of households, the closing of urban schools while new schools are being built in the exurbs, and the need for more services for older persons.

In addition, the Midwest is sharing in the migration events that have led to notable geographic variation in population growth. Significant exurban growth is taking place on the fringes of virtually every metropolitan area in the region. The exurban movement, rooted deeply in the preference of the middle and upper-middle classes for living in small towns or bucolic environments, is not likely to halt in the 1980s, unless major energy shortages severely constrain automobile commuting.

The Midwest, too, possesses established and still-growing amenity areas: the Missouri Ozarks and the northern portion of lower Michigan, plus emerging amenity areas in northern Wisconsin/Minnesota and southern Ohio/Indiana/Illinois. Just as growing job opportunities in the sunbelt plus the ties of many midwesterners to the South will draw many midwesterners outside of the region, the ties of midwestern metropolitan residents to these developing amenity areas will keep many people within the region.

The areas that are experiencing major population declines within the region are of two types: a steadily diminishing number of agriculturally dependent counties in all parts of the region, and a few counties that contain large central cities. The overall decline of the former will gradually wane as such areas sink to their population minima. The decline of the central city counties may wane too, but the more important trend of the 1980s will be the increased diversification of their populations. Minority populations will continue to reside primarily in central cities; upper-middle-class whites, including many young singles and couples, will continue to migrate into central cities; and the immigrant population will continue to be drawn to central city destinations.

Thus, in terms of fundamental population trends and their impacts, the Midwest is in many ways a microcosm of the United States as a whole. Internal variations in the geographic patterns of growth and decline are substantial in both cases. While the Midwest as a whole will continue to grow slowly in population, many areas within the region will encounter the varied problems that accompany rapid growth, decline, or changing population composition and distribution.

Notes

1. Detailed discussions of the reasons can be found in Morrison and Wheeler (1976), Roseman (1977), Morrill (1978), and DeAre and Long (1981).

2. Migration efficiency, E_{ij}, is computed as follows:

$$E_{ij} = N_{ij}/(M_{ij} + M_{ji}) \times 100$$

where M_{ij} = gross migration from region i to region j
M_{ji} = gross migration from region j to region i
$N_{ij} = M_{ij} - M_{ji}$

3. It must be noted, however, that while there may be little numerical net effect in this situation, there can be considerable qualitative effect; e.g., the demographic structure of the two opposing streams could be different, impacting the current population composition and future population growth rates of each area differentially.

References

Beale, C. L., and G. V. Fuguitt. 1981. Demographic perspectives on midwestern population redistribution. In C. C. Roseman et al., eds., *Population redistribution in the Midwest*. Ames: University of Iowa, North Central Regional Center for Rural Development.

Beyers, W. B. 1979. Contemporary trends in the regional economic development of the United States. *Professional Geographer* 31 (Feb.):34–44.

Carlson, A. U. 1973. Recent immigration, 1961–1970, a factor in the growth and distribution of the United States population. *Journal of Geography* 72:8–18.

DeAre, D., and L. Long. 1981. Meet the average American. *American Demographics* 3 (Apr.):22–27.

Fuguitt, G. V., and J. J. Zuiches. 1975. Residential preferences and population distribution. *Demography* 12:491–504.

Immigration and Naturalization Service. 1970–79. *Annual report*. Washington, D.C.: U.S. Government Printing Office.

Lonsdale, R. E. 1981. Industry's role in nonmetropolitan economic development and population change. In C. C. Roseman et al., eds., *Population redistribution in the Midwest*. Ames: University of Iowa, North Central Regional Center for Rural Development.

Morrill, R. L. 1978. Population redistribution, 1965–1975. *Growth and Change* 9:35–43.

Morrison, P. A. 1981. The transition to zero population growth in the Midwest. In C. C. Roseman et al., eds., *Population redistribution in the Midwest*. Ames: University of Iowa, North Central Regional Center for Rural Development.

Morrison, P.A., and J. P. Wheeler. 1976. Rural renaissance in America? The revival of population growth in remote areas. *Population Bulletin: 31*. Washington, D.C.: Population Reference Bureau.

Numbers News. 1981. Supplement to *American Demographics*. 16 Mar.

Rogers, K. D., et al. 1974. *The state of economic and social development in the North Central region of the United States*. Ames: University of Iowa, North Central Regional Center for Rural Development.

Roseman, C. C. 1977. *Changing migration patterns within the United States*. Washington, D.C.: Associaton of American Geographers, Resource Paper 77–2.

Roseman, C. C., S. M. Ives, and F. M. Shelley. 1980. An AID analysis of factors associated with contemporary net migration in the United States. *Geographical Perspectives* 45 (Spring):15–24.

Roseman, C. C., and J. D. Williams. 1980. Metropolitan to nonmetropolitan migration: A decision-making perspective. *Urban Geography* 1 (Oct.–Dec.):283–94.

U.S. Bureau of the Census. 1963. State of birth. *Census of population: 1960*. Washington, D.C.: U.S. Government Printing Office, Final Report PC (2)–2A.

———. 1973. Mobility for states and the nation. *Census of population: 1970*. Washington, D.C.: U.S. Government Printing Office, Final Report PC(2)–2A.

———. 1981a. U.S. summary, final population and housing unit counts. *1980 census of population and housing*. Washington, D.C.: U.S. Government Printing Office, Advance Reports PHC 80–V–1.

———. 1981b. Population profile of the United States. *Current population reports*. Washington, D.C.: U.S. Government Printing Office, Series P–20, No. 351–360.

———. 1981c. Geographic mobility: March 1975 to March 1980. *Current popula-*

tion reports. Washington, D.C.: U.S. Government Printing Office, Series P-20, No. 368.

Wiseman, R. F. 1978. *Spatial aspects of aging*. Washington, D.C.: Association of American Geographers, Resource Paper 78-4.

3

Energy Costs and Land Use Patterns in Metropolitan Chicago

ARTHUR GETIS

In the United States the population flight out of cities has continued unabated from just after World War II to the present. Except during several recessions, the rate of movement has been remarkably steady. Initially, people moved to the far reaches of the central city and to the inner suburbs, but today the inner suburbs have joined the central city as an origin area of outmigration. The destinations for those who leave American metropolitan areas are both the outer suburbs and other regions of the country. The forces at work to bring about this movement have changed from time to time, but the results have been uniform: a vast abandonment of central cities in all parts of the country. Some observers have suggested that the small but increasing numbers of returning migrants represent the vanguard of a reversal in migration patterns and that as energy costs increase, the process of suburbanization will end and new patterns of urban development will begin to appear. This chapter examines these suppositions by looking at the effects of increased energy costs in intra-urban migration, using the foremost metropolis in the Midwest, Chicago, as a case study.

The nature of the outmigration of people from Chicago between 1945 and 1973, the year of the first energy crisis, is well known. As in all of the older metropolitan areas of the country with high inner city population densities, Chicago's suburban migration was fostered by postwar increases in real income and in family size, by the availability of automobiles, by the improved highway system, and, not least, by the white response to the black immigration to the central city. After 1960 improved industrial technology freed many manufacturers from urban rail links, congested old plants, and urban suppliers so that many firms also moved to the suburbs, thus reinforcing the residential movement pattern already underway. By the 1970s industrialists counted access to suburban workers as an added incentive to relocate, and so the suburbanization of industries accelerated.

In the first intra-urban migration wave of the 1960s, such inner suburban communities as Addison, Bellwood, Chicago Heights, Cicero, Des Plaines, Evanston, Franklin Park, Maywood, Melrose Park, Niles, and Skokie became workplace foci for the growing numbers of people in those communities and in the nearby residential communities of Arlington Heights, Berwyn, Calumet City, Downers Grove, Elmhurst, Harvey, Lombard, Mount Prospect, Oak Lawn, Park Ridge, and many smaller suburbs (Figure 1).[1] For the first time reverse commuting from Chicago to the suburbs became noticeable. In the 1970s the outer suburbs of Bolingbrook, Buffalo Grove, Wheeling, Hoffman Estates, Schaumburg, Hanover Park, Glendale Heights, Wheaton, Naperville, Woodridge, Orland Park, and Tinley Park were the chief recipients of the outmigrants. These communities, like those in the first group, form a giant half-oval around Chicago. The mean distance at its narrowest point for the inner suburbs is only about 12 miles from the Loop, while the distance to Wheaton, for example, in the outer suburbs is about 25 miles. The questions that suggest themselves are these: Have energy costs affected the outmigration of people, industry, and commerce? Do energy costs affect the rate at which the suburbanization process takes place? As energy costs increase, will the process of suburbanization in the Chicago area end and new patterns of urbanization take form? What effect will higher energy costs have on Chicago's central business district?

The General Effect of Higher Energy Costs on Migration

Before considering Chicago specifically, we shall look at migration and its relation to energy costs in two ways. First, we will consider the simple and somewhat artificial case in which transportation expenses are the only rising costs in both household and entrepreneurial budgets. Second, we will consider rising energy costs in the context of actual life, where individual people can take steps to alleviate their effects.

In the first instance individuals weigh the costs of moving against the loss of income engendered by increased commuting costs. When the balance favors moving, these people will obviously consider relocating closer to their workplaces. For industries, however, the process is not so straightforward. Because corporations must usually devote a larger portion of their total costs to transportation than individual workers do, entrepreneurs will consider closely the increased expenses for material shipments, but they also will take into account the cost of having

Figure 1. Chicago Standard Metropolitan Statistical Area.

workers commute to the firm's site. If most workers live in the suburbs, it may be in the firm's best interests to relocate near them. This would be the case for certain commercial activities, especially those dependent on skilled labor or intensive managerial inputs. For most firms, however, the tendency would be to remain as close to suppliers, shippers, and transportation terminals as possible. When most firms follow this pattern, the result will be a compact, high-density urban area in which workers commute relatively short distances. Two studies add credence to this assertion. Romanos (1978) subjects higher energy costs to utility analysis and concludes that their effect will probably be the establishment of residential areas sited closer to employment locations. He suggests that future development will take the form of more compact development around suburban nuclei, with lower densities in the areas between centers. Waymire and Waymire (1980), although not in complete agreement with Romanos, conclude from their analysis and modification of various well-known urban models that a rise in energy prices will generate centralizing urban adjustments.

In the second, more realistic instance, energy consumption patterns are more complicated than in the first case. The two largest consumers of energy in the United States are automobiles (fuel) and residences (heating and cooling). Clearly, as energy costs increase, individuals will take many steps to alleviate the cost pressure before they consider a move (Small, 1980). As an alternative to a change in location, individuals adjust to higher energy costs by changing their driving habits, becoming more careful about speeding and about accelerating too quickly. They reduce the number of nonessential trips and combine purposes to maximize the usefulness of a single trip. As pressure builds, they make arrangements for carpools or, if public transit is available at a reasonable cost—and this includes an intangible inconvenience cost—they might utilize it. Another solution is to purchase a fuel-efficient car. Although a "downsize" car may increase gas mileage by 50 percent, the high cost of automobiles must also be considered in this solution. Since 1973 rises in the cost of fuel have been significantly greater than the inflation rate, compelling people at this state of the adjustment process to calculate closely the benefits of greater fuel efficiency. Since 1977 gasoline prices have tripled, auto costs have risen with the inflation rate (about 50 percent), and fuel efficiency for cars on the road has risen by about 30 percent. Extending Small's analysis, let us suppose that these trends persist for the next four years. (The federal government has mandated a new car standard of 27.5 miles per gallon for 1985 model cars.)

Table 1 presents data that make it possible to compare the costs of work trips over time for three types of automobiles. The figures in the

Table 1. Work-trip Costs for Fuel by Year

Round-Trip Distance	Type of Automobile	1977	1981	1985
40 miles	A (14 mpg)	$ 686	$1,029	$1,372
	B (19 mpg)	$ 505	$ 758	$1,010
	C (25 mpg)	$ 384	$ 576	$ 768
30 miles	A (14 mpg)	$ 514	$ 771	$1,029
	B (19 mpg)	$ 379	$ 568	$ 758
	C (25 mpg)	$ 288	$ 432	$ 576
20 miles	A (14 mpg)	$ 343	$ 514	$ 686
	B (19 mpg)	$ 253	$ 379	$ 506
	C (25 mpg)	$ 192	$ 288	$ 384
10 miles	A (14 mpg)	$ 171	$ 267	$ 342
	B (19 mpg)	$ 126	$ 189	$ 252
	C (25 mpg)	$ 96	$ 144	$ 192

body of the table represent the total gasoline expenditure in one year that includes 240 round trips for each of four distances between home and workplace. The three automobiles represent the typical cars in 1977 (Type A: 14 miles per gallon), 1981 (B: 19 mpg), and forecasted for 1985 (C: 25 mpg). Using constant 1981 dollars, a value of $1.00 per gallon for fuel is assigned in 1977, $1.50 for 1981, and $2.00 for 1985. Thus in 1981 a person who drove a car getting 19 mpg would spend $568 per year for commuting 30 miles round trip to work. A number of conclusions can be drawn from Table 1:

1. If one "downsizes" (increases auto mileage) over time, the rise in fuel costs is minuscule.

2. If one does not downsize, the greatest increase in commuting costs is an average of $340 per year during the period 1977-85, and that is for the 40-mile round trip. Long-distance commuters could save a good deal by purchasing a fuel-efficient car and can be expected to downsize.

3. If one does not downsize and has a relatively short commuter trip (10 miles round trip), the average increase in costs is less than $100, hardly a strong incentive to change autos.

4. A person with a C-type car in 1981 who travels 40 miles round trip would save $430 per year by moving to a place only 5 miles from the workplace. However, this saving does not cover moving costs or all of the other tangible and intangible costs associated with moving. When one takes the expense of a move into account, one might conclude that

the fuel savings would have to be greater to make up for these expenses. The difference between a 40-mile and a 10-mile round trip is an extreme case; other cases would bring fewer savings.

These conclusions and others that can be drawn from Table 1 show that increased gasoline costs alone provide relatively little incentive to move. When one includes the adjustment mechanisms mentioned above, there would be even less incentive to move unless home heating and cooling costs were rising rapidly or unless one belongs to certain vulnerable population categories to be discussed in the next section.

As with gasoline costs, a number of measures can be taken to lower household energy costs before relocation becomes necessary. Such adjustment mechanisms as lowered thermostat settings, use of insulated drapes, furnace and water heater insulation, and general house insulation are all strategies that one can employ before deciding on a different type of housing. These measures are very likely to offset appreciable increases in the cost of household energy. From the foregoing it seems evident that higher energy costs will not significantly affect the suburbanization process.

Groups Particularly Sensitive to Increased Energy Costs

As is true in most cases, there is a range of responses to any stimulus. The analysis outlined above fails to take into account certain large and significant groups of people who are especially vulnerable to even small increases in the cost of energy. What are these groups, and what are the effects of these higher costs on their homeplace location?

People on Fixed Incomes

Those on fixed incomes are, for the most part, retirees who are sensitive to housing costs but not to work-trip costs. In the Chicago SMSA 8.5 percent of residents receive social security income. Many of these older people are torn between their desire to live close to relatives and friends in the city and their need to find cheaper living arrangements elsewhere, often in a region of low energy use. One of the forces at work in energy-related migration is the continued movement of retirees to the sunbelt. Those who remain in the metropolitan area seek fuel-efficient apartments in safe neighborhoods. In a recent study Neels shows that fuel efficiency in new, carefully designed buildings rises dramatically as the number of units increases from one to four (1982). The great bulk of those units built with dwellers of moderate income in mind are in the suburbs, not in the central city. Older, renovated units can be found in the city, but these tend to be more expensive and are inhabited by people who are better off than most retirees.

People with Low Incomes

The poor can be divided into two groups: those who work and those who depend heavily on government assistance. In the Chicago SMSA about 9 percent of the people are below the poverty level and about 3 percent receive public assistance or welfare. For those in the first group, relocation to housing farther from their workplaces would be out of the question. In fact, this group is tied to the lowest-cost mass transit and cannot easily consider moving away from areas served by public transportation. As more and more potential employers leave the city, these people become stranded in a city without opportunity. Higher energy costs tend to restrict the movement of the poor further. Those dependent on government assistance weigh the benefit package in their city against benefits in other possible areas for settlement. Higher energy costs may provide an incentive for welfare recipients, as for the elderly, to move to cheaper areas, but, unlike retirees, those on welfare are often not free to do so.

People Forming New Households

This group of people is in the relatively enviable position of being able to minimize energy costs by selecting their household units with economic considerations in mind. Savings of several hundred dollars per year would be a significant consideration for individuals of relatively low income. In the Chicago SMSA 14 percent of the people are between 20 and 29 years old. Even if only a modest proportion of them are forming new households, in terms of numbers their market effect would be considerable. Perhaps more than any other group, these people, in the face of high energy costs, locate their residences so as to reduce these costs. Because their households usually consist of only one or two people, the demand is for apartments near workplaces rather than near schools, playgrounds, or parks.

These three groups, then, which constitute approximately 20 percent of the metropolitan area population, are greatly affected by higher energy costs, but only half of them are in a position to select a homeplace to lower these costs. Of these perhaps a total of 250,000 people will move close to a workplace location in the next few years. To determine the areas within the metropolitan area that they seek, more research about recent trends in job location would be helpful.

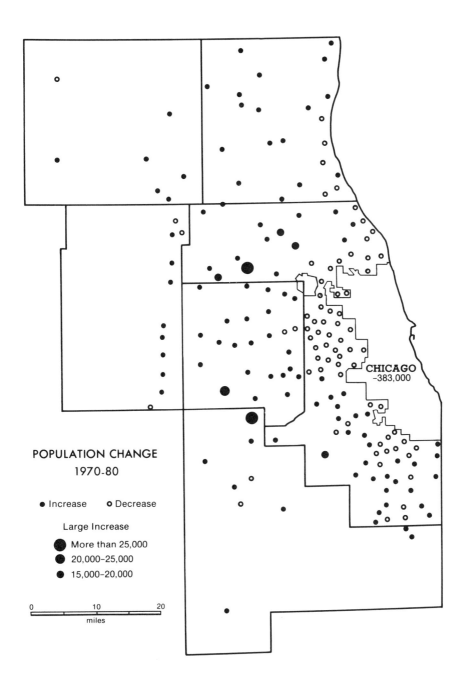

Figure 2. Population change, 1970–80.

Changing Population and Industrial Location Patterns
of the Chicago SMSA

Between 1970 and 1980 the city of Chicago lost 364,000 people, or 10.8 percent of its population. This tremendous loss is balanced by the gain in population in the remainder of the Chicago SMSA of 492,000 people (U.S. Bureau of the Census, 1981c). That the entire SMSA grew by only 128,000 persons implies that, in addition to a declining natural increase in population, many people are leaving the region for other parts of the country. Within the region there are vast differences in population increase and decrease. Not only is the city of Chicago losing population, but the inner suburbs have lost as well. For example, in the northern inner suburbs Evanston, Skokie, Morton Grove, Niles, and Park Ridge have lost 9 percent of their collective population since 1970 (Figure 2). In the western inner suburbs Franklin Park, Elmwood Park, Oak Park, Berwyn, and Cicero lost 10 percent; in the southern inner suburbs Evergreen Park, Calumet Park, Blue Island, Riverdale, and Dolton lost 10 percent of their population.

The situation is far different, however, in the outer suburbs. The seven communities that have gained the most population have increased collectively by 148,000 people and account for 30 percent of the suburban increase. These are Mount Prospect, Hoffman Estates, Schaumburg, Hanover Park, Naperville, Bolingbrook, and Orland Park. The first four of these are within 10 miles of O'Hare Airport. The enormous growth is in a nearly perfect concentric ring around Chicago ranging from 18 to 30 miles from the Loop. The growth is heaviest in those parts of the ring associated with O'Hare, the Northwest Tollway (Interstate 90), and the East-West Tollway (Route 5).

This pattern is further exemplified by the change in numbers of housing units. Figure 3 shows the change in the number of housing units between 1970 and 1980. Again, it is the area beyond the inner suburbs that has undergone the greatest change. The communities with the largest absolute increases in housing units are Schaumburg (15,000), Bolingbrook (10,000), Mount Prospect (9,000), Hoffman Estates (8,000), Naperville (8,000), and Hanover Park (7,000).

From these patterns that indicate a population much more spread out than ten years ago, one might infer that journeys to work have lengthened considerably. Such is not the case, however. The Chicago Area Transportation Study (1980) reports that from 1970 to 1979 the average one-way journey-to-work distance increased from 6.0 to 6.2 (airline) miles for workers who reside in Chicago and from 7.9 to 8.0 miles for workers in the SMSA outside of Chicago. These changes are very small,

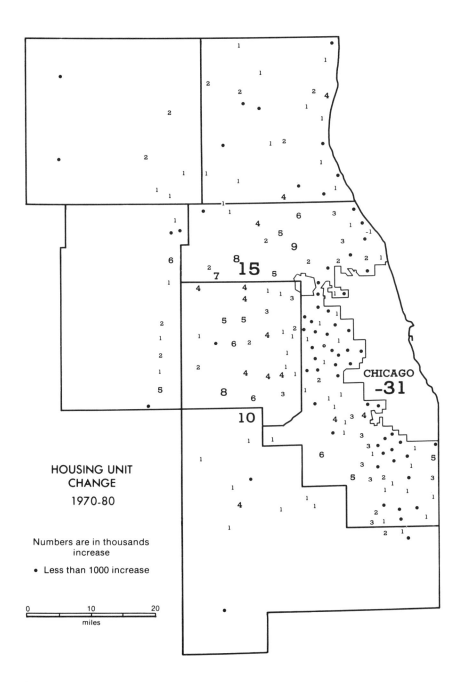

Figure 3. Housing unit change, 1970–80.

considering the great changes in new housing location and population patterns during these years. The conclusion, of course, is that industries and other workplaces must be moving to the suburbs as well.

A recent study for Chicago's Continental Bank (1978) shows that the pattern of journeys to work has not changed appreciably in 20 years. Most workers, whether central city or suburban, travel rather short distances to work, and the great bulk of suburban workers live in contiguous communities. Apparently, increased energy costs have not constricted the area from which labor is pulled to particular industries.

An analysis of the changes in manufacturing workplaces clarifies much of the current economic structure of the Chicago SMSA. The forces affecting the location of industries also bear on the location of housing, retail and wholesale sales, and office buildings. Let us consider the changes in industrial location for three five-year periods beginning in 1963. Figures 4 to 6 show the location of changes in the number of manufacturing establishments having 20 or more employees for three different time periods.

In the period 1963–67 the city of Chicago began to lose industries, though not at as high a rate as in the next ten years (Figure 4). From 1963 to 1967 the increases were most evident in the inner suburbs, but by 1972 new plants were being built in both the inner and outer suburbs (Figure 5). By 1977, after the first energy crisis, there were losses in the inner suburbs and a tremendous growth in the northern and western areas, particularly around O'Hare International Airport (Figure 6). During this final period the southern suburbs, both inner and outer, had a mixed development rate. The depressed state of South Chicago and the relative decline of the heavy industrial base in South Chicago and the southern suburbs offset, to some extent, suburbanization tendencies. Industries are essentially blocked from entering communities on the North Shore either because of zoning restrictions or because of the lack of available land. Thus the pressure for the establishment of industrial parks is in the west, from northwest to southwest. Analysis of the overall figures leads one to the conclusion that the city of Chicago's industrial base is being eroded rapidly and that those Chicago residents who depend on it are forced to consider workplaces in the outer suburbs or in other communities. In addition to the negative factors related to congestion and deterioration, the combination of the following positive factors appears to be instrumental in this process: availability of modern facilities in industrial parks, access to freeways, availability of parking space for employees, closeness to homeplaces of firms' chief officers, availability of an adequate diversified labor force, and proximity to O'Hare Airport for

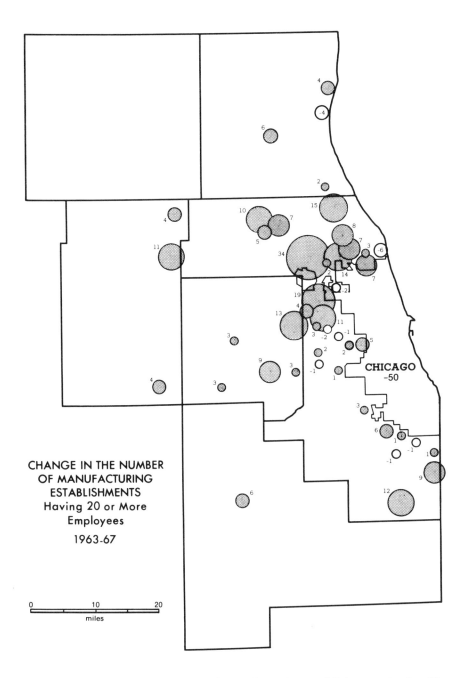

CHANGE IN THE NUMBER
OF MANUFACTURING
ESTABLISHMENTS
Having 20 or More
Employees
1963-67

CHICAGO
-50

0   10   20
            miles

Figure 4. Change in the number of manufacturing establishments having 20 or more employees, 1963–67.

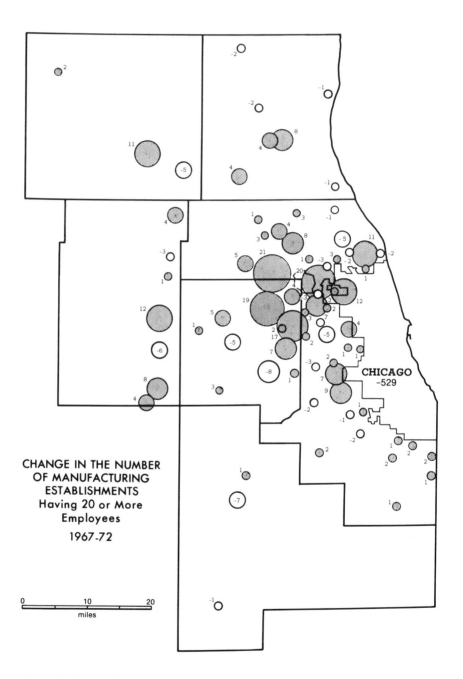

Figure 5. Change in the number of manufacturing establishments having 20 or more employees, 1967–72.

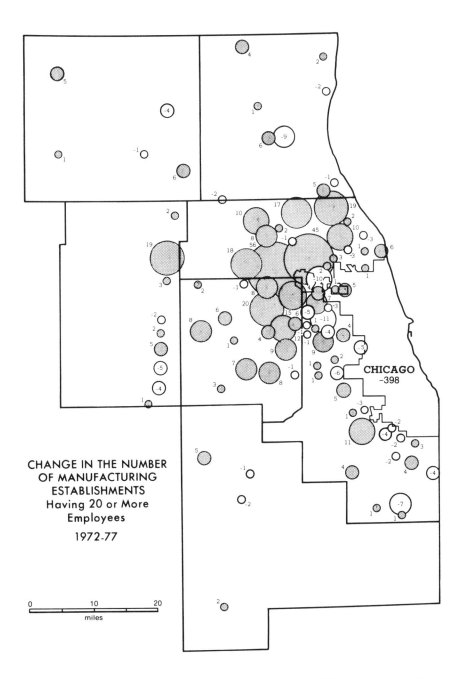

CHANGE IN THE NUMBER OF MANUFACTURING ESTABLISHMENTS
Having 20 or More Employees
1972-77

```
0        10        20
|____|____|____|
      miles
```

Figure 6. Change in the number of manufacturing establishments having 20 or more employees, 1972–77.

convenient transport of goods and of sales representatives to other major commercial centers.

There is additional evidence that suburbanization has continued in spite of higher energy costs. Since 1970 commercial space in the metropolitan area has doubled. Of this increase of 70 million square feet, 30 million is in downtown Chicago and 40 million is in the suburbs. Figure 7 shows the distribution of these workplaces by square feet. It shows that central Chicago is still a vibrant office work focus. Four areas of the suburbs are especially noteworthy as office sites: the Edens Expressway corridor that parallels the North Shore, the O'Hare Airport area, Schaumburg (west of O'Hare), and Oak Brook (west of the Loop). Eleven percent of the floor area of the suburban developments is in buildings that have O'Hare in their names. The O'Hare area is clearly emerging as a major focal region in the SMSA, surpassed only by the central business district of Chicago.

Conclusion

Although increased energy costs have apparently influenced the choice of home location for certain segments of the population in the Chicago SMSA, the vast majority of people have apparently taken other steps to reduce energy costs. Allowing for overlap among the three groups mentioned above—the retirees, the poor, and the young workers—perhaps 15 to 20 percent of the population are deeply affected by higher energy costs. Of these, we can deduce that perhaps 3 to 5 percent of the population in recent years have moved to housing units that minimize energy costs. Although this is not a large proportion of the population, it does represent 200,000 to 350,000 people—a figure that, when translated into housing and industrial location changes, represents significant alterations of the landscape. It represents both an increase in the rate of inner city redevelopment and an increase in the rate of apartment building near O'Hare Airport. Office construction in central Chicago has not abated, and as long as this process continues there will be a strong desire to redevelop neighborhoods close to workplaces.

One might now consider O'Hare as the transportation hub of a remodeled Chicago, just as the train terminals helped make the Loop the most important urban focus in the past. The new Chicago can be thought of as having two main foci—one in the inner city and one in the suburbs. The difference, of course, is that the former is marked by high densities and is dependent on mass transportation journey-to-work trips while the latter depends on automobiles and airplanes. Because growth is uneven throughout the outer suburbs, one can discern rings around

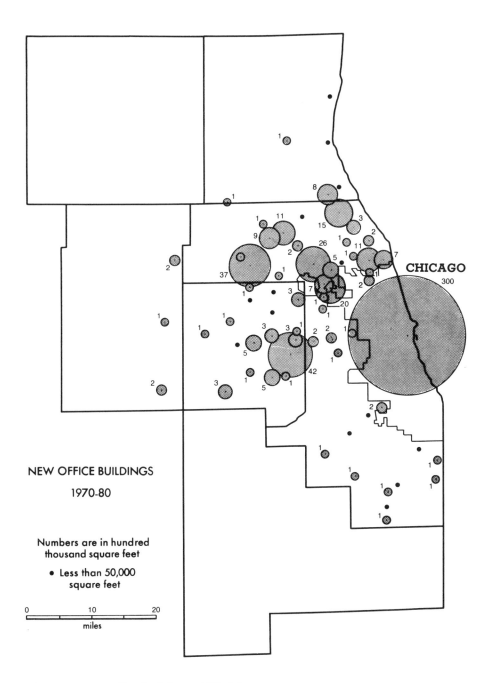

Figure 7. New office buildings, 1970–80.

O'Hare, much like the famous Burgess rings that are synonomous with presuburban Chicago. Near O'Hare, including the Schaumburg area, are several massive shopping centers, a tremendous concentration of industry and offices, and modest densities of apartment houses. Farther to the west and north these densities decline. For the immediate future we can expect the O'Hare area to become more of a focus because higher energy costs do not seem to prevent suburbanization, and there is no evidence to suggest that development in the suburbs will abate.

It is noteworthy that suburbanization trends in other midwestern metropolitan areas are roughly similar to those of Chicago (Muller, 1981). The suburban portion of Chicago's SMSA population increased 6.0 percent between 1970 and 1980 (from 51.7 to 57.7 percent). For Detroit this figure is 6.5 percent, for St. Louis 6.6 percent, for Cleveland 6.2 percent, and for Minneapolis–St. Paul 7.6 percent (U.S. Bureau of the Census, 1981c). It is likely that analysis of these major metropolitan areas would reveal patterns of land use similar to those in Chicago.

Note

1. Figures 1 through 7 were compiled by the author using data from the *State of Illinois statistical abstract 1980* (Illinois Bureau of the Budget, 1980), *Economic profile of counties* (Illinois Department of Business and Economic Development, 1978), *1967 census of manufacturers* (U.S. Bureau of the Census, 1970), *1970 census of population* (U.S. Bureau of the Census, 1973), *1972 census of manufacturers* (U.S. Bureau of the Census, 1976), *1977 census of manufacturers* (U.S. Bureau of the Census, 1981a), *1980 census of population and housing* (U.S. Bureau of the Census, 1981b), *1980 census of population* (U.S. Bureau of the Census, 1981c), and *Employment and earnings, states and areas, 1938–78* (U.S. Bureau of Labor Statistics, 1979).

References

Chicago Area Transportation Study. 1980. *1979 travel and household characteristics survey.* Chicago.

Continental Illinois National Bank, Area Development Division. 1978. *Industrial labor sheds: Suburban area of metropolitan Chicago.* Chicago.

Illinois Bureau of the Budget. 1980. *State of Illinois statistical abstract 1980.* Springfield: Illinois Bureau of the Budget, Office of Planning.

Illinois Department of Business and Economic Development. 1978. *Economic profile of counties.* Springfield: Illinois Department of Business and Economic Development, Office of Research.

Muller, P. O. 1981. *Contemporary suburban America*. Englewood Cliffs, N.J.: Prentice-Hall.

Neels, K. 1982. Families, houses, and the demand for energy. *International Regional Science Review* 7 (May):69-82.

Romanos, M. C. 1978. Energy-price effects on metropolitan spatial structure and form. *Environment and Planning A* 10:93–104.

Small, K. A. 1980. Energy scarcity and urban development patterns. *International Regional Science Review* 5 (Winter):97–117.

U.S. Bureau of the Census. 1970. *1967 census of manufacturers*. Washington, D.C.: U.S. Government Printing Office.

———. 1973. *1970 census of population. Vol. 1: Characteristics of the population*. Washington, D.C.: U.S. Government Printing Office.

———. 1976. *1972 census of manufacturers*. Washington, D.C.: U.S. Government Printing Office.

———. 1981a. *1977 census of manufacturers*. Washington, D.C.: U.S. Government Printing Office.

———. 1981b. *1980 census of population and housing: Illinois preliminary population and housing unit counts*. Washington, D.C.: U.S. Government Printing Office.

———. 1981c. Standard metropolitan statistical areas and consolidated statistical areas: 1980. *1980 census of population*. Washington, D.C.: U.S. Government Printing Office, PC80-SI-5.

U.S. Bureau of Labor Statistics. 1979. *Employment and earnings, states and areas, 1939-78*. Washington, D.C.: U.S. Government Printing Office.

Waymire, B., and E. Waymire. 1980. Effects of rising energy prices on urban space. *Regional Science and Urban Economics* 10:407–22.

4

Images of Place: Symbolism and the Middle Western Metropolis

JOHN A. JAKLE

This photo-essay on the metropolises of the Middle West plays on several basic assumptions. First, it is assumed that the Middle West has bonafide metropolises. I have skirted this question by looking only at the region's metropolitan areas with more than one million people, in the belief that if a million people cannot make a metropolis, no one can. Second, it is assumed that the region's millionaire cities are visually significant and that this significance is somehow rooted in the region's identity as America's hinterland. It has thus become my purpose to sort through the place imagery of the Middle West's largest cities to see what, if anything, has made them both similar and different. In this essay I focus not on the realities of the Middle West's metropolises but on their images as reflected in landscape symbols.

Images of place—and this includes images of cities—are combinations of belief, attitude, and icon. Beliefs about the nature of places and the positive and negative feelings that are associated with these beliefs attach themselves to icons that represent or typify these places. Whereas beliefs and attitudes are usually expressed in words, icons are usually known through visual images—in the modern age, most often photographs. People look at cities in stereotyped ways. One has only to mention Chicago or Detroit for certain stereotyped pictures to come to mind: a skyline, landmarks that may include key monuments or important buildings, ceremonial spaces such as central plazas, key street-scapes, especially the "Main Street," and perhaps special districts that have a distinctive look. Cities are also known from bird's-eye views, as, for example, the view from the top of Chicago's Sears Tower. Although central business districts present the most imageable cityscapes, cities are also known for their prevailing urban fabric—Detroit's automobile plants—beyond the downtown area.

Belief and Attitude

What are some of the words middle westerners attach to their metropolises? Adjectives are particularly expressive of beliefs and attitudes about place, especially when a poet sets out to personify an urbanscape. To Carl Sandburg, Chicago was "a tall bold slugger set vivid against the little soft cities," the "City of the Big Shoulders" (1950, p. 3). Julian Street wrote, "Chicago is stupefying...an Olympian freak, a fable, an allegory, and incomprehensible phenomenon...monstrous, multifarious, unnatural, indomitable, puissant, preposterous, transcendant... throw the dictionary at it!" (1947, p. 359). Chicago is also readily associated with crime, vice, and graft. Anselm Strauss, in *Images of the American City*, writes of Chicago's "two poles: gigantic enterprise and tremendous violence" (1961, p. 41). Corruption may be a necessary accompaniment of enterprise in Chicago, a city of hustlers. Even the designation "Windy City" suggests a restless, shifty thing.

Detroit abounds with superlatives: "Detroit the Dynamic," "City of Opportunity," "Arsenal of Democracy," "Automobile Capital of the World," "Motor City," and "Motown." Detroit is synonomous with mass production and symbolizes both corporate management and organized labor. Detroit is a fusion of men and machines. Strauss, however, writes that Detroit appears to scorn its history as the embodiment of twentieth-century drive and energy (1961, p. 25). Since the automobile industry chose the city as its center of enterprise, the city has come up with a progression of "New Detroits," each one promising to be better than the last. A blue-collar city, Detroit is "home-loving" and "sports-minded." Robert Sinclair writes, "Most Detroit families own homes, take pride in them, and appear to spend an extraordinary amount of time in them. Perhaps this explains the apparent lack of life in public places" (1970, p. 11). Sports, both amateur and professional, absorb much of the city's energy. Strauss writes: "Cities whose range of economic functions is exceedingly narrow seem frequently to lack variety of social style and suffer from deficiencies in 'culture' and civic virtues esteemed in most towns" (1961, p. 117). Robert Sinclair and Brian Thompson conclude, "A sameness, monotony and lack of sophistication pervade much of Detroit's life, suggesting that auto industry principles have spilled over into many walks of life" (1976, p. 289).

Detroit is a city of sharp social contrasts and extremes. Since the 1967 riots the city has become a symbol of the ills of American urban society. Plagued by street violence, the city was called the "homicide capital" in the 1970s. In a city filled with recent rural migrants, rural images also abound. The "City of Homes" is also the "City of Trees," just as Chicago is sometimes still called the "City of Gardens" and the "Prairie City." In the past century Detroit, as the "Great Lakes City," was considered one of the nation's most attractive resorts: "the City Beautiful." Willard Glazier, in *Peculiarities of American Cities*, wrote, "She sits like a happy princess, serene, on the banks of her broad river, guarding the gates of [Lake] St. Clair" (1884, p. 193). City boosters could write as late as 1917 of a "city possessing a mysticism of charm and a delightful natural beauty, accompanied by a practical industrial phase" (*Beautiful Detroit,* 1917).

St. Louis can no longer claim to be "first in shoes, first in booze, and last in the American League." The production of airplanes and other space-age technology far overshadows shoes and beer, and the St. Louis Browns have moved to Baltimore. St. Louis is a diversified city—its industry built on a broad commercial base that resembles Chicago's rather than Detroit's. Hutton, in *Midwest at Noon,* found St. Louis to be a mature city, its cultural life vigorous and "spread more generally over its citizens" (1946, p. 156). John Gunther found St. Louis "seasoned, with a wealth . . . deeply entrenched; it gives a sense of civilization like that of Cincinnati, grave and mature" (1947, p. 350). St. Louis faces south and east and has always done so. The city's steamboats oriented her to New Orleans, and its railroads turned her to Baltimore even before the Browns began to play baseball. Once the outfitting and administrative center of the Southwest, St. Louis served as a window not for easterners looking west but for westerners looking east. St. Louis was a gateway city to the industrial Northeast. The basic geography textbooks said so before St. Louis boosters confused matters by building the arch commemorating a "Gateway to the West." St. Louis was long known as the "Mound City" by way of emphasizing her native American antiquity. (The Cahokia or Monk's Mound still lies across the Mississippi River.)

Cleveland, once called the "Forest City," is an industrial metropolis located on Lake Erie's south shore. The city's descriptors are varied, although today its ethnicity seems to dominate. Whereas every middle western metropolis contains different racial and ethnic groups (Chicago, for example, claims to be the world's second largest Polish city), Cleveland has made the most substantial fuss over its ethnic diversity. Czechs, Germans, Poles, Italians, Yugoslavs, Hungarians, Russians, and, most recently, blacks have imprinted the city's personality. The Cleveland Cultural Gardens with their nationalistically inspired memorials symbolize this cultural pluralism: one community of many communities, communitas communitatum. Rooted in a Yankee past (Cleveland was the economic and cultural capital of Connecticut's Western Reserve) the city has been seen to mix capitalism and idealism. Graham Hutton wrote, "There is something of a religious quality in the atmosphere of Cleveland lacking in most other big Midwest cities. Mammon is not quite everything . . . and religion seems . . . to be more than ritual or good form" (1946, p. 152). Recently, the city's ethnic and racial diversity has crystalized in confrontation politics that set much of the earlier idealism aside and invite some derision. To boosters in Columbus and Cincinnati, Cleveland has become the "Mistake by the Lake," the blighted Cuyahoga "Flats" symbolizing a pluralistic industrial society in crisis.

Minneapolis and St. Paul constitute the "Twin Cities," or simply "the Cities" to people in their hinterlands. No other descriptors seem appropriate except insofar as each city seeks to debunk the other. Minneapolis, the larger place, seems to exude more vigor and vitality, whereas the smaller, older St. Paul appears to progress cautiously. Some Minneapolitans claim that they set their watches back 50 years when they go to St. Paul (Hutton, 1946, p. 361). Hutton wrote in the 1940s, "St. Paulites disguise their jealousy of their neighbor's taller buildings, large size, and spruce image with smugness and the unmistakable impression that they are cultured and urbane while Minneapolitans are bumptious philistines" (1946, p. 361). Today St. Paul is seen as a mature "eastern" city but less sophisticated than its younger "western" neighbor. "Minneapolis is a margarita after a soccer game; St. Paul is a cold beer after mowing the grass" (Ziemba, 1980, p. 7). Minneapolis has developed a reputation for clean, effective government. Crime rates are low and the city is relatively free from urban blight. The city sits near the top of every nationwide survey that rates the quality of city life.[1] Unlike Cleveland, the Twin Cities do not offer the same smorgasbord of ethnic groups, although there is a Scandinavian flavor to Minneapolis and German and Irish flavor to St. Paul.

Germans made Milwaukee famous for its beer, "Brewtown" in today's street parlance. But the Scots and Irish contributed early to the city's distinctiveness as have the Poles more recently. Hutton observed, "The stately homes on the northern bluffs have an uncanny mixture of north German and Scottish features in the architecture: Bremen combines with Balmoral." In the blue-collar residential sections, he continued, "you might as well be in Poland" (Hutton, 1946, p. 154). Milwaukee is pictured as mature and its citizens as "sober, thrifty, comfortable, and prosperous" (Strauss, 1961, p. 26). Richard Davis observed, "Consider dear old Lady

Thrift. That is, the plump and smiling city of Milwaukee, which sits in complacent shabbiness on the west shore of Lake Michigan like a wealthy old lady in black alpaca taking her ease on the beach" (1947, p. 189). Milwaukee exudes stability and conservatism. Much of the old city has survived intact, and urban blight is a relatively minor problem.

Longfellow called Cincinnati "the Queen City of the West" and the "City by the Beautiful River" (1859, p. 130). (The French had called the Ohio River "La Belle Rivière.") Most people agree that Cincinnati, despite her dowdy appearance, has charm. An old red and yellow brick city, Cincinnati sweeps up from its waterfront across the flat terraces and over and beyond the hills that encircled the nineteenth-century town. Cleveland, St. Louis, and St. Paul share a similar terrain that is in sharp contrast to the flat, monotonous plains upon which Chicago, Detroit, and Indianapolis are built. Like Rome (and Kansas City), Cincinnati claims to have been built on seven hills. Cincinnati also is a gateway city—a gateway connecting a vast southern hinterland with the industrial Northeast. Perhaps, like St. Louis, and certainly like nearby Louisville, Cincinnati could be considered as much a southern as a middle western city. As in Milwaukee and to a lesser extent in St. Louis, a large population of German descent adds a cosmopolitan dimension to the city.

Kansas City claims to be the "Gateway to the West" but, unlike St. Louis, Kansas City never built an arch to prove it. A friendly, open, and restless city, Kansas City shares the same vitality that characterizes Minneapolis. It seems to be a place that works as its designers intended. Although civic graft has been as much a part of the history of Kansas City as of Chicago, city government even in the corrupt years created a quality urban fabric. The city contains some 150 miles of tree-lined boulevards (more than in any other American city) and some 9,400 acres of parks (Gapp, 1980b, p. 1). The city maintains hundreds of fountains (many enhanced with elaborate sculptures) and thus calls itself "the City of Fountains." As in Oscar Hammerstein's lyric, "Everything is up to date in Kansas City." The place is no longer a wild cowboy town, the springboard to wide open spaces like Oklahoma. Indeed, Kansas City has become typically American. According to George Perry, "Kansas City is a kind of interior American crossroads and melting pot where the Southerner, the Northerner, the Easterner, and the Westerner meet to become plain John American. . . . It is not only America's approximate geographical heart, but the center of gravity for her taste and emotion" (1961, p. 106).

Hoosiers know their capital city by various nicknames. The euphemisms "Circle City" and "Monument City" acknowledge the unique street pattern that focuses on the downtown Soldiers and Sailors Monument; "Nap Town" and "Indy" are shortened versions of the full name, Indianpolis. For one month each year the city becomes the "auto racing capital of the world," a legacy of the past when Indianapolis rivaled Detroit as a center of automobile manufacture and heavy industry. During the other eleven months many residents see their city as "Indianoplace." The city seems to have no decisive personality and no clear image. Like Columbus, Indianapolis is seen to be a large, overgrown town, "provinical, countrified, and deadly dull" (Perry, 1961, p. 188). Perhaps, unlike Columbus, which calls itself "the biggest small town in the U.S.," Indianapolis has yet to admit to the facts (Gapp, 1980a, p. 1).

Some readers may question whether Columbus even deserves to be called a metropolis. Paul Gapp recently wrote, "Columbus has the sleepy ambience of an overgrown county seat. It is neat, snug, provincial, and slow to accept change" (1980a, p. 1). And yet Columbus is as large as other American cities, such as New Orleans, Dallas, and Portland, that have a clear metropolitan stamp. Columbus is a world-ranking center of scientific and technological research and data dissemination. Such activities, however, attract little attention and are tucked quietly away in neat suburban industrial parks. In down-home fashion Columbus is a city that refuses to be pretentious. Like Indianapolis, Columbus is typically American, although such a designation is also frequently applied to other cities in the region, especially, as noted above, Kansas City. Columbus, Indianapolis, and Kansas City are firmly rooted in the rural hinterland of the Middle West. The bulk of their residents are recent rural transplants from the small towns and farms of a region that is not only at the geographic heart of the nation, but that possesses many of those middle-class traits thought to be typical of the American way of life (Strauss, 1961, p. 107). Because these sites can claim relatively few distinctions, they content themselves with lesser assertions of typicality.

Icons

Yi-Fu Tuan suggests that cities develop personalities represented by signatures or icons in the landscape (1978, p. 234). Personality, he says, has two principal dimensions—one commands awe and the other affection. Clearly, some middle western metropolises are more awesome than others and command respect for their sheer size, economic muscle, and vigor of growth. These are pretentious cities constantly on the make. Other cities are more easily loved for their down-home qualities, their

(a) Chicago

(b) Detroit

Figure 1. Skylines.

(c) Minneapolis

(d) Cincinnati

stability, or their sense of timelessness. These cities, like old friends, are comfortable. Some cities seem to present a curious mixture of moods, to have split personalities.

We read a city's personality by looking at its face. To know a place is essentially to recognize, interpret, and respond to the icons by which the place is identified and made understandable in terms of associated beliefs and attitudes. Icons, as public symbols, offer coded, shorthand expressions to comprehend diversity in place, and to separate differences and similarities from place to place. What, then, are the icons of landscape that give substance to the Middle West's metropolises? What do we see of meaning in the face of the middle western city?

Skylines

Skylines say where a city has been and where it is going. Skylines command awe. Tall buildings that compete for dominance are the most pretentious statements of city power yet devised, more important even than domed stadia with "big-league" teams, "international" airports with flights to other continents, art museums, symphony orchestras, and the other paraphernalia of civic pride. Skylines separate the "tall bold sluggers" from the "little soft cities." No city possesses a skyline more impressive than Chicago's (Figure 1a). Chicago is said to have invented the skyscraper, although it was New York City that created tall pointed towers of steel frames. Chicago has beaten New York at its own game. Witness the Sears Tower, the world's tallest office structure, and the Standard Oil and John Hancock buildings, which are nearly as tall. Chicago's skyline is so sprawling that its entire sweep can only be captured by camera from a distance of several miles.

Detroit's skyline speaks less of power and more of change. Today there is still another "New Detroit" (Figure 1b). Renaissance Center, looking like the "City of Oz" (or, as local pundits have it, "Henry Ford's bowling trophy"), looms over the older business district. Whereas Chicago's skyline speaks of constant accretion over time, Detroit's speaks of disjuncture. Renaissance Center is a clear rejection of the city's post-riot image. It stands as a phoenix risen from the ashes of an older business district which, in fact, is not totally dead. (Whether Renaissance Center will draw the remaining breath from the older downtown is yet to be resolved.) The Minneapolis skyline also displays disjuncture (Figure 1c). The IDS Tower soars upward to dwarf the older city crouched at its feet. Minneapolis is clearly a city on the make. Cincinnati has placed its confidence in other symbols (Figure 1d). The towers of commerce hide behind the new riverfront stadium. The "Queen City's" skyline is nonassertive.

(a) Chicago

(b) Indianapolis

Figure 2. Bird's-eye views.

(a) St. Louis

(b) Chicago

Figure 3. Landmarks.

(c) Chicago

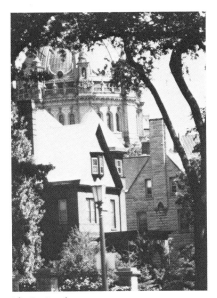

(d) St. Paul

Bird's-eye Views

Skylines, whatever their intrinsic messages, represent a significant way of looking at cities, what Grady Clay has called a "fix" or a rigidly conditioned point of view (1973, p. 23).[2] The bird's-eye view is another kind of fix. As with the view of skylines, an overview pulls the spectator back from the city. Generalization is encouraged as detail in landscape is lost. Chicago presents the most spectacular view from above (Figure 2a). In the 1940s Graham Hutton advised, "Go to the remarkable observatory on top of the Board of Trade Building, above the 'wheat pit,' and walk all round looking out for miles across railyards, stockyards, great public buildings, hotels, skyscrapers . . . and as far as you see . . . are the evidence of hectic activity: producing, transforming, packing, merchandising, printing, transporting, financing, selling, advertising, bustling, jostling, hurrying" (1946, p. 154). Today one can go to the top of the 120-story Sears Tower, which is three times higher. But the view from the 28-story City-County Building in Indianapolis is equally as interesting (Figure 2b). The Monument Circle with its surrounding curved facades presents an intimacy of scale more human in its portent than any view from a highrise in Chicago. The state capitol building in the distance lends a home-town aura not unlike a court house in a small Indiana county seat. Community is clearly symbolized. Indianapolis appears still to be the sedate overgrown town many admire.

Landmarks

Nothing makes a city quite as imageable or as clearly visible as widely advertised landmarks. Landmarks may be latent in a landscape, like the capitol building and the monument in Indianapolis. Such structures are comfortable to view, so well integrated are they in a city's historic fabric. Other landmarks are assertive. They stand in stark contrast to their surroundings and demand total attention. The Gateway Arch at St. Louis is such a structure (Figure 3a). The arch is awe-inspiring. It attracts more tourists than any other man-made object in the United States not owned by Walt Disney Productions (Trillin, 1980, p. 108). The arch has the general import of the "heavenly dome": a universal symbol that far outshines the "gateway" function contrived for the Jefferson National Expansion Memorial where the arch is located. However, many St. Louisians still have difficulty taking the arch seriously. A local joke places a statue of a huge croquet player in East St. Louis posed to hit a huge ball. Nonetheless, most agree that the arch does have a visual effect that symbolizes the whole of St. Louis in one grand gesture.

(a) 1956

(b) 1963

Figure 4. Detroit's Kennedy (Cadillac) Square.

(a) Cincinnati

(b) Cincinnati

Figure 5. Ceremonial open spaces.

(c) Detroit

(d) Detroit

Chicago's landmarks are a curious mixture of old and new. The water tower, a survivor of the great Chicago fire, symbolizes continuity with the past, whereas the John Hancock Building close by symbolizes the city of continual growth and modernity (Figure 3b). Chicago is a city conscious of its landmarks even when there is frequent disagreement about what is historically significant. Recently threatened, but now saved, was the elevated railroad that gave its name to downtown—the "Loop." People take to new landmarks with astonishing ease. Horace Sutton writes in the *Chicago Tribune*, "Get in a cab and ask to see the Picasso, and the driver will take you straight to Daley Plaza. The Picasso—there seems to be no other name because nobody knows what it is—weighs 162 tons and stands 50 feet tall. It has two huge wings, but it also has a pair of eyes. To some it is a bird, to others it is the face of a woman" (Sutton, 1979, p. 2). Perhaps, Picasso saw Chicago as an enigma, a true amalgam of adjectives (Figure 3c).

Some cities adopt specific landmarks for lack of viable alternatives. The Roman Catholic Cathedral in St. Paul gloats over Summit Avenue as a symbol of city conservatism (Figure 3d). Abler writes, "Local wags often remark how fitting it is that the St. Paul Cathedral stands higher and is more imposing than the State Capitol building for that is, or at least was, an accurate reflection of the relationships between the powers the edifices memorialize" (Abler et al., 1976, p. 362). Some cities are known for the landmarks they destroy. Detroit's old city hall on Cadillac Square was long the city's focal point (Figure 4a). Not only was the building torn down in favor of an underground parking garage, but the historically vital square was renamed Kennedy Square following President Kennedy's assassination (Figure 4b). The city clearly turned its back on its past and denied its own history. The area has become a disaster zone. Several adjacent blocks have been cleared and have been awaiting redevelopment for over a decade.

Ceremonial Open Spaces

Cincinnati has preserved and elaborated Fountain Square, the traditional center of its downtown (Figure 5a). Like Minneapolis and St. Paul, the city has invested in pedestrian walkways that link downtown blocks by second-story skyways over streets (Figure 5b). The walkways focus at the Tyler Davidson Fountain and thus make this subtle landmark more noticeable and elaborate greatly the ceremonial role of its surrounding open space. Although Detroit has destroyed its traditional heart, that city has sought to re-establish a semblance of ritual space in its new Civic Center on the Detroit River (Figures 5c and 5d). But here

(a) Cleveland

(b) Detroit

Figure 6. Ceremonial enclosures.

(a) Chicago

(b) Cincinnati

Figure 7. Streetscapes.

(c) Milwaukee

(d) Milwaukee

the expressway has replaced the pedestrian plaza, and automobiles have replaced pedestrians. Jefferson Avenue, which feeds two city express-ways directly, separates the Civic Center from the rest of downtown, and most of the Civic Center is given to underground and rooftop parking lots. Truly, here is the "Motor City."

Ceremonial Enclosures

Downtown redevelopers have rediscovered the shopping arcade. Downtowns, stripped of retailing by suburban shopping centers, have learned to fight back. Cleveland's nineteenth-century arcade survives as a visually arresting model (Figure 6a). But the new shopping plazas with their atriums, caged elevators, and files of escalators now steal the show as they do in Detroit's Renaissance Center (Figure 6b). So attractive are these enclosures that cities covet such plazas as ceremonial centers. A new Cadillac Square was recently proposed for the damaged part of Detroit's downtown.

Streetscapes

Obviously, a city's personality is reflected in its public ways. Enclosed malls under private ownership cannot replace the public streets and sidewalks as a city's true measure of worth. Every city has its symbolic streets. In Chicago Michigan Avenue leads the list of distinguished thoroughfares (Figure 7a). But mention State Street, La Salle Street, Rush Street, or Outer Drive and vivid pictures come to mind. Every city has a "Main Street," sometimes, as in Kansas City, even called Main Street. Here the principal department stores are located and sometimes the principal theaters and hotels as well. In Indianapolis it is Washing-ton Street, in Minneapolis it is Nicholet Street (recently outfitted as an outdoor mall), and in Cleveland it is Euclid Avenue. Cities have an interest in preserving the integrity of their principal streets by encourag-ing diversity and human scale. Cincinnati's Race Street retains its integ-rity, having been improved as a pedestrian space (Figure 7b). Mil-waukee's Wisconsin Street retains most of its twentieth-century charm, despite the intrusion of modern office towers (Figures 7c and 7d). The Wisconsin Street Bridge, a key downtown landmark, has recently been reworked to perpetuate the twist where the avenue crosses the Milwau-kee River. Here the regularity of the grid of streets, common to every middle western city, is disrupted in a visual delight.

(a) Chicago

(b) Detroit

Figure 8. Movement in the city.

(a) Kansas City

(b) Columbus

Figure 9. Special districts.

(c) St. Louis

(d) St. Louis

Movement

Movement brings a city street to life. Nowhere is the excitement of movement more evident than in Chicago beneath the nation's last downtown elevated railroad (Figure 8a). Every middle western city except Cleveland has eliminated its streetcars, and in Cleveland only the Shaker Heights suburban commuter line survives. But in Detroit the trolley cars are back, if only to carry tourists to and from the civic center (Figure 8b). This is curious, for industrial Detroit, more than any other force in recent history, rid the nation's cities of its streetcars in favor of automobiles and buses. Every city has become a "motor city," and downtown streets have lost much interest. Gone is the squeal of metal on metal, the hum of traction motors, and the ringing of bells. In Chicago the drama continues above the streets on the soon-to-be-renovated "el."

Special Districts

Downtown is a special district within every city. Here much of a city's personality as a place is seen to focus. Here the landmarks and ceremonial spaces cluster. Here street scenes are most vivid. Some middle western cities have begun to develop and promote the imagery of outlying areas as special districts. Kansas City's efforts date from before World War I when the Country Club Plaza was conceived (Figure 9a). Today the plaza with its distinctive Spanish-styled architecture of tile roofs, mosaic walls, towers, and turrets is the city's principal retail section. In Columbus, district making has preserved the German Village area, a former blue-collar, ethnic neighborhood (Figure 9b). German Village finds its equivalents in Cincinnati's Mount Adams, St. Louis' Lafayette Park, and Chicago's New Town and Lincoln Park areas. Some special districts refuse to die. Despite the virtual elimination of old St. Louis beneath the Gateway Arch, old sentiments persist along the waterfront. Wharfboat restaurants and theaters and a remnant cluster of old warehouses (resuscitated as "La Clede's Landing") reinforce the arch's tourist appeal (Figures 9c and 9d). Here periodically arrives Cincinnati's floating landmark, the Delta Queen.

Prevailing Urban Fabric

The large cities of the Middle West share a general form. A business district sits near a river or lakefront (Indianapolis might be considered an exception). Here focus the city's railroads, major thoroughfares, and expressways. Industrial plants surrounded by mile after mile of anti-quated housing spread outward from the city center (Figure 10a and 10b). Major thoroughfares are lined with businesses, relics of the street-car in older sections and creatures of the automobile in newer sections (Figure 10c). Where urban renewal of the 1950s and 1960s dominates, public housing makes an institutional presence: Pruitt-Igoe in St. Louis or the Taylor Homes in Chicago (Figure 10d). At the edge of the metropo-lis the new city grows (Figure 10e). A spread-out fabric, this new city is the least imageable of all, although elite neighborhoods oriented to lake beaches, rolling terrain, and other amenities do attract attention and, like downtown, symbolize the city's good life, as in Cleveland's Shaker Heights, Kansas City's Mission Hills, and Detroit's Grosse Pointe (Figure 10f). Such outlying scenes may dominate a city's total image, especially when the central business district is small and relatively undistinguished.

Conclusion

Like metropolises everywhere, middle western cities show diversity. Each metropolis has sought to promote a distinctive image for itself even where typicality has seemed the prevailing characteristic. Each city's future growth and well-being will depend to some extent upon the success of such continued image making. Middle western cities share many things in common just by being middle western. Future prosper-ity will also depend upon the positive reinforcement of shared regional stereotypes. Most Americans view the Middle West as a rich agricultural heartland that is the essence of rural, small-town America. This bucolic vision has obscured the cities as metropolitan places. Many Americans see the Middle West's metropolises as little more than overgrown factory towns, as processors of agricultural raw materials (milling, packing, brewing) and manufacturers of goods for regional consumption (iron and steel for tractors and plows). That these cities are also financial and commercial centers with sophisticated "space-age" industries serving national and international markets is often obscured from view.

Few Americans view the Middle West's metropolises as cosmopolitan places, as truly diversified centers that equal the cities of the Eastern Seaboard or the regional centers of the South and West. When recog-nized as producers of steel, chemicals, automobiles, airplanes, or computers, middle western cities loom primarily as work places, as "blue-collar" towns. Other functions such as communications, ad-ministration, education, art, and science are seen to overlay the region's

(a) Detroit

(b) Detroit

(c) Chicago

Figure 10. Prevailing urban fabric.

(d) Chicago

(e) Chicago

(f) Detroit

industrialism only thinly. This lack of diversity seems to be incorporated into the city's very design. The Middle West's metropolises are primarily of the late railroad era, modified by automobile technology. There is a high degree of standardization on the grids of streets as interrupted by the railroad lines and the new expressways. Middle Western urbanscapes are seen to pack few surprises and contain little novelty outside their downtowns.

Too much of the perceived diversity distinguishing the middle western metropolises is lodged in their central business districts. Most of this distinction has been very recently contrived. Mammoth skyscrapers, such as the Sears Tower, and new ritual places, such as the Daley Plaza, dominate the current view of Chicago. In Detroit it is the Renaissance Center. In St. Louis it is the Gateway Arch. Icons of the past count for little or nothing. Newness and progress have been integrally linked inside business districts as if to counterbalance the physical decay beyond. The positive valuing of a diversity that is rooted in relic landscapes has been slow to develop even in the more conservative cities like Milwaukee and St. Paul, where old houses in old neighborhoods still prevail. The molders of city images have sought to strike too much awe, and not enough affection, in the eye of the beholder.

Image making in middle western cities should be linked to landscape. Promoters should not be afraid to be visually aware, to expend thought and money on the icons of place that make a city imageable and attractive. The boosters of the Middle West's metropolises have not been blessed with the warm winter climates or soaring mountain backdrops that are associated with the boom towns of the South and West. Nor do middle western city promoters have available the wealth of tradition possessed by Eastern Seaboard centers. Nonetheless, boosters in the Middle West do have substantial economic and social diversity with which to work, a diversity that is rooted in the American "heartland" of rural and small-town ideals, ethnic origins, and industrial power. City images should be carefully rooted in the total fabric of landscape and not imposed artificially in the isolation of partially abandoned and partially remade central business districts. As Detroit was once "the City Beautiful" for its tree-lined residential streets, so can it be again. As Chicago was once the "Garden City" for its emphasis on residential quality, so can it be again. Future metropolitan promotion in the Middle West should reach out into the neighborhoods to plumb the positive aspects of ethnic diversity and to emphasize the quality of life. Middle western cities should be made to stand for what is best in the American way of life.

Notes

1. Perhaps the most widely known of the recent polls was reported in Louis (1975).

2. "Fixes" are rooted in the perspective tradition of visual representation whereby the three-dimensional landscape is presented on a two-dimensional surface.

References

Abler, R., J. S. Adams, and J. R. Borchert. 1976. The twin cities of St. Paul and Minneapolis. In J. S. Adams, ed., *Contemporary metropolitan America*, vol. 3. Cambridge: Ballinger.

Beautiful Detroit. 1917. Detroit: Detroit Convention and Tourist Bureau.

Clay, G. 1973. *Close-up: How to read the American city.* New York: Praeger.

Davis, R. S. 1947. Milwaukee: Old lady thrift. In R. Allen, ed., *Our fair city.* New York: Vanguard Press.

Gapp, P. 1980a. Columbus, quintessentially middle America. *Chicago Tribune,* 29 Mar., p. 1.

———. 1980b. Kansas City, what all the fuss is about. *Chicago Tribune,* 27 Mar., p. 1.

Glazier, W. 1884. *Peculiarities of American cities.* Philadelphia: Hubbard Brothers.

Gunther, J. 1947. *Inside U.S.A.* New York: Harper and Brothers.

Hutton, G. 1946. *Midwest at noon.* Chicago: University of Chicago Press.

Longfellow, H. W. 1859. Quoted in C. MacKay, *Life and liberty in America.* London: Smith, Elder.

Louis, A. M. 1975. The worst American city. *Harper's Magazine* 254 (Jan.):67–71.

Perry, G. S. 1961. Quoted in A. L. Strauss, *Images of the American city.* New York: Free Press.

Sandburg, C. 1950. Chicago. *Complete poems of Carl Sandburg.* New York: Harcourt, Brace, and World.

Sinclair, R. 1970. *The face of Detroit: A spatial synthesis.* Detroit: Wayne State University, Department of Geography, and U.S. Office of Education, National Council for Geographic Education.

Sinclair, R., and B. Thompson. 1976. Detroit. In J. S. Adams, ed., *Contemporary metropolitan America*, vol. 3. Cambridge: Ballinger.

Strauss, A. L. 1961. *Images of the American city.* New York: Free Press.

Street, J. 1947. Quoted in J. Gunther, *Inside U.S.A.* New York: Harper and Brothers.

Sutton, H. 1979. New Chicago image: City of art, gentility. *Chicago Tribune,* 9 Dec., p. 2.

Trillin, C. 1980. U.S. journal: St. Louis, Mo., regional thoughts from atop the Gateway Arch. *New Yorker,* 16 June, pp. 104–9.

Tuan, Y. F. 1978. Space and place: Humanistic perspective. *Progress in geography,* vol. 6. London: Edward Arnold.

Ziemba, S. 1980. St. Paul a thriving revival. *Chicago Tribune,* 31 Mar., p. 7.

II

Problems and Issues

5

Capital Punishment for Midwestern Cities

ALFRED J. WATKINS

In May 1981 Tom and Debbie Lowell said good-bye to their family and friends in Detroit and moved to Houston, a city they had never seen and where they knew no one. The decision to move was painful, but they felt they had no choice. For the past several months they had been subsisting on welfare payments of $34.50 every two weeks from the state of Michigan, $70 a month in food stamps, and whatever additional money they could beg and borrow.

Debbie had quit a well-paying job as a machinist in early 1979 in a futile effort to save an earlier marriage. But with Detroit's economy sinking fast because of the long gas lines and skyrocketing energy prices that followed the 1979 Iranian revolution, finding a new job became impossible. She had been unemployed for more than two years when she told her parents she was moving to Texas. Tom was also a victim of Detroit's sagging economy. He had been laid off from his job as a plumber in March 1980 and had not been able to find employment since then. By the time Tom and Debbie finally left Detroit, unemployment in the Motor City was 14.7 percent, and Mayor Coleman Young estimated that 60 percent of the city's population was receiving some form of public assistance (Lemann, 1981).

Houston is a natural destination for recession-weary migrants from Michigan. Many families have already made the long trek south, and they are sending a clear message to their former neighbors: high energy prices may have decimated Detroit's automobile-based economy, but they are a boon to Houston's petrochemical industrial complex. Houston "is the new Detroit, the new New York. This is where the action is," exults former Houston Mayor Fred Hofheinz (Sterba, 1976, p. 24). So as word filters back, the migration to Texas gathers momentum. By mid-1981 the *Houston Chronicle* reported it was selling 4,200 papers in Michigan every Sunday. Twenty-one percent of the 1981 engineering graduates of Michigan State University found jobs in Michigan; 22 percent took jobs in Texas. Houston radio station KILT has become the self-proclaimed official station for transplanted people from Detroit. And at Gilley's, the suburban Houston honky-tonk where John Travolta conquered the mechanical bull in the movie *Urban Cowboy*, the country and western bands regularly dedicate songs "for all you people from DEE-troit." The cheers from the homesick midwesterners on the dance floor are usually deafening.

More than a century before Tom and Debbie left Detroit, Texas was the favorite destination for another group of down-and-out migrants. After the Civil War southerners headed west in such numbers that when they left, they simply scrawled the initials G.T.T. across the front of their shacks; everyone knew that this meant they had "gone to Texas." Most were sharecroppers and tenant farmers fleeing land exhausted by years of cotton farming and a usurious crop lien system. For these earlier migrants Texas represented a second chance, an opportunity to start over, unencumbered by the financial domination of banks and merchants. Some made fortunes in oil, cattle, real estate, and banking, but many found themselves back in a state of penury. In Texas, much to their chagrin, they found the banks and merchants as dominant as they had been in other parts of the South. In no mood to move a second time, and perhaps realizing that migration could never solve problems caused by the financial and marketing arrangements that dominated all of southern agriculture, they formed the Farmers Alliance and spearheaded the Populist movement (Goodwyn, 1978; Woodward, 1951).

Today's migrants to Texas and other sunbelt states are primarily blue- and white-collar workers fleeing Northeast and Midwest urban centers. Nevertheless, they have much in common with their nineteenth-century predecessors. As business moves elsewhere and multinational corporations close profitable factories because they hope to receive even higher rates of return in new locations or new endeavors, midwestern cities are becoming economically exhausted. Their residents seem to have no choice but to move to less depressed regions and pray that the same forces that disrupted their lives once will not disturb them again. Some are prospering in their new homes, but many are finding the sunbelt less than hospitable. Wages in the predominantly non-union factories and offices are much lower than in the industrial Northeast and Midwest. Worse yet, unemployed steelworkers and autoworkers often discover their skills and experience are in low demand. "Workers in computer technology and the health sciences and bilingual teachers stand the best chance right now of making it in Houston," according to Don Horn, secretary-treasurer of the Houston area AFL-CIO (Jolidon, 1981, p. 59).

Those without these valued skills "find that the economy has little more use for them here than in the North. So they wind up with minimum-wage jobs, barely above poverty, and stay; or disillusioned, they go back north. In either case, they cannot seem to find a home in a post-industrial economy that no longer offers a leg up to those of low education and low skills" (Stevens, 1981, p. B11).

Whether these disillusioned migrants will foment another radical insurgency—either in the sunbelt or in their old hometowns—remains to be seen. But at this point, at least three things are certain. First, the shift of population and jobs from the Midwest and Northeast to the sunbelt reached landslide proportions during the 1970s. Second, these demographic and employment patterns have sparked a heated debate among policy analysts. On one side are those who consider these trends both ineluctable and beneficial. They advocate terminating all government programs that inhibit the free and unfettered movement of people and jobs and replacing them with new programs that facilitate interregional migration. Arrayed against them is a second group of policy analysts, business executives, and financiers who argue that abandoning Midwest cities is both economically foolish and politically unnecessary. Rather than encouraging migration, they believe the current midwestern malaise and aura of desperation is a golden opportunity for businessmen and politicians to cooperate in revitalizing U.S. industry and the Midwest's decaying cities. But, this second group argues, the restoration of a good business climate in the industrial heartland cannot be accomplished with business-as-usual policies. Therefore, they are demanding fundamental political reforms and dramatic changes in municipal government structures as a prerequisite for restoring midwestern cities to some semblance of their former economic structure.

Finally, no matter which side emerges victorious in the current policy debate, many current and former residents of midwestern cities will find their plight similar to that of nineteenth-century migrants who discovered that their choices lay between poverty in their old homes or poverty in Texas. Residents of midwestern cities confront a similar Hobson's choice: move to the sunbelt and face the prospect of lower wages, fewer fringe benefits, less safe work environments, and reduced social services, or stay put and face either continued unemployment or take possible new job opportunities that provide a reduced standard of living.

The Anatomy of Urban Decline

If it is true, as Tiebout (1956) suggested in a different context, that people vote with their feet, then many from the Midwest and Northeast are electing the sunbelt. Between 1975 and 1980 the Northeast census region had a net outmigration of approximately 1.5 million people while the North Central region had a net outmigration of nearly 1.2 million. During the same period the South and West, by comparison, had a net gain of 1.8 million and 0.9 million migrants respectively (U.S. Bureau of the Census, 1981a). Of the nearly 2.6 million people who left the Northeast between 1975 and 1980, 1.5 million settled in the South, 727,000 in the West, and approximately 412,000 in the North Central region. Of the 3.2 million migrants leaving the North Central region between 1975 and 1980, 1.7 million settled in the South and 1.2 million relocated to the West (U.S. Bureau of the Census, 1981a).

Even with this flow of migrants to other regions, North Central population grew by 2.3 million between 1970 and 1980. But midwestern central cities, and indeed entire metropolitan areas, have not kept pace with this growth. Central city population decline is a comparatively well-documented and long-standing phenomenon. Nationwide, 56 central cities lost population during the 1950s, 95 during the 1960s (Lowry, 1980), and 192 during the 1970s (U.S. Bureau of the Census, 1981b). In the Midwest the cumulative effect of, in some cases, more than 30 years of unrelenting year-after-year population declines has taken its toll on central cities. As of 1980, 36 of the 106 central cities in Midwest SMSAs had lost more than 10 percent of their peak population. Among the big losers were St. Louis (47.1 percent), Cleveland (37.3 percent), Battle Creek (36.2 percent), Detroit (34.9 percent), Youngstown (31.4 percent), East Chicago (31.0 percent), Minneapolis (28.9 percent), Cincinnati (23.5 percent), Dayton (22.4 percent), Flint (19.0 percent), Canton (19.0 percent), Akron (18.3 percent), South Bend (17.2 percent), Chicago (17.0 percent), Hammond (16.1 percent), Gary (14.8 percent), Milwaukee (14.2 percent), and St. Paul (13.8 percent) (U.S. Bureau of the Census, 1981b).

Until the mid-1970s many analysts viewed these central city population declines with equanimity. From their perspective, only a portion of the metropolitan area was considered to be sick; the vitality of the entire metropolitan area was rarely questioned. In fact, the decline of central cities along with what was perceived as a corresponding shift of population and wealth to the suburbs was frequently viewed as either a beneficial process or, at worst, something to be accepted stoically. Banfield typifies the former approach: "The overall gain of wealth by building in the suburbs may more than offset the loss of it caused by letting the downtown deteriorate" (1973, p. 5). Harrison, who normally could be expected to disagree with Banfield on most issues, also accepts central city population declines with fatalistic complacency: "Thus, suburbanization is, in and of itself, neither unexpected nor does it necessarily reflect some socioeconomic pathology in the central city. Urban areas may simply be undergoing an evolutionary change of form" (1974, p.4).

In retrospect, these statements seem exceedingly optimistic. Although the initial problems in midwestern metropolitan areas may have first appeared confined to central cities, most recent data suggest that the cancer of economic decline has spread to the point where it is engulfing the entire metropolitan region. One of the eight SMSAs in the North Central census region experienced absolute population declines between 1970 and 1980. Even more ominously, most of the SMSAs have experienced net outmigration since 1970. Between 1970 and 1978, Chicago with a net loss of 355,500 migrants, Detroit with 305,000 net outmigrants, Cleveland with 204,000 net outmigrants, and St. Louis with a net migration loss totaling 141,000 led all Midwest SMSAs, but in relative terms migration losses seem to have affected large and small SMSAs with equal severity. Only ten midwestern SMSAs had net inmigration during the 1970s. Most of them were small college towns or state capitals, areas whose economic base is hardly representative of the heavy manufacturing so typical throughout the region (U.S. Bureau of the Census, 1980).

In some circumstances population declines may prove beneficial. For example, if the number of jobs available in the SMSA remains constant or declines more slowly than population, the ensuing tight labor market should enable those who remain to command higher wages and more rapid promotions. Unfortunately, these balmy conditions did not prevail during the 1970s. According to the U.S. Department of Housing and Urban Development:

> In central cities with declining employment, the rate of job loss often exceeded the rate of population loss. The 20 largest cities that lost jobs most rapidly from 1970 to 1977 saw their employment base shrink by an average of two percent a year; population in those cities also declined, but at a rate of 1.5 percent a year, a one-fourth lower rate. Where the number of jobs increased, the rate of job expansion tended to exceed the rate of population growth. In the 20 largest cities where employment grew most rapidly from 1970 to 1977, jobs increased almost three times as fast as population. (1980, pp. 3–4)

This unfavorable relationship between employment and population growth rates is especially noticeable for the manufacturing sector. Sternlieb and Hughes (1977) show that between 1960 and 1975 population in the Northeast grew by 10.7 percent while manufacturing jobs declined by 13.0 percent. Similarly, for the North Central region, population during the 15-year interval grew by 11.7 percent, far exceeding the 4.2 percent increase in manufacturing jobs. The South, on the other hand, had an extremely favorable relationship between population and manufacturing employment growth. In that region manufacturing employment growth exceeded population growth by a 41 to 35 percent margin.

The Mischievous Hand?

In view of these trends, it is not surprising that so many midwestern migrants continue to move to regions promising better employment opportunities. Most midwestern cities grew to prominence during the industrial revolution of the late nineteenth and early twentieth centuries (Watkins, 1980b); since then their employment prospects have been strongly tied to the fortunes of the now-declining industries that dominate their economies. It is surprising, however, that so many policy analysts believe the nation would be best served by accelerating and facilitating the exodus from midwestern metropolitan areas. In perhaps the best known of these studies, the President's Commission for a National Agenda for the Eighties (1980) argues that manufacturing-based cities must now adapt to a new constellation of postindustrial activities. Unfortunately, this transition is being resisted, the commission suggests, because sentimental social scientists and policy makers insist that these cities "should be largely permanent and unchanging" (President's Commission, 1980, p. 2). In contrast to this misguided perception, the commission argues that cities "should be allowed to change in step with widespread changes in the larger society. This report seeks to underscore the long term *inevitability* and desirability of this transformation [to a postindustrial economic base]" (p. 3).

Because the commission views the transition to postindustrial society as inevitable, it asserts that "special efforts to lure manufacturing industries back to older central cities" must fail (p. 15). "Policy makers should neither seek to restore the industrial city to its former form and function, nor force urban society to perform tasks in ways and in locations that are no longer appropriate" (p. 16). Instead, the commission suggests "that the principal role of the federal government should be to assist communities in adjusting to redistributional trends . . . by removing barriers to mobility that prevent people from migrating to locations of economic opportunity, and by providing migration assistance to those who wish and need it" (p. 5).

Although the commission report elicited predictable howls of outrage from many municipal officials—New York City's deputy mayor Nathan Leventhal characterized its recommendations as "dumb," and the *New York Times* reported that Mayor Koch's reaction was "unprintable"

(Haberman, 1980, p. 1)—its analysis and conclusions are not new. Eight years earlier Sternlieb (1971) declared, "The major problem of the core areas of our cities is simply their lack of economic value" (p. 15). He concluded, "The city as we have known it, and the forms of economic and social organization which characterized it are simply irrecoverable" (p. 21). In a similar, although slightly more ominous vein, Baer (1976) announced that efforts to resuscitate many central city economies were hopeless. Urban scholarship and domestic public policy, he asserted, have been characterized by a "refusal to admit that older cities or neighborhoods can die; they may be 'sick' or 'deteriorating' but the belief is nevertheless held by experts and politicians alike that with proper treatment those areas will recover and live forever" (p. 3). Instead of refusing to face reality, Baer argues, the time has finally come for us "to contemplate the various aspects of urban death and to suggest what may be done to ameliorate its consequences. Contemplation is meant to be just that: a considered exposition that treats urban death as very much in the natural order to things, to be taken in stride—not an apocalyptic pronouncement" (p. 4).

These arguments all rest on the assumption that there are "natural" and "inevitable" processes afflicting metropolitan areas. It is almost as if some mischievous hand were guiding the destiny of these unfortunate cities, heaping troubles on the downtrodden and bestowing benefits on those rapidly growing cities that least need them. The analyses are filled with sentences that have no human subjects or actors. Bankers, corporate executives, financiers, and the legions of MBAs whose daily work involves deciding where new factories should be built, which facilities should be closed, and which "populist" mayors should be denied loans to roll over maturing debt never enter their discussions. Instead, the President's Commission, for example, tells us that economic problems in older industrial cities result from "economic opportunities . . . migrating out of cities" (p. 19). The problem is compounded because "industrial innovation that spawns new industry [has] dispersed away from central areas" (p. 24), leaving "cities, metropolitan areas, and even regions . . . awash with international economic trends and influences." These international trends and influences seem especially ominous. The commission notes that they are "stark testimony to the power and inevitability of the deconcentration forces at work" (p. 27).

By attributing all problems to natural and inevitable process, those who propose to abandon older metropolitan areas absolve themselves of responsibility for identifying crucial actors and the potentially critical variables that public policy may influence. More important, as long as inanimate forces are blamed for the cities' woes, victims of central city decline have no choice but to accept their fates passively. After all, it is rather difficult to fight migrating job opportunities and international trends and influences.

Despite its flaws, the commission report almost inadvertently identifies at least one factor—corporate executives' investment decisions—which may explain why midwestern cities are having so many problems. The commissioners note that "the shifting intrametropolitan, interregional, and transnational investment patterns of private industry often demonstrate remarkably little allegiance to political jurisdictions" (President's Commission, 1980, p. 41). They attribute this to the quest of private industry for a better business climate and to lack of corporate concern for the social consequences of their actions: "Despite the necessity to encourage and enforce a measure of corporate social responsibility . . . economic development policies seldom appreciate that private sector relocation decisions often are more responsive to the non-economic business climate than to vacillating cost differentials. The term 'business climate' often suggests the absence of constraints and restrictions rather than the presence of anything specific" (p. 43). Finally, they imply that corporate executives will continue to flee midwestern cities as long as elected municipal officials pay more attention to their constituents' needs for social services than to corporate demands for a better business climate: "The package of urban services offered by some jurisdictions has become too elaborate to be maintained into the future. Service trimming, therefore, is often suggested as a means of reflecting the shrinkage of the tax and population bases. However, political constraints have traditionally militated against lowering service levels or dropping certain services altogether" (p. 45). They add that municipal officials "should be encouraged to give careful attention to the reality and image of their business climate. By projecting an attractive business climate (albeit subjective and amorphous), they can increasingly compete for primary investment and secondary expansion under certain conditions" (p. 48).

Capital Punishment

The threats by business executives to devastate local economies and discredit mayors who resist their entreaties for a better business climate have contributed both to the rise of the sunbelt and to the mid-1970s rhetoric about the "second war between the states" (Goodman, 1979; Harrison and Bluestone, 1980; Watkins, 1980a). Recent corporate behavior indicates that these threats should not be taken lightly.

In Cleveland, for example, a consortium of six local banks, led by Brock Weir, chairman of the Cleveland Trust Company, set out to defeat Dennis Kucinich, the populist mayor who campaigned against property tax abatements for large corporations and against selling the municipal electric system (Muny). Their weapon was simple: on 15 December 1978 the banks refused to roll over $15.5 million of Cleveland debt and plunged the city into bankruptcy.

Two events seem to have precipitated the immediate crisis. First, in the days preceding default, Kucinich and city council president George Forbes could not agree on the precise details of a financial rescue ordinance. Forbes, acting in concert with Weir, insisted the city sell Muny; Kucinich refused. Second, like many other financially strapped cities, Cleveland had been balancing its budget only with the aid of all sorts of financial gimmicks. At the end of 1978 the banks refused to roll over old deficits until they were assured the city would put its finances in order.

On closer inspection, however, Cleveland's default cannot be blamed on paralyzing political rivalries and accounting sleights-of-hand. In the first place bank officials had known of the city's financial problems and accounting gimmickry for at least five years preceding default. A congressional committee staff study of the Cleveland bankruptcy found:

> The problems highlighted in 1978 were not new.... These activities were known not only to city officials but generated discussion in the community at large. The business/banking community was clearly aware of the city's problems as the 1973, 1974, 1975, 1977, and 1979 reports of the Greater Cleveland Growth Association suggest. These reports commented on city deficits or potential deficits, supported increasing the income tax rate, supported the sale of city assets, and questioned reliance upon short-term borrowings. (U.S. Congress, 1979b, p. 838)

Second, Kucinich was taking steps to restore Cleveland's financial solvency. He proposed increasing the city income tax rates, reducing the city work force, and halting the practice of using capital improvement funds to supplement the city's expense budget. In addition, he asked the First Boston Corporation to serve as the city's financial advisor and Ernst and Ernst, a major New York City accounting firm, to audit all city finances. Ernst and Ernst recommended additional financial safeguards, which Kucinich accepted without complaint. The Federal Reserve Board studied the Cleveland default and found: "The city indicated its willingness to implement these recommendations and, as stated in the Ernst and Ernst report, was in the process of initiating these recommendations" (U.S. Congress, 1979b, p. 130).

Still the banks were not satisfied. Why? Weir indicates that the Cleveland banking and business community wanted to punish Kucinich for his anticorporate stance. Earlier in 1978 they had bankrolled a recall campaign. When that failed, they decided to take more drastic actions. Five months after the default Weir admitted Cleveland's financial problems were "rather small." "The real problem," he asserted, "has been the social-political climate" (U.S. Congress, 1979b, p. 35). Weir noted that previous administrations had similar financial problems but, he explained, "We weren't asking the type of questions of them that we are asking this administration. There are a couple of reasons why. First New York happened. That taught us all a lesson about asking questions. The second reason is the attitude of the Kucinich administration. The Perk administration was not as antagonistic toward the business community and the banking community as to precipitate a showdown." On another occasion he declared, "We had been kicked in the teeth for six months. On December 15 we decided to kick back" (U.S. Congress, 1979b, p. 34). Less than 24 hours before the city defaulted, Weir wrote, "I believe the well publicized enmity of the city administration towards Cleveland bank officials has been completely unjustified and is from my viewpoint, a product of raw political power. I for one do not intend to take these allegations lying down" (U.S. Congress, 1979b, p. 34).

Not surprisingly, an analysis prepared for the House Committee on Banking, Finance, and Urban Affairs concluded that it was not dispassionate financial analysis but rather the bank's desire to humiliate Kucinich that precipitated the Cleveland default:

> The interlocking relationship of Cleveland Trust Company and some of the other banks with much of the corporate community, and the deep animosities and political cross-currents in which some bank officers became involved suggest the strong possibility that factors other than pure hard-nosed credit judgments entered the picture. At a minimum, it is impossible to conclude that key bankers donned green eye shades, locked themselves in their board rooms, and made dispassionate decisions based solely on computer runs. (U.S. Congress, 1979b, p. 839)

In his congressional testimony Kucinich charged that Cleveland's bankruptcy was a prime example of "capital" punishment. "A documented instance of the use of credit as a political lever, the withholding of credit as corporate extortion or corporate blackmail, is what emerges from any objective analysis of Cleveland's default," he explained (U.S. Congress, 1979b, p. 8). He concluded by charging that engineering municipal bankruptcies was only one of many weapons in the corporate arsenal. "Business officials exercise far greater power than any single politician. They decide whether to lend money to a city and on what terms. They decide whether to close a plant and put thousands of people out of work. They decide when, where, and how to invest billions of dollars of profit they have accumulated from the labor of working people. The people of America are beginning to demand that big business be held accountable for its decisions" (U.S. Congress, 1979b, p. 12).

Although Kucinich and his allies are demanding strict business accountability and an end to "corporate arrogance," congressional inaction has allowed corporate executives to wreak havoc in another midwestern city, Youngstown, Ohio. In September 1977 Youngstown Sheet and Tube closed its Campbell Works, putting 4,200 steelworkers on the unemployment rolls. Two years later United States Steel closed its McDonald Mills and Ohio Works, Jones and Laughlin announced the final closing date for its Campbell Works blast furnaces and Brier Hill facilities, and Republic Steel announced layoffs of 400-500 people. Altogether, the Youngstown metropolitan area lost 10,000 steel industry jobs in a two-year period.

The steel industry was quick to blame these closings on low profitability caused by EPA regulations and on cheap foreign steel being dumped in the United States by government-subsidized Japanese steel firms. Congressional hearings, however, indicate that other motives may have prompted these steel company decisions.

Bill Knoel, the president and chief executive officer of Cyclops Corporation, one of the nation's top ten steel firms, presented the industry story to Congress. He told them, "If new investment is to be made in the steel industry in this country, it should be the result of improved profitability. If we have reasonable profits, we will attract the capital we need in the competitive money markets of this country. And you will need no guarantees from the industry that we will invest in steel" (U.S. Congress, 1979a, p. 122). He attributed the low profitability to unfair trade practices and "de facto price controls at least since the Kennedy-Blough confrontation in the early 1960s." Yet Knoel also admitted:

> In spite of this, the steel industry in the United States is the most profitable in the world. Hear what I said. We are all concerned about the lack of adequate profitability of our domestic steel industry, but it is the most profitable in the world. . . . Let me point out it isn't a recent phenomenon. For the five years 1971 through 1975, the Japanese earnings averaged 1.7 percent on assets. And the European industry was .2 of 1 percent! During the same period, the United States steel industry's earnings were 5 percent. (U.S. Congress, 1979a, p. 120)

If the U.S. steel industry is as profitable as Knoel asserts, why have there been so many steel mill shutdowns? Ray Marshall, then Secretary of Labor, may have provided the answer. In an interview several weeks before leaving office, he recounted how he asked Japanese steel officials why they continue to invest in such a low-profit industry. After recovering from the shock of such a foolish question, they told him, "If we don't invest in steel, who will?" When Marshall raised the same issue with U.S. steel executives, they replied, "We don't make steel. We make money" (Sweeny, 1980, p. 18).

This attitude on the part of U.S. steel executives helps to explain the situation in Youngstown. As far back as 1969 government economists predicted that if Lykes Brothers Steamship Company, a New Orleans–based conglomerate, was permitted to purchase Youngstown Sheet and Tube, the steel mills would close within ten years. They reasoned that Lykes would have huge demands for cash to service the loans it took out to acquire Youngstown Sheet and Tube and to prop up other subsidiaries that had an insufficient cash flow. These cash demands would prevent needed investments and modernization, ensuring the steel works' eventual obsolescence. Such behavior is not limited to Lykes. Between 1977 and 1980 United States Steel increased its steel assets by 13 percent; their nonsteel assets grew by 80 percent. While its steel assets were growing more slowly than inflation, United States Steel built new petrochemical plants, searched for oil in South America, built a new test facility for jet aircraft, expanded its mining operations, and invested in real estate (U.S. Congress, 1980). In other words, steel corporations and conglomerates were refusing to invest in steel mills, even though they were profitable, because they believed they could earn a higher rate of return doing something else. These other investments may have improved their bottom line, but that is small consolation for the thousands of Youngstown steelworkers who suddenly found themselves out of work.

Despite this documented pattern of disinvestment, U.S. steel companies continue to ask Congress for import restrictions, tax preferences, and other forms of government assistance. Congress has received their requests favorably. Yet when the Youngstown Ecumenical Council requested government grants and loan guarantees to purchase Youngstown Sheet and Tube and reopen it as a community-owned venture, the Economic Development Administration drafted its denial even before the request was formally submitted. When another group of workers offered to purchase the unwanted steel mills from United States Steel, the corporation refused to consider the offer. This prompted then Senator Donald Stewart to remark:

Recently, United States Steel announced that it would not consider selling its Youngstown operations to the workers there, saying that the company recently asked Congress for a package of new programs to help maintain domestic steel production. How can the company ask Congress to help an industry keep up production when it refuses to sell a plant that conceivably could not continue to produce steel? The company, in any event, argues that the plant cannot compete. If this is true, then what does United States Steel have to fear? (U.S. Congress, 1980, p. 2)

Making Cities Safe for Corporations

In reality, big corporations have a great deal to fear from such proposals. Quite simply, their plans to revitalize midwestern cities could be destroyed if these more progressive alternatives prove viable. Instead of supporting community ownership and workplace democracy, they are declaring that midwestern cities will never regain their former stature as manufacturing centers in the industrial heartland while they are dominated by militant unions and mayors like Kucinich who advocate anticorporate policies. And as long as corporations retain control over investment policy, they will have the power to punish cantankerous mayors and to wrest concessions from unruly unions.

In a recent speech in Great Britain, Walter Wriston, the chairman of Citicorp, clearly and forcefully explained what political officials must do to prevent capital from fleeing to more hospitable climes. Although his remarks focused on the international movement of capital, they apply equally to mayors and prime ministers:

As a last resort, all the multinational company can do in its relations with a sovereign state is to make an appeal to reason. If this fails, capital, both human and material, will leave for countries where it is more welcome. Whether or not there is a shortage of capital is the subject of debate, but no one asserts there is a surplus. Since men and money will in the long run go where they are wanted and stay where they are well treated, capital can be attracted but not driven. In the long run it all comes down to this: the future of the global economy in any one area will be determined by the degree to which a particular government is willing and able to sacrifice the material well-being of its citizens to non-economic factors. Everything we've discussed thus far will be resolved almost automatically when our nation-states make up their minds concerning this one basic question. (Friedmann, 1978, p. 32)

Wriston's comments have recently been echoed, although in somewhat less candid form, by numerous urban policy analysts. For example, Peterson suggests that cities have no choice but to levy regressive taxes because they "best strengthen the local economy" (1979, p. 160). London notes perceptively that decaying cities are "waiting for people to come and do the investing." But it will be like waiting for Godot, he concludes, unless we "give politicians support when they vote against a nice hospital or more short-term aid because we need other things—to make this region grow" (1978, p. 189). Starr argues that local elites must become "environmentally indifferent," "marginally compassionate," tolerant of "growth inequality between persons," and willing to remove growth issues from the political process. Once the elites adopt these new attitudes, declining metropolitan areas "with adequate land, all sewered streets, electric lights available, with labor that's been reduced to desperation, will look like a promising place in which to undertake economic activities" (1978, p. 196).

But Wriston's "appeal to reason" and call for improving the "non-economic factors" suggest that these changes as well as such currently popular remedies as tax abatements, enterprise zones (Kemp, 1980), and subminimum wage scales will not be sufficient to revitalize cities. Although these policies would surely be greeted enthusiastically by multinational corporations and viewed as evidence that the local citizenry has seen pitfalls of anticorporate militancy, Wriston's speech suggests that capital will not be satisfied with anything less than a wholesale revamping of the local political system. After all, big business will not want to reinvest in places like Youngstown or Cleveland and then discover that voters have elected an unfriendly city council. Instead, it is demanding guarantees that the business climate has been permanently improved.

In Third World nations the International Monetary Fund serves to improve the business climate and impose austerity without first getting voter approval. In New York City businessmen serving on the Municipal Assistance Corporation (MAC) and Emergency Financial Control Board (EFCB) serve the same function. The EFCB, for example, was granted authority to impose a municipal employee pay freeze for the duration of the fiscal crisis and was empowered to seek jail sentences for any city official who interfered with the board's budget-cutting plans. Not surprisingly, Felix Rohatyn, the architect of the financial rescue plan that turned New York City into the private fiefdom of the banks, believes this political intervention should be imposed on other economically distressed cities in the Northeast and Midwest. In a 1979 speech in Austin, Texas, Rohatyn explained:

The influence that the private members of MAC and EFCB exerted was on the political process itself. . . . The direction and philosophy of a large unit of government was fundamentally and permanently changed as a result of the involvement, some would say intrusion, of the private sector in government. In my judgment, this is a principle that is applicable to a vast array of national problems for reasons not too dissimilar to the New York City experience. . . . The United States today in many ways is similar to New York City in 1975. (Watkins, 1981)

Conclusion

Wriston, Rohatyn, Weir, and their corporate allies clearly recognize that fundamental political reforms offer a tidier sort of austerity, one that will be less disruptive than episodic municipal bankruptcies and messy regional economic collapse. And by refusing to invest in certain cities, closing factories in others, and failing to extend loans to unfriendly mayors, they have the power to beat their political opposition into submission. For residents of midwestern cities, therefore, the choice is simple: barring any victories along the lines of worker ownership and economic democracy, their only options are migration to states like Texas that already have a "good business climate," or submission to the dictates of big business.

The stakes are high. At issue is not only the economic viability of these metropolitan areas but the future of democracy and self-government. These issues could not be more clearly highlighted than in the contrasting statements of Brock Weir and the Reverend Charles Rawlings, leader of the Youngstown Ecumenical Council.

In an interview conducted by a local radio station Weir announced, "I'm not elected by the public. I'm elected by private enterprise. I have obligations first and foremost to a bunch of individual private depositors and borrowers and to individual and collective groups of shareholders" (U.S. Congress, 1979b, p. 50).

Several months after Weir's candid admission, Rawlings told a congressional investigation:

It is not just Youngstown that is at stake in this hearing, as I am sure the committee members know. Rather, is is the possibility for economic recovery and survival in countless industrial cities that is challenged by the present course of events. The United States Steel Corporation's insistence on the right to neglect and then close a plant when coupled with the exercise of power to block others from buying the facilities and resuming production is an exercise of control over the life and welfare of communities that has not been given by this country's constitution to anyone—for such exercise of power is clearly injurious to the common good and public welfare. (U.S. Congress, 1980, p. 71)

References

Baer, W. C. 1976. On the death of cities. *Public Interest* 45 (Fall):3–10.

Banfield, E. 1973. *The unheavenly city revisited*. Boston: Little, Brown.

Friedmann, J. 1978. On the contradictions between city and countryside. *Comparative Urban Research* 6:1–41.

Goodman, R. 1979. *The last entrepreneurs*. New York: Simon and Schuster.

Goodwyn, L. 1978. *The populist movement*. New York: Oxford University Press.

Haberman, C. 1980. Koch administration attacks idea of United States aid for sun belt migration. *New York Times*, 29 Dec., p. 1.

Harrison, B. 1974. *Urban economic development*. Washington, D.C.: Urban Institute.

Harrison, B., and B. Bluestone. 1980. *Capital and communities*. Washington, D.C.: Progressive Alliance.

Jolidon, L. 1981. The long road south. *Houston City* 5 (Sept.):56–59, 160–65.

Kemp, J. 1980. Greenlining urban America: Enterprise zones for economic growth. *Commentary*, July, pp. 3–6.

Lemann, N. 1981. Gone to Texas. *Texas Monthly*, Sept., pp. 142–47, 260–74.

London, P. 1978. Revitalizing the Northeast: Making redevelopment politically acceptable. In G. Sternlieb and J. Hughes, eds., *Revitalizing the Northeast*. New Brunswick, N.J.: Rutgers University, Center for Urban Policy Research.

Lowry, I. 1980. The dismal future of central cities. In A. Soloman, ed., *The prospective city*. Cambridge: MIT Press.

Peterson, P. 1979. A unitary model of local taxation and expenditure policies. In D. Marshall, ed., *Urban policy making*. Beverly Hills, Calif.: Sage Publications.

President's Commission for a National Agenda for the Eighties. 1980. *Urban America in the eighties*. Washington, D.C.: U.S. Government Printing Office.

Starr, R. 1978. The intellectual ambience of decline. In G. Sternlieb and G. Hughes, eds., *Revitalizing the Northeast*. New Brunswick, N.J.: Rutgers University, Center for Urban Policy Research.

Sterba, J. 1976. Houston as energy capital sets pace in sun belt boom. *New York Times*, 9 Feb., p. 1.

Sternlieb, G. 1971. The city as sandbox. *Public Interest* 25 (Fall):14–21.

Sternlieb, G., and G. Hughes. 1977. New regional and metropolitan realities of America. *Journal of the American Institute of Planners* 43 (July):227–41.

Stevens, W. 1981. Unskilled northerners find sun belt job climate cooling. *New York Times,* 18 Aug., p. B11.

Sweeny, P. 1980. Ray Marshall on the Carter record, American industry, the days ahead. *Texas Observer,* 26 Dec., p. 17.

Tiebout, C. 1956. A pure theory of local government. *Journal of Political Economy* 64:416–24.

U.S. Bureau of the Census. 1980. Estimates of the population of counties and metropolitan areas: July 1, 1977 and 1978. *Current population reports.* Washington, D.C.: U.S. Government Printing Office, Series P-25, No. 873:Table 1.

———. 1981a. Geographic mobility: March 1975 to March 1980. *Current population reports.* Washington, D.C.: U.S. Government Printing Office, Series P-20, No. 368.

———. 1981b. Standard metropolitan statistical areas and consolidated statistical areas. *Census of population.* Washington, D.C.: U.S. Government Printing Office, Supplementary Report PC80–51–5:Table 1.

U.S. Congress. 1979a. *Problems in steel trade and the competitiveness of the American steel industry.* Field hearings before the Subcommittee on Trade of the Committee on Ways and Means, House of Representatives, 96th Cong., 1st sess., 30 Nov., 27 Dec.

———. 1979b. *Role of commercial banks in the financing of the debt of the city of Cleveland.* Hearing before the Subcommittee on Financial Institutions, Supervision, Regulation, and Insurance of the Committee on Banking, Finance, and Urban Affairs, House of Representatives, 96th Cong., 1st sess., 10 July.

———. 1980. *Effects of steel industry closing on small businesses and local communities.* Hearing before the Select Committee on Small Business, Senate, 96th Cong., 2d sess., 5 Feb.

U.S. Department of Housing and Urban Development. 1980. *The president's national urban policy report.* Washington, D.C.: U.S. Government Printing Office.

Watkins, A. 1980a. Good business climates: The second war between the states. *Dissent,* Fall, pp. 476–84.

———. 1980b. *The practice of urban economics.* Beverly Hills, Calif.: Sage Publications.

———. 1981. Felix Rohatyn's biggest deal. *Working Papers for a New Society* 8 (Sept./Oct.):44–52.

Woodward, C. V. 1951. *The origins of the new South: 1877–1913.* Baton Rouge: Louisiana State University Press.

6

Capital Infrastructure Deterioration and Planning in Midwestern Cities

CARL V. PATTON

The capital infrastructure of many midwestern cities is decaying. Streets, highways, bridges, water systems, sewers, public buildings, and the very nuts and bolts that hold midwestern cities together and make them livable are in disrepair.[1]

This urban crisis has many faces. First there is deterioration. Many older facilities, although properly designed, have declined because of deferred maintenance. Second, some capital facilities are inadequate because changing needs, demands, and technology have made them obsolete. These facilities, which were sufficient when constructed decades ago, cannot meet today's standards or handle the demand from population increases. Third, some communities have failed to install needed capital facilities as service needs expanded or as technology changed. Finally, some capital facilities function badly today because their original designs were deficient. All four problems exist in the Midwest, although the bulk of the region's capital facility problems spring from deterioration and lack of maintenance.[2]

The dilapidation of midwestern cities has made national headlines (Alexander, 1981; Associated Press, 1981). In Cleveland, as an example, internal rusting in water pipes has cut water supply drastically, and service has been interrupted many times. In 1978 a state judge ordered the city to relinquish control of the water system to another authority because "a state of emergency exists" (Mitgang, 1979, p. D–2). The city-owned water system needs $250-500 million in replacement and renovation, and an additional $340 million is needed to halt sewer system flooding of basements. Thirty percent of the city-owned bridges are unsatisfactory or deteriorated and need more than $150 million in major repairs. Likewise, 30 percent of the street system needs to be resurfaced or repaired (Humphrey et al., 1979b).

Infrastructure deterioration is not limited to the major cities of the Midwest. Smaller cities such as Decatur and Urbana in Illinois need to replace major portions of their outmoded sewer systems. In East St. Louis three-fourths of the city schools do not meet the state's health and life safety codes (Bahl, 1978). Even rural areas in the Midwest have experienced infrastructure deterioration. Miles of rural roads and hundreds of rural bridges are in desperate need of repair (Bunker and Hutchinson, 1979).

Continued neglect of capital facilities will place large financial burdens on future generations, hasten the outmigration of residents and industry, increase the likelihood of facility abandonment, reduce the chance of replacing the capital infrastructure in the future, and diminish the financial capacity of midwestern cities.

The purpose of this chapter, then, is to describe the infrastructure problem in the metropolitan Midwest, to identify approaches being taken to solve this problem, and to outline action that cities and towns in the Midwest might take to reverse their physical deterioration. Attention is focused on problems, policies, and programs rather than on an accounting of costs.[3] Furthermore, since local governments will bear the primary responsibility for repair, the steps they can take will be stressed. Even if federal funding becomes available, municipalities will have to establish priorities and develop planning, programming, and financial mechanisms to rebuild their infrastructures.[4]

Investigating the Problem

To begin this study, we identified cities that have recognized the existence of capital facility deterioration and have made efforts to solve the problem. We limited the search for such cities to the Midwest not only because of the focus of this book but also because many severe infrastructure problems are found within this region. In addition, the Midwest, as a microcosm of the nation, contains cities that exhibit the full range of urban problems; it thus provides an excellent stage on which to conduct this investigation. Finally, many midwestern cities are "on the brink"; they still have a reasonable chance to solve their capital stock problems.

We selected seven cities for study: Joliet, Illinois; Milwaukee, Wisconsin; Lansing, Michigan; Kansas City, Missouri; Indianapolis, Indiana;

Figure 1. Storm-water drainage problem—deteriorated roadway.

Figure 2. Deteriorated road surface on bridge.

Figure 3. Narrow bridge.

Figure 4. Structural deterioration of bridge.

Figure 5. Crumbling bridge sidewalk.

St. Paul, Minnesota; and Dayton, Ohio. They represent a range of cities located throughout the Midwest.[5] Like other researchers, we were stymied by the absence of comparable inventories and record-keeping systems for the cities under study. Nonetheless, with the assistance of professionals in the seven case cities, we developed an approximation of capital facility deterioration and needs for the major types of capital facilities, including sewer and water systems, roads, and bridges.[6] Data reported in the following case studies are drawn from personal interviews conducted during 1980 and 1981, unless otherwise noted. It is too early to evaluate case city efforts to solve the capital deterioration problem. Nonetheless their recognition of the problem and systematic attempts to deal with it provide valuable lessons for other cities.

Joliet

The home of the Checker Cab Company and the Joliet Livestock Marketing Center (a successor to the Chicago stock yards), Joliet experienced recent rapid growth to reach its current population of 78,000. According to the director of public works, Joliet has serious problems because some components of the infrastructure "don't exist or weren't built properly in the first place." For example, the city has annexed areas that had not been developed under the city's subdivision regulations and thus did not have proper infrastructure systems. Streets were often constructed without flexible pavement at intersections and without curbs and gutters. Some sections that were built without storm sewers now experience flooding and erosion.

Joliet's chief planner cites the combined storm and sanitary sewer system as the city's largest infrastructure problem. Over half of the developed area of the city is served by combined sewers (City of Joliet, 1979), and all of the sewers built before 1960 are combined. Sewer backups have caused widespread basement flooding so that the city of Joliet has had to bypass combined sewage directly into local streams and rivers during heavy rains. Backup problems have been so severe in some areas that street drainage catch basins have been cemented shut, resulting in flood damage to the streets they were to drain.

In addition, both of the city's sanitary sewer treatment plants need expansion and updating to meet federal wastewater requirements. The city's west-side plant and major west-side interceptors were built only five years ago, before the most recent capital improvement plan was established, but the interceptors are already inadequate.

The city also faces a long-range water supply problem. Joliet relies primarily on deep aquifer wells, and the city has determined that a new water source will be needed before the end of the century to augment the ground water.

Joliet has responded to these problems through a Capital Improvement Plan (CIP) process that was started in 1977, one of the newest and most basic of those examined. The preparation of Joliet's five-year CIP is essentially an administrative process; the city's capital improvements coordinator (who is also the city's chief planner) compiles the CIP and oversees its production. The process begins when the coordinator sends project proposal forms to the heads of departments that might undertake capital improvement projects during the next five years. The form asks for a brief description of the proposed project, its location, an estimate of its total cost, sources of funding, an estimate of the project's effect on operating costs and revenues, and an evaluation of its positive and negative impacts. The form also asks departments to determine how consistent each project is with other current or proposed projects and with city plans and policies. Finally, the department must assign each proposed project a priority ranking.

The capital improvements coordinator reviews each department's list to ensure that the proposed projects are consistent and that they do not conflict with city plans and policies. The director of the Finance Department then reviews the projects to make sure that the funding sources identified by the departments can accommodate their proposals. With this information the coordinator compiles a first draft of the CIP, which is then returned to department heads for comments.

The plan commission must then approve the proposed CIP. The commission, with the city council, holds a public meeting on the proposed CIP. It is also sent to the city manager for evaluation, and the recommendations of the plan commission and the city manager are forwarded to the council. After the city council reviews and makes amendments to the proposed CIP, it approves the CIP by passing an ordinance. The first year of the completed CIP then forms the basis for the development of the capital improvement budget for the next year. The city council adopts the capital budget with the city operating budget during the annual budget cycle.

Direct citizen participation in the development of the CIP is minimal and has consisted of poorly attended public hearings. Current efforts in Joliet are concentrated on ensuring support of the new process within the city staff. For the moment this is taking precedence over encouraging increased public participation. Joliet has developed a technical CIP process that is able to respond to rather concrete, clearly defined capital needs. However, the mayor and other local officials are concerned that Joliet will not be able to maintain its capital infrastructure because of increasing project costs and public unwillingness to support tax increases and special assessments.

Milwaukee

The "beer city" of the "Dairy State," Milwaukee has a population of 630,000, making it the largest city in Wisconsin. The Milwaukee area, which is located on Lake Michigan and drains into several major rivers, faces extensive, costly renovation and repair of its sewer and water systems. In 1975 the state of Wisconsin sued the Milwaukee Metropolitan Sewerage District, charging that overflows from Milwaukee's sewer system spilled untreated sewage into Lake Michigan and thereby violated water quality standards and endangered health. Deteriorated sewer facilities and combined sewers were named as the major causes of the system's overflow problem. In May 1977 the circuit court ordered Milwaukee to eliminate virtually all overflows from its sewage system and to treat all its sewage. A federal court, in a parallel suit, also decided against Milwaukee later that year. The federal court order required a higher level of overflow abatement than the state court ordered, but this decision has since been overturned by the U.S. Supreme Court.

The Master Facilities Plan, developed in response to the circuit court order, describes cracked, deteriorating, and leaking sewers in a system that is more than a century old. According to the plan, 13 percent of the clear water problem (entry into the system of water that does not need treatment) can be eliminated through sewer rehabilitation, an $86 million program that includes a sewer evaluation study, the repair of collapsed and broken sewer lines, and the disconnection of sources of clear water inflow (Laszewski, 1980). The plan also calls for the elimination of overflow from combined sewers by the construction of two major new interceptor sewers for inline storage plus underground cavern storage. Solving the combined sewer problem will cost approximately $328 million.

One of the district's two treatment plants has also proved inadequate. Major plant rehabilitation, improvement, and expansion are necessary at the 1920s Jones Island plant to meet wastewater treatment needs and federal and state pollution regulations.

Both Milwaukee Metropolitan Sewerage District and city officials stated that by undertaking the sewage rehabilitation project they have seriously jeopardized their ability to tackle other needed capital improvement projects. Overall, Milwaukee's capital infrastructure is in good repair, although bridge maintenance and replacement have apparently not kept pace with need. The city is now faced with financing a stepped-up bridge replacement program; four bridges were replaced in the last five years and even this appears less than is needed. Milwaukee's other infrastructure problems include deteriorated alleys, aging harbor dock walls, and improperly installed water mains.

A staffed body made up of engineers, planners, and financial experts, which operates independently of any agency or department, prepares Milwaukee's Capital Improvement Program. The annual process of producing the CIP, which has evolved since the 1940s, begins when the capital improvements committee, comprised of the commissioner of public works, commissioner of city development, and comptroller, requests departments and agencies to project capital needs for the next year and the five following years. Departments use engineering data, citizens' complaints, and similar information to decide on projects and establish priorities among them. The departments submit the project requests to the committee staff along with data on need, facility life, capital cost, impact on the city operating budget, and potential revenues.

The projects then go through a two-cycle decision process. The technical subcommittee evaluates each project and program by holding hearings in which departments present and justify their proposals. From the information gathered at these hearings and from their independent examination of projects the subcommittee prepares a proposed six-year CIP.

In a second round of hearings departments present and defend their proposals, and the capital improvements committee reviews the findings of the subcommittee and amends the subcommittee's proposed six-year program. The technical subcommittee then assigns an overall priority ranking to each project in the amended program.

After the capital improvements committee reviews these priority ratings, it is finally ready to establish a planned six-year Capital Improvement Program. A capital budget, based on the initial year of the CIP, is evaluated by the Department of Budget and Management Analysis, which holds hearings and makes its recommendations to the mayor. The mayor includes the capital budget in his proposed annual executive budget, holds public hearings, then submits his executive budget to the common council for its review and approval. After the council adopts the executive budget, the capital budget is established as the first year of the six-year program.

The relatively good condition of Milwaukee's capital plant can be attributed to the city's well-developed, reliable CIP process and a CIP publication that serves as a working document rather than a "wish list." In fact, the first year of the CIP becomes the capital budget. The independent CIP committee is also seen as a way to assure that decisions are made in the best interests of the community. Of course, the recent wastewater treatment court orders have overshadowed the CIP process. Furthermore, the commissioner of public works has stated that the city faces a "tremendous struggle" to maintain capital facility quality because of increased costs and decreased funding.

Lansing

The capital of Michigan, Lansing is also the site of the largest Oldsmobile plant in the nation. It is perhaps ironic, then, that street maintenance in this city of 130,000 is a major problem. Each year a street inspection is conducted to augment a detailed 1977 survey, and although only 80 percent of the update was complete at the time of our study,

approximately 300 miles of local streets were rated as in need of immediate resurfacing in 1980. In 1979, however, the year before the most
recent update, the city had been able to afford to resurface only 9 miles of
local streets. The condition of major streets is also dismal; out of approximately 100 miles of major streets, 13 miles need immediate resurfacing,
but the city had funds to resurface only 5 miles in 1979.

Bridges, too, suffer from deterioration. A consultant's study of bridge
renovation, which included an evaluation of general condition, strength,
steel supports, concrete, and weight restrictions needed, indicated that
16 of the 21 bridges surveyed needed major repair or maintenance (Snell
Environmental Group, 1980). Visual inspection of one bridge, which
was recently restricted to passenger cars only, showed rusted steel support girders, collapsing sidewalks, and a severely deteriorated street
surface with holes so large that the river below could be seen through
them. Visual surveys of other bridges revealed similar conditions.

The city also has a combined sewer problem; one-third of the city is
served by combined sewers. The overflow of untreated sewage into local
drainage courses has created friction between the city and the state of
Michigan's Department of Natural Resources (DNR), which has
authority to approve expansion of sewer systems within the state. For six
months development in Lansing came to a standstill because the DNR
refused to allow the city to add new sewage customers until it moved to
meet EPA guidlines and to stop overflow discharges into the river. The
DNR currently grants Lansing permission to add new customers as
existing discharges are reduced.

The city of Lansing is mandated by state law and by city charter to
prepare a six-year capital program annually. Responsibility for producing the Capital Development Program (CDP) lies with the City Planning Department and with its advisory body, the Planning Board.

To prepare and update the CDP, the staff of the Planning Department
solicits information throughout the year from city agencies and departments about needed capital improvement projects and the priorities to
be assigned them. Additional information is secured when the proposed
CDP is submitted to the departments for their review and comment.
Projects and programs entered into the CDP are derived not only from
city agencies and departments but also from the previous year's CDP,
from a review of the previous year's budget appropriations, from the
capital budget requests for the upcoming year, and from city plans and
ongoing planning programs. In addition, the Planning Department
submits the CDP for review to 50-75 neighborhood organizations and
citizen's groups. At a public hearing held by the Planning Board, these
groups and other interested individuals and organizations comment on

the CDP and on other needed projects. In selecting projects for the CDP, the Planning Department is guided by a statement of budget policies and priorities issued by the city council, as required by the city charter.

Once the Planning Department has updated the CDP, it is submitted both to the Planning Board and to the mayor for approval. The plan goes to the city council at the same time that the mayor sends his proposed annual budget to the council, so that the CDP can guide the council's budget considerations (although Planning Department staff stated that the actual use of the CDP for this purpose is minimal). The council holds a joint public hearing on both the CDP and on the proposed city budget. After making any desired amendments the council adopts the budget and the CDP.

The CDP plays a small role in determining what projects eventually appear in the capital budget. Departments do not see the CDP as a planning tool and, once completed, it is "out of sight, out of mind." The lack of interaction between the planning and other departments during the preparation of the CDP impairs its value as a tool for maintenance and repair of capital facilities. The Planning Department hopes that by working more closely with departments in the development of the CDP, and possibly by simplifying it, the CDP may become a more viable document.

Kansas City

A "buying and selling" town of 450,000 people along the old Santa Fe Trail and the Missouri River, Kansas City remains an important distribution center for midwestern agricultural products. As a transportation center, the city depends on good roads and bridges. Unfortunately, most of the bridges in the city were built before 1920 and are, in the words of the director of public works, "antiquated." The majority were not designed for current traffic levels, and several informants stated that they have not received adequate maintenance since their construction. City officials estimate that bridges carry 20 to 30 percent of total daily traffic in Kansas City and note that the city's industrial areas are especially dependent on the bridge network.

The city engineer reported that 22 bridges require "immediate" replacement. A 1978 bridge condition survey determined that two-thirds of the 307 bridges evaluated needed more than routine maintenance, and that more than $10 million in bridge work was necessary. Several hazardous bridges have been closed to traffic, affecting the traffic patterns of thousands of Kansas City residents.

In addition, many streets are so damaged that they cannot take current traffic loads or levels. The city budget officer stated that the city has spent

$5.5-7 million per year on its street resurfacing program and added that these expenditures are "just not sufficient to get the streets to where they should be." According to the director of the Department of Public Works, $20 million is needed to pay for curb and gutter replacement.

Sewer system problems also exist. Of the 316 square miles of the city, 80 square miles are served by combined sewers that date back 80 to 125 years (City of Kansas City, 1979). According to the city engineer, flooding is a common problem; a thousand Kansas City households regularly get water in their basements after only an inch of rainfall. Although the director of public works referred to the deficient storm drainage system as the city's biggest infrastructure problem, and although the lack of an adequate system has caused erosion and pollution in some watersheds, he stated that because a "dramatic amount of dollars" is needed to deal with the problem, no systematic effort has been undertaken to separate the sewers.

Kansas City does have a method to plan capital improvements that was established in the early 1970s under the federal 701 Planning Grant Program. Departments essentially produce their own CIPs by using engineering data and other information to ascertain their needs for the next budget year and for the subsequent five years. Several departments have sophisticated mechanisms to inventory and determine needs. Departments submit their plans to the city budget officer on project request forms, providing a basic description of each project proposal, a brief justification, a breakdown of costs by year, and priority ratings. Guided generally by departmental priority ratings, the budget officer produces a six-year inventory of capital improvement needs and selects projects to be included in the annual capital improvements program budget. The budget is reviewed by the Department of City Development for development implications and is then submitted to the city manager, who in turn reviews it and submits it to the mayor and city council. The council makes the final decisions on projects depending upon resources. Although they are free to select projects, they tend to respond to department priorities.

Officials and politicians in Kansas City feel that the city has exhausted pay-as-you-go financing for capital improvements, and that the city's ability both to maintain and update the infrastructure and to provide badly needed new capital facilities has begun to suffer. The city manager estimates that recent annual capital expenditures have met only 10 percent of the annual need, and there is wide recognition that a mechanism to increase the chance of voter approval of bond issues is urgently necessary. Between 1970 and 1980 only 6 of 39 bond issues were approved. In response, the Citizen's Advisory Committee (CAC) on

Capital Improvements was formed by the mayor in 1980. The CAC, which reports to the mayor and council, determines Kansas City's capital improvement needs independently and separately from city departments. In evaluating plans, the committee does not consider financing, other than to identify projects that require bonding. City officials hope that when citizens themselves determine the city's needs, voters will be more willing to pay for them.

Indianapolis

The home of the Indy "500" and the capital of the state, Indianapolis is known for its consolidated city-county government. This town of 700,000 also has a bridge maintenance problem. The director of the Department of Transportation has estimated that 50 of the city's 489 bridges are in "dire" need of repair and should be closed to traffic and replaced immediately. The city has already shut down several bridges. Although a strong demand for bridge replacement and renovation in the next decade is foreseen, the availability of funding is doubtful (City of Indianapolis, 1980).

Street maintenance has also fallen behind. The director of the Department of Metropolitan Development (DMD) stated that the city should be repaving 300 miles of streets every year, so that each street would be repaved every ten years. He added that the city "had never hit 300 miles." The most ever achieved was 260 miles in one year, but ten years ago the city was repaving as little as 50 miles per year. According to the director of the DMD, curbs, gutters, and sidewalks have also been neglected and are rapidly deteriorating.

Indianapolis, like other cities in this study, is served in a large part of its central city by combination sanitary/storm sewers that flood regularly and discharge sewage into rivers and streams. This situation will almost certainly continue, because, as the director of the Division of Planning in the DMD states, "There has not been a deliberate or conscious effort or attempt to set up a program that would systematically replace the combined sewer system with a separate system because costs are just astronomical. There is no way it could be done." The city is attempting to separate the combined systems as new development or redevelopment occurs, but the sewage eventually flows back into the combined system.

Indianapolis's parks are also in trouble. A property tax freeze has prevented park support from being increased, and revenue is not available for long-term capital programs or even for routine maintenance of the existing park system. Parks, a low-priority item, operate on a budget smaller than that of five years ago. The result is serious deterioration of park infrastructure.

As part of the effort to resolve these problems, the Department of Metropolitan Development produces a five-year CIP entitled the Capital Expenditure Program (CEP), which serves as input into the annual budget process. The DMD invites operating departments that are likely to need capital improvements to a meeting at which DMD personnel lay out the CIP ground rules. Departments then submit capital requests on DMD forms, basing their project proposals primarily on engineering data and funding availability. Departments set their own priorities, and there is little interdepartmental coordination.

The DMD reviews the proposed projects to determine consistency with growth and development objectives. In actual practice, this review, although it varies from year to year, has never been very extensive. After review by the DMD, the final capital expenditures document is submitted to the Metropolitan Development Commission, the advisory body for the DMD. The commission recommends which projects should be undertaken and sends the CEP to the mayor, who officially transmits it and the staff and commission recommendations to the city-county council (city and county governance is unified under the Indianapolis Unigov System). The CEP is to be used by the council as a guide when making annual budget appropriations. The use of this document for that purpose has been minimal, however, because most funds are dispensed in lump sums on a departmental rather than project basis, and because council members prefer to rely on their own judgment in approving budget proposals.

A growth policy, under development for four years and seen as likely to be adopted, represents a new effort to provide policies by which capital projects can be evaluated on a more sophisticated level. A DMD spokesman sees the growth policy as a "keystone from which capital budgeting and programming can become an analytical rather than a cataloging, inventorying tool." Upon adoption by the council, the growth policy would provide, according to the proposed policy document, "a common base from which to make capital facility, amenity and land-use decisions regarding future urban development" (Greater Indianapolis Progress Committee, 1980, p. 45).

St. Paul

St. Paul, the capital of Minnesota, and Minneapolis, its twin city, are frequently cited as examples of progressive governance because of the metropolitan council, an areawide planning and coordinating body for the region. In spite of this enlightened government, there remain unsolved capital deterioration problems in the twin cities.

For example, St. Paul, a city of 270,000 in this metropolitan area of 2 million, needs to undertake extensive and costly sewer maintenance and rehabilitation. The useful life of most sewer pipes is 70 to 100 years. Today, over three-fourths of the sewers in St. Paul are at least 50 years old, and some are more than 100 years old. The city is currently assessing sewer conditions and has begun to plan a systematic rehabilitation program. Additional difficulties are caused by the fact that St. Paul is served by a combined sanitary and storm-water sewage system with insufficient capacity that causes sewer backups into homes, businesses, and streets. Since 1955 the city has spent approximately $2 million per year for storm sewer construction, and as yet, only 30 percent of the city's sewer system is separated.

St. Paul has also been unable to maintain adequately or rehabilitate the 36 percent of the city's bridges for which it is responsible. Approximately 15 percent of the city bridges have a federal sufficiency rating below 50, indicating that replacement is necessary. Another 30 percent score between 50 and 80 on sufficiency ratings that show the need for extensive repair. The city Public Works Department has developed a priority list for bridge repair and replacement. Between $3 and $4 million are allocated annually, and the city repairs the worst bridges first.

There are approximately 300 miles of arterial streets and 400 miles of residential streets in St. Paul. A 30-year replacement cycle for arterial streets would require an annual expenditure in current dollars of approximately $7 million, but the current annual allocation for replacement of arterial streets falls between $5 and $5.5 million. A 50-year replacement cycle for residential streets would require an annual expenditure in current dollars of approximately $5 million, but St. Paul is allocating only $1 million per year for residential street replacement. Altogether, the city is short approximately $6 million each year for street replacement (Aichinger, 1980).

St. Paul is responding to its capital facility needs through a two-year capital budgeting and programming process. The process begins with a citizen task force review of Capital Allocation Policies (CAP), a statement of policies for evaluating capital improvements proposals. Project proposals from operating departments and city organizations are reviewed by the planning commission to assure conformance to adopted plans and allocation policies. The budget office then holds meetings with departments to identify conflicts between the proposed projects and the CAP or other city plans or policies. With this information, the budget office conducts a preliminary review of projects, eliminating those that are clearly inappropriate. After reviewing any changes in their lists, departments submit formal project funding requests to the city budget director, who then sends all project requests to the capital improvement budget committee.

The committee consists of 18 citizens appointed by the mayor to evaluate project proposals and recommend a capital budget. It performs its duties primarily through three task forces, each one dealing with a specific functional area. The task forces establish priorities among projects by using rating sheets that are designed to ensure both that capital allocation policies play the primary role in setting priorities and that all projects conform to city policies. Each project is rated on a number of items: the project's contribution to the repair or replacement of obsolete facilities, the adequacy of its programming and phasing, and its effect on energy consumption and operating and maintenance costs.

The capital improvements budget committee then merges the priority lists of the task forces into a draft budget for each funding source and holds hearings where citizens can support or oppose its budget recommendations. After the hearings the committee develops a recommended capital budget for the upcoming two years and a CIP program for the five ensuing years. Both the mayor and the city council review the committee's recommended budget. The mayor also holds a public hearing and then proposes his version of the two-year budget. The mayor's proposed capital budget and the committee's five-year program are submitted to the city council, which holds two public hearings and then adopts budget appropriations for the capital projects.

St. Paul's capital fund allocation process and its extensive citizen involvement grew from an attempt to secure a more stable flow of capital improvement funds. Instead of seeking voter authorization for capital project bonds, St. Paul is allowed by the state of Minnesota to issue a set amount of general obligation bonds without voter referendum. The county delegation to the state legislature oversees the city's capital allocation procedure, under which citizen involvement in the budget process is substituted for voter approval. This arrangement notwithstanding, funding for capital improvements falls short of need.

Dayton

Located in southwestern Ohio's Miami Valley, Dayton, the fourth largest city in the state, is the home of National Cash Register, Continental Data Systems, and numerous machine tool companies. An old city, Dayton has many major capital facilities that were built in the late 1920s and are now wearing out all at once. As a consequence, major renovation and replacement of capital facilities are currently taking place in this city of 200,000 persons.

Street maintenance and repair are the most urgent priorities. Forty-two percent of Dayton's thoroughfares are more than 50 years old, and 52 percent of these thoroughfares have not been resurfaced within the past 21 years, even though the average expected life of resurfacing is 17 years. The need for maintenance and repair of thoroughfares, residential streets, bridges, and signals in Dayton has forced the city to allocate the largest portion of its 1981 CIP budget to its surface transportation system.

Capital improvements are also needed in some areas of the city to alleviate backup of wastewater into home basements, a situation caused by residents having tied stormwater drainage into the sanitary sewer system. Drainage problems also occur during heavy rains when debris collects at storm sewers. Replacement and maintenance costs for sanitary sewers, storm sewers, sewer support, and wastewater treatment are estimated at $650 million, but only about $34 million have been allotted for sewer maintenance and replacement in the 1981 CIP budget.

Dayton's bridges also need repair. One hundred of the city's 157 bridges are considered to be in need of minor repairs and ongoing maintenance to extend their useful lives. Thirteen bridges are at "minimal tolerable limits," meaning that repair or rehabilitation is essential for safety (City of Dayton, 1981, p. 13). Dayton has a five-year bridge maintenance program in which bridges are scheduled for repair either by the city work force or by contract.

In the mid-1970s it became apparent to Dayton officials that deferred maintenance was not the most economical long-term CIP policy. This realization led to a total revision of the budget document from a line item to a program document. The budget now presents, program by program, the community conditions, the city services provided to meet these conditions, and the cost of providing these services. It attempts to interrelate city service goals, community problems, program objectives, performance criteria, and program budgets. During 1980 the city council identified general community goals and objectives and adopted them by formal resolution. They are now used as the foundation for plans, strategies, and resource allocation decisions.

Dayton's city council has aggressively pursued a program to increase intergovernmental revenues. After the city council made a commitment to increase investments, the administration put in a new system to evaluate each project request according to its impact on the approved allocation framework. Participants in the evaluation process include department directors, members of the capital investment committee (CIC), and citizen representatives. The greater the impact and the more priorities affected, the higher the rating a project receives. Projects that contribute the most to the achievement of city goals are selected.

The CIC, appointed by the city manager, consists of the assistant city managers, the budget and planning officers, and the department director responsible for public works contracts. This committee is charged with developing Dayton's CIP and has spelled out the priorities to be used in evaluating project requests. Factors for setting priorities include city goals, approved plans and strategies, departmental and citizen goals, budgetary impacts, and capital facilities impacts.

The CIP process begins when departments and elected neighborhood priority boards are sent project request forms by Dayton's OMB. The OMB submits the completed forms to the CIC's technical advisory committee, which evaluates and ranks each project. The CIC selects those projects to be considered for inclusion in the capital budget and notifies departments and priority boards of its decisions. Departments and priority boards can appeal to the OMB. The CIC undertakes a second evaluation of proposed projects and makes a final recommendation to the city manager. The capital budget is then combined with the operating budget into an integrated program budget for consideration and approval by the city council. Although Dayton has a one-year capital budget, long-term maintenance and replacement schedules mean that the city also has a long-term capital expenditure commitment.

Dayton's capital budgeting process now gives increased consideration to infrastructure maintenance. The city has changed its funding priorities to assure that maintenance programs are adequately financed and uses part of its municipal income tax for capital improvements. Dayton has also developed a basic inventory of capital conditions and a repair and replacement schedule. The city is making what its budget manager calls "a serious effort to keep the replacement schedules on track."

Generalizations

The seven case cities have recognized the importance of capital improvement programming to arrest deterioration, and each city has devised a method for producing an improvement plan. The CIP processes can be classified as technical, fiscal, political, and citizen review models, although the four models do not describe particular cities and are not mutually exclusive. The four models do, however, clarify the procedures that have had some success in the case cities. All models share the basic stages of the CIP process: projects are proposed, a master list is compiled, and projects are analyzed by staff, reviewed by council, placed in priority, and eventually approved and implemented.

The technical model is distinguished by the reliance both on technical recommendations from department heads and on short-term financial analysis. The fiscal model involves not only more sophisticated longer-term financial analyses but also greater coordination among city departments and greater consideration of long-range development objectives. The political model is characterized by the setting of spending priorities primarily by politicians. Although all models provide for some citizen input, the citizen review model is marked by the incorporation of citizen input at several steps in the CIP process.

The technical model centers around project review and is driven by technical priorities. Individual departments compile a list of projects they deem to be needed, and the city's budget officer determines which of these projects can be included in the city budget in light of continuing operating budget requirements. The budget officer then submits a capital budget along with the regular operating budget to the mayor. Capital projects make their way into the mayor's budget because they are rated high by individual departments, are well documented by the requesting departments, and provide necessary, basic services.

The fiscal model has evolved in those cities that have a more complex fiscal setting and the capacity for long-range budget planning. The project review process is preceded by an estimate of fiscal capability for forthcoming years. This revenue estimate provides the basis for both the general operating budget of the city and project priorities for individual department budgets. One or more committees, most often an administrative committee comprised of department heads, the mayor or chief administrative officer, and other city staff members responsible for fiscal matters, then review project requests from the individual departments for consistency and technical and political feasibility. These project requests are also scrutinized by the planning or development department or a similar city division to help assure consistency both with long-range plans and with the plans of nearby jurisdictions and independent agencies such as water and school districts. These committees then submit their findings and recommendations to the mayor through the budget officer, who reconciles the recommendations with a revised revenue estimate and operating budget needs. By this time the list of capital projects has been shortened substantially and becomes an element of the mayor's annual budget.

In contrast to the technical and fiscal models, capital budgets under the political model tend to be made by council. City departments submit individual project requests to the budget review officer, who examines them for fiscal accuracy. The projects may be compiled in a draft budget that is submitted to council for review. Department heads and citizens alike may petiton council for favored projects. The council may seek advice from the planning department, but the council makes the final decision about projects to include in the city budget.

A more complex and lengthy process has evolved in the case cities that need capital improvements but have not been able to convince citizens to vote for tax increases. Under the citizen review model citizens are brought into the capital facility planning process at several points, but special efforts are made to involve them at the beginning. General priorities are generated early in the CIP process through an annual citizen survey or through communitywide meetings. Citizens may enter the process again to comment on specific proposals by city departments, and they may also go over the completed budget. Under the citizen review model, departments may combine citizen input with technical data in order to generate proposals. These projects, which usually number more than could ever be funded, may then undergo citizen evaluation in order to measure support for them, to reveal conflicts among them, and to clarify the preferences of city neighborhoods. The city budget officer also examines the proposed projects for cost and consistency. This official ascertains the number of projects to be included in the operating budget, the number that require other types of financing, and the sources of funding available. The budget officer is again responsible for assembling a proposed budget for council and citizen review, and the final product becomes the mayor's budget.

Each model has its advantages and disadvantages. The most compli- cated one, the citizen review model, is not necessarily the best. The most desirable model for a particular city depends on that city's prior experi- ence in capital programming, its fiscal status, its ability to project revenues and expenditures, and its technical capacity to conduct facility inventories. The historic relationship among city participants in plan- ning and policy development is also significant.

Where no CIP process exists, the technical model would be the easiest to adopt, since the departments responsible for the capital projects are responsible for identifying needs, and these projects are selected on the basis of technical need within a fixed budget. The fiscal model, on the other hand, would be more appropriate for cities with a number of spending departments and a relatively high level of technical ability. The technical model might be adopted as a step toward implementing the fiscal model. The political model may be the most widely used CIP method. Because it tends to spread capital projects throughout a city, it has worked well in past years when funds for cities have been adequate. In a future where targeting may be essential if limited funds are to make an impact, the political model may well be insufficient.

Finally, the citizen review model, despite its time-consuming attributes, may be essential to convince citizens to finance capital improvements. This model increases the stake of participants in the CIP process and at the same time informs them about capital facility shortcomings that fall between or cut across individual neighborhood needs. Communities that adopt this model seek to expand the parochial views of neighborhoods and other interest groups in order to generate support for communitywide capital improvements.

These case cities have sought to place authority in the Capital Improvement Program by converting the CIP report from a "wish list" into a working document that sets forth a city's priorities. In this way they attempt to transform the CIP process from a mere inventory procedure to a decision-making one. Projects are not simply listed in the CIP but are also subjected to technical and political analysis so that those projects eventually included are feasible. Cities also build confidence in the CIP process and CIP documents by establishing a clear relationship between the budget for the first year of the CIP and the city's annual budget. Attempts are being made to assure that Capital Improvement Programs, especially in their first two years, provide guidance to private developers and public agencies.

Some case cities are also making conceptual changes in their project planning processes. Emphasis on policy is replacing an individual project orientation, and a neighborhood focus is replacing the citywide orientation of many city departments. Efforts are also being made to coordinate projects among city departments and between the city and other jurisdictions more carefully. Much of this activity, however, is merely rhetoric. The number of staff members devoted to CIP preparation and implementation, and the financial resources available, remain limited.

Lack of funds is perhaps the greatest impediment to solving the capital deterioration problem. In all these cities the level of local and state funding for capital improvements has stagnated or declined. Some cities have also found it increasingly difficult to raise funds through bonding.[7] In addition, federal assistance has not kept up with need. Most current observers do not hold great hopes for a reversal of these trends in the near future.[8] Even if Congress provides funds for rebuilding decaying infrastructure, major needs will remain.

The public's failure or inability to recognize deterioration contributes to infrastructure decline. "Out of sight, out of mind" applies to most capital facilities, especially sewer and water systems, but also to such "invisible" items as bridge supports and building safety systems. Furthermore, many citizens who have rejected bond referenda argue, "It's really not as bad as they say. Nothing has happened yet, and every year they say it's ready to collapse." One informant summed up the difficulty of generating support for capital replacement by his comment: "Sewers don't have constituencies."

It is, however, too easy to blame the condition of capital facilities on the lack of citizen support, for politicians and public officials have also been remiss. Their failure derives not only from the notorious short-term view of politicians and the absence of public pressure but also from a lack of basic information about the extent of deterioration. In many cases those who are knowledgeable about deterioration have not communicated this information to others. Furthermore, some officials and politicians hold an "I don't want to know" attitude. They argue that the problem is virtually unsolvable, so there is little reason to think about it! Moreover, public officials and politicians apparently have a good grasp of the public's view toward deterioration and spending. Many citizens are apparently willing to live with poor conditions that do not affect them directly if doing so will eliminate or postpone a tax increase.

The cities in our study are among those in the Midwest that have recognized that capital improvement planning and programming are crucial to arrest deterioration, yet even these cities have experienced problems in developing and maintaining citizen interest in their CIP procedures. Attitudes toward the CIP process vary. It is sometimes seen as an infringement on the authority and prerogatives of individual departments and as a way to disguise the politics of capital facilities planning. But because of the dire consequence of failure, politicians and officials in these midwestern cities seem to support the CIP process and are undertaking strong implementation efforts.

Prospects

If communities continue to postpone capital expenditures, the costs in the future will certainly exceed today's costs. Capital replacement today thus means that less will have to be spent in future years. The need is so great, however, that midwestern cities are not likely to catch up if today's expected level of services is to be continued. Already midwesterners are learning to live with deterioration. Triage may have to be practiced in the future. Capital facilities in very poor condition may have to be abandoned to save the rest of the municipal body. Minimal maintenance may have to be given those facilities in good condition, and the bulk of resources will have to be spent to restore sound but deteriorating facilities.

Expectations may also have to be lowered. Midwesterners may have to accept a reduced number of municipal services and a reduced level of service from those municipal facilities that remain. Not all residents will be willing to accept these reductions, so we are likely to witness the establishment of assessment districts for the provision of neighborhood or sub-area services and the expansion of user fees for other services.[9] Funding will certainly be a primary issue, and midwestern communities should expect to absorb more of the costs of financing through local taxes, new forms of bonding, and such techniques as tax increment financing.[10] Planners in the case communities know that the bulk of funding in the long run will have to come from local jurisdictions, and some are attempting to open the eyes of politicians, officials, and the public to the severity of the problem. In concert with this effort, they are working to convince community leaders that it is important to establish a realistic CIP process. To achieve these goals, these planners are becoming more involved in the political aspects of capital facility decision making.

Because fewer projects will be funded, more accurate, detailed studies of proposed CIP projects will be required. Even more attention will have to be given to analyses of conditions, to the possible effects of continued neglect, and to alternative development patterns. Greater stress on long-range factors in the CIP process, and a greater linkage between the general planning process of communities and the project planning of city departments, will be essential.[11] Emphasis must be shifted from individual projects to policies designed to guide the selection of groups of projects that, in combination, will bring the greatest return on the limited capital facility dollar.[12] Determining such policies demands not only more informed citizen participation but also better project analysis by professional staff so that meaningful alternatives are provided for the public's choice.

For the most part, municipalities appear virtually unorganized in their attack on the capital deterioration problem. Few cities know how others develop inventories, measure the extent of deterioration, and estimate the cost of replacement. At a minimum there must be an exchange of experience. Some information is available from such research groups as the Urban Institute (Peterson, 1979–81) and the American Planning Association (1980b, c), but cities could also benefit from a program of information exchange and expertise sharing. Midwestern cities might also organize to lobby at state and federal levels in an effort to demonstrate the seriousness of the capital deterioration problem.

Conclusion

Midwestern cities face a large task in redressing the capital facilities deterioration problem. Declining populations, lowered densities, shrinking budgets, and reduced federal aid all spell difficulty. Furthermore, population expansion in the sunbelt is beginning to tax capital facilities there. With the shift of congressional power to the South, it seems unlikely that northern and midwestern cities can expect preferential treatment for capital reinvestment.

What can midwestern cities do? Those interested in replacing capital facilities must establish a data base to determine the extent of deterioration. Citizen priorities must be gauged to determine the level of services demanded and the priorities among them. Municipal debt must be scheduled to determine which improvements can be afforded and how much can be undertaken on an annual basis. Citizen opinion data and fiscal data can be combined to ascertain the level of replacement that can be supported. Above all, if improvements are to be made, the attitudes of elected officials and voters must change. Citizens and officials alike must decide that the future of the Midwest is worth investing in today.

Notes

1. Financial support for this study was received in part from the Research Board of the University of Illinois at Urbana-Champaign. Karen L. Chinn and Keith Mitchell assisted with research and contributed to earlier drafts of this chapter. Generous assistance and helpful observations were provided by city officials and other persons in the case cities. Comments on earlier versions of this chapter were provided by Barry Checkoway, Gerard Froh, Judith Getzels, Leonard Heumann, and Gretchen West Patton.

2. Information about the capital deterioration problem in a number of major U.S. cities can be obtained in Peterson (1979–81), American Planning Association (1980b, c), American Public Works Association (1980), and Choate and Walter (1981). Capital infrastructure, as discussed in this chapter, excludes such items as police and fire service equipment that some cities include in the capital budget. These areas also provide examples of the failure to maintain and upgrade over the years. Including these services would, of course, push up the estimate of capital replacement costs in these case cities.

3. Others have found these numbers nearly impossible to derive; refer to Peterson (1979–81). Whether cities can afford the repairs is another issue. For information of fiscal capability, see Howell and Stamm (1979). The costs of repair and replacement are increasing dramatically, aided by the impact of delay (Choate, 1980).

4. Most local governments have little idea of what they can do to help them-

selves. This chapter, then, partially fills the requests of local officials who, during our research, asked to learn about the methods and techniques used in midwestern cities that have begun to address capital replacement needs.

5. These cities were selected as a result of the author's involvement in a nationwide study of a related topic (American Planning Association, 1980b, c). Dayton and St. Paul were included in the earlier study, and data collected then were updated for use in this chapter.

6. Without a major and expensive data collection effort, there is no way to determine whether the conditions in our case cities are representative of the other cities in the Midwest. This chapter was meant not to provide a detailed report of the case cities but, rather, to provide an overview of the problems and attempted solutions throughout the Midwest. For each of the case cities we provide a brief description of that city's more severe capital facility problems.

7. Much of the capital improvement work in smaller cities is funded on a pay-as-you-go basis from the general fund. Most cities have used bonding or other types of borrowing to finance their larger projects. Some cities also have revolving funds from which to finance capital improvements. Community Development Block Grant funds have been used to finance capital improvements primarily in CDBG target areas within cities. Most recently, cities have begun to charge developers for at least a share of the capital improvement costs, and techniques such as tax increment financing have begun to attract the interest of these communities. For a case study of municipal debt financing, see Schilling et al. (1980).

8. For information on the impact of the decline in federal support for cities, see Levine and Rubin (1980).

9. For the pros and cons of user fees, see Straussman (1981); see also Baxter (1980).

10. For ideas about local financing, see Schilling et al. (1980) and So (1979). For details on bonding, see Snyder (1977). For the pros and cons of tax increment financing, see Harbit (1975).

11. Wilson (1980) suggests that the Dallas model might be emulated by other cities. Cincinnati has been cited as an older city with a well-maintained capital plant as a result of good management (Humphrey et al., 1979a).

12. For work on this topic, see Wacht (1980) and American Planning Association (1980).

References

Aichinger, T. J. 1981. City budget analyst, City of St. Paul, office of the mayor. Letter of 3 Sept.

Alexander, C. 1981. Time to repair and restore. *Time*, 27 Apr., pp. 46–49.

American Planning Association. 1980a. *Allocating capital funds: Some new approaches for local governments.* Chicago.

—— 1980b. *Local capital improvements and develoment management: Anal-*

ysis and case studies. Washington, D.C.: U.S. Department of Housing and
Urban Development, Office of Policy Development and Research.

———. 1980c. *Local capital improvements and development management: Executive summary.* Washington, D.C.: U.S. Department of Housing and Urban
Development, Office of Policy Development and Research.

American Public Works Association. 1980. The decline of public works investments. *American Public Works Association Reporter,* July, pp. 7–11.

Associated Press. 1981. Crisis in cities: Ailing urban areas losing battle to reverse
declining trends. *Champaign-Urbana News Gazette,* 11 May, p. A–10.

Bahl, R., ed. 1978. *The fiscal outlook for cities: Implications of a national urban
policy.* Syracuse, N.Y.: Syracuse University Press.

Baxter, R. 1980. Initiating user fees for a drainage utility. *American Public
Works Association Reporter,* July, pp. 20–21.

Bunker, A. R., and T. Q. Hutchinson. 1979. *Roads of rural America.* Washington, D.C.: U.S. Department of Agriculture, Economic, Statistics, and Cooperative Service.

Choate, P. 1980. *As time goes by: The costs and consequences of delay.* Columbus, Ohio: Academy for Contemporary Problems.

Choate, P., and S. Walter. 1981. *America in ruins: Beyond the public works pork
barrel.* Washington, D.C.: Council of State Planning Agencies.

City of Dayton. 1981. *City of Dayton, Ohio capital budget.* Dayton, Ohio.

City of Indianapolis. 1980. *1980 capital expenditure program.* Indianapolis,
Ind.

City of Joliet, 1979. *Capital improvement program 1980–1984 (draft).* Joliet, Ill.

City of Kansas City. 1979. *Capital improvements program budget 1979–1980.*
Kansas City, Mo.

Greater Indianapolis Progress Committee. 1980. *Revised version of the growth
policy to the Metropolitan Development Commission.* Indianapolis, Ind.

Harbit, D. A. 1975. *Tax increment financing.* Washington, D.C.: National
Council for Urban Economic Development.

Howell, J. M., and C. F. Stamm. 1979. *Urban fiscal stress: A comparative
analysis of 66 U.S. cities.* Lexington, Mass.: Lexington Books.

Humphrey, N., G. E. Peterson, and P. Wilson. 1979a. *The future of Cincinnati's
capital plant.* Washington, D.C.: Urban Institute.

———. 1979b. *The future of Cleveland's capital plant.* Washington, D.C.: Urban
Institute.

Laszewski, E. J. 1981. City engineer, city of Milwaukee, department of public
works. Letter of 15 Oct.

Levine, C. H., and I. Rubin, eds. 1980. *Fiscal stress and public policy.* Beverly
Hills, Calif.: Sage Publications.

Mitgang, L. 1979. Byways, bridges in sad condition. *Champaign-Urbana News-
Gazette,* 30 Dec., p. D–2.

Peterson, G. E., gen. ed. 1979–81. *America's urban capital stock.* 6 vols.
Washington, D.C.: Urban Institute.

Schilling, P. R., T. E. Griggs, and J. Ebert. 1980. Wisconsin municipal debt finance: An outlook for the eighties. *Marquette Law Review* 63 (Summer):540–92.

Snell Environmental Group. 1980. *Renovation study of the Washington Avenue, Elm Street and Shiawassee Street bridges.* Lansing, Mich.

Snyder, J. C. 1977. *Fiscal management and planning in local government.* Lexington, Mass.: Lexington Books.

So, F. S. 1979. Finance and budgeting. In F. S. So, ed., *The practice of local government planning.* Washington, D.C.: International City Managers' Association.

Straussman, J. D. 1981. More bang for fewer bucks? Or how local governments can rediscover the potentials (and pitfalls) of the market. *Public Administration Review* 41 (Jan.):150–58.

Wacht, R. F. 1980. *A new approach to capital budgeting for city and county government.* Atlanta: Georgia State University, Business Publications Division, College of Business Administration.

Wilson, P. 1980. *The future of Dallas's capital plant.* Washington, D.C.: Urban Institute.

7

Residential Patterns in a Midwestern City: The St. Louis Experience

ROBERT E. MENDELSON and MICHAEL A. QUINN

Real estate markets are closely tied to economic conditions; cities with high levels of unemployment experience softness in real estate prices while property values escalate in boom towns (Burchell and Listokin, 1981). St. Louis is a nongrowth area, the classic example of a declining urban region. In a listing of 30 Standard Metropolitan Statistical Areas (SMSAs), St. Louis had a May 1980 unemployment rate exceeded only by Buffalo and Detroit (Wagman, 1981b). Prices for resale homes reflected this economic stagnation. St. Louis and Detroit ranked second and third of 15 areas in lowest average prices in a mid-1981 survey. In comparison, San Francisco and Houston, with relatively strong economies and low unemployment rates, were among the top four in highest average prices (Evans Teeley, 1981).

Like many older regions in the Midwest and Northeast, the population and commerce of St. Louis have left the central city. Between 1970 and 1980 St. Louis's population decline exceeded (in percentage terms) that of any large American city (*St. Louis Post-Dispatch*, 1980). With few immigrants to replace those departing the city, new homes built on the periphery have resulted in abandonment of units in the core (Mendelson, 1976). Large tracts of land on the city's near north side have become a wasteland inhabited by a declining number of poor black households. In contrast, sunbelt areas, because of their rapid growth, have sufficient demand for all housing, and decentralization does not necessarily create decay and disinvestment (Williams, 1973).

Racial segregation, too, has helped shape residential patterns in St. Louis; racial discrimination and prejudice have had a fundamental impact on the operation of local housing markets. St. Louis remains among the most segregated of major midwestern central cities. While there has been substantial black suburbanization during the past 15 years, attempts to achieve housing dispersal of low-income blacks typically have encountered fierce resistance.

The impact on St. Louis residential patterns of each of these factors—economic conditions, land use dispersion, and racial segregation—is documented in the sections that follow. We then conclude with public policy recommendations to encourage urban revitalization and a more equitable distribution of housing throughout the region.

The Economic Fortunes of St. Louis

Cities go through cycles of popularity. Eighty years ago St. Louis was the fourth largest American city and had a booming economy. Now, however, technological and product obsolescence have crippled its economy and have caused a population exodus and a decline in city real estate values, most notably in the last two decades. Regions that are currently in vogue and booming might well heed the history and fortunes of St. Louis.

Established as a fur trading post in 1764, St. Louis grew because of its midwestern location near the confluence of two large rivers, the Mississippi and the Missouri. Commerce and people traveled the rivers, and the city became a major port and supplier for the industrial East and the developing West. After the 1817 arrival of the first steamboat, river traffic increased and, with it, the importance of the city. St. Louis was even mentioned as a future U.S. capital (Kirschten, 1960). Packet boats, which were both luxurious passenger and functional cargo carriers, flocked to St. Louis, the 1850 national leader in river shipping tonnage (Kirschten, 1960). Between St. Louis's incorporation in 1809 and the Civil War, its population exploded from 1,200 to 160,000 (Leven et al., 1976). The city remained a transportation center after the railroads reached East St. Louis in 1856. For 20 years freight and passengers were ferried to the St. Louis side, until in 1876 the first major bridge over the Mississippi was completed. St. Louis's population rose to 600,000 in 1900,[1] and the city hosted the elaborate 1904 World's Fair. Over 1,300 new structures and the third modern Olympiad attracted visitors to the fair from all over the world.

By the time of the fair, however, St. Louis had lost the long competition with Chicago both for control of railroad traffic and for economic domination of the Midwest. The city continued to expand, but no longer at a rapid pace. St. Louis attained its population peak of 857,000 in the early 1950s; at this time there remained little unused land within its 61 square miles. In the late 1950s the area had a diversified economy, with leather goods and apparel declining and transportation equipment, particularly railroads and autos, increasing. St. Louis was the world's second largest railroad center (after Chicago) and the second largest U.S. truck center (Metropolitan St. Louis Survey, 1957).

Nevertheless, in the 1950s St. Louis industry had begun to suffer from functional obsolescence. Those companies that constituted a diversified employment base before World War II started to leave after the war. Although St. Louis was still the U.S. shoe capital in 1960, many of its manufacturing operations had already moved to small towns where labor was cheaper and less organized (Kirschten, 1960). Soon after this, foreign competition came to control shoe production. In 1959, 7 percent of national hog slaughtering took place in the St. Louis area, but in the next two decades meat packers closed their plants and moved to rural areas close to the livestock (Kirschten, 1960; Wagman, 1981c). Textile and apparel firms also shut down during the 1960s and 1970s. Today only one of 30 breweries remains in the city.

Aeronautical and auto assembly companies took up the postwar employment slack in St. Louis, but these highly volatile replacement industries proved to be a mixed blessing. By 1972, 40 percent of St. Louis area manufacturing employment was in aero-related companies (*St. Louis Post-Dispatch,* 1972). The region became heavily reliant on one industry and one aircraft company, McDonnell-Douglas, whose expansion obscured for some time the deterioration in other aspects of the local economy (Long, n.d.). In addition, energy price escalation and increased foreign competition have crippled the automotive industry, producing an economic disaster for the city. Until recently the St. Louis area was second only to Detroit in the production of American cars. In the last few years Carter Carburetor has closed, and General Motors has moved its Corvette plant and some other assembly operations out of St. Louis.

The expansion of employment in the defense and aerospace industries between 1940 and 1960 was reflected in a St. Louis metropolitan growth rate that was higher than that in the United States as a whole. During the 1960s, however, population growth in the St. Louis area fell behind that of the nation, and between 1970 and 1980 the rate of growth in the United States was 11.5 percent while the St. Louis SMSA *declined* 2.3 percent (Ferguson, 1981).

Population and employment losses in St. Louis are impressive even by midwestern standards. During the past decade the central city's population and nongovernment employment fell by 27 and 22 percent respectively. Among other major midwestern central cities, only Cleveland and Detroit approximated St. Louis's rate of population decline, while St. Louis stood virtually alone in employment losses between 1970 and 1976, with a percentage drop more than double that of its nearest competitor, Detroit (U.S. Bureau of the Census, 1980).[2] From 1970 to 1980 the city's population fell from 622,000 to 453,000, and the future looks discouraging. It is anticipated that between 1979 and 1990 St. Louis will have the 99th lowest annual population growth rate of 108 U.S. metropolitan areas. In 1990 the St. Louis area is expected to rank 54th among 108 metropolitan areas in per capita income, down from 38th in 1978 (Wagman, 1981a). When city officials protested the preliminary 1980 census results, a Bureau of the Census employee advised them to be more realistic: "If they don't wake up and acknowledge the exodus, they're going to lose it all. They ought to get out of their offices and drive through north St. Louis. A lot of it looks like a ghost town. When we come back to count in 1990, it may not even be a city. It may be a village" (Shirk, 1980).

Both demographically and economically, the city of St. Louis has become a smaller part of the SMSA. In 1950 it contained about 47 percent of the metropolitan population; 30 years later, only 19 percent. Physically, the city comprises about one-fiftieth of the SMSA, which also includes four counties each in Missouri and Illinois. Until 1876 the city was a part of St. Louis County but withdrew when residents sought freedom from rural domination (Kirschten, 1960). Locked in by the Mississippi River on the east and St. Louis County on the other three sides, the city cannot expand. The county population, fed by major suburban growth after World War II, has swollen to twice that of the city. Attempts to incorporate the city into St. Louis County have been resisted by voters.

The Real Estate Market

A good part of the city's housing was built between 1900 and 1930. Most units are brick, and construction is of high quality. Brick and stone mansions abound, particularly in west and south St. Louis neighborhoods (Drummond and Eschbach, 1976; Leven et al., 1976). Visitors are frequently surprised by the beauty of the housing and the relatively low selling prices.

Much can be learned about housing in St. Louis by examining the careers of city real estate entrepreneurs between 1920 and 1980. These investors have been important in the St. Louis market, buying and selling single-family houses and holding for investment the bulk of the residential units available to the poor and near-poor. Many of the real estate operators in the 1910s and 1920s were Irish, German, or Jewish immigrants or their descendants. They purchased properties in the neighborhoods where they lived and continued to own them when other ethnic groups moved in. The low-income property business was not considered respectable until middle- and upper-class people began to engage in it as part of the recent back-to-city movement. In the past the industry was left to immigrants, who were happy to find any enterprise, for widespread bias in St. Louis and other places prevented them from moving into socially approved professions and businesses (Glazer and Moynihan, 1963). Many immigrants and their descendants made fortunes during the 1920s, lost them during the Depression, regained them after World War II, and lost them again in the 1960s.

Both the Depression and World War II contributed to housing shortages in St. Louis. The high unemployment levels during the Depression forced families to share dwellings, and when defense industries expanded in the late 1930s, rural migrants flocked to the city for work. By then, however, wartime shortages had restricted new construction. The impact on the city of the exodus to the suburbs, which began in the 1920s, was softened by rural job-seekers eagerly seeking vacant units (Leven et al., 1976). Property in all parts of the city was valuable both during and immediately after World War II. Abandonment, so much a part of St. Louis land use patterns in the late 1960s and early 1970s, rarely took place. In 1950 the city of St. Louis had a residential vacancy rate of 1.69 percent, the eighth lowest of the 32 largest central cities in the United States. By 1960 the rate had risen to 5.23 percent and was the 15th lowest; ten years later the rate was 9.63 and the highest of the group (Leven et al., 1976).

When World War II rent controls were abolished in 1953, there was a rush to acquire city property for investment. Purchasers had little trouble securing financing from individuals and savings and loan institutions; leverage was obtained through high loan-to-sale-price first mortgages and through secondary and tertiary financing. Investors in and out of the real estate business competed to buy multifamily structures. Physicians, lawyers, and merchants, many of them unfamiliar with ownership and management, put funds into dwellings occupied by low- and moderate-income families. Later, when suburban construction reduced housing shortages and made many city neighborhoods unpopular, these novices watched their incomes and equities on these highly leveraged properties erode.

By the mid-1960s investment in housing had become unprofitable in large portions of St. Louis. Entire districts were abandoned as middle-class blacks joined whites in fleeing the city; neighborhoods filtered down so far that only unwanted structures remained. No group followed the last wave of poor blacks into many parts of north St. Louis. Confined by racial segregation, the city's low-income black residents found themselves trapped in the neighborhoods with the highest abandonment rates.

During the late 1960s vandalism became rampant in north and west St. Louis. When structures became vacant, thieves stripped them of heating and plumbing equipment and sold the metals for a few dollars; many owners, reluctant to put money into their buildings, did not replace these stolen items (Liebert, 1976). Both amateur and professional investors became disenchanted with city real estate. Properties were foreclosed under deeds of trust and tax liens; owners felt fortunate when they lost only their equities and did not also face deficiency judgments against them by mortgagees. Not only were profits reduced or eliminated, but property management became difficult and hazardous, as delinquencies, vacancies, vandalism, and racial hostilities increased. Some lucky landlords found other work before the market slipped badly in the mid 1960s—one became a high official with the Federal Housing Administration (FHA), another a professor of urban affairs, and a third a developer of federally assisted low- and moderate-income housing.

> Some [landlords] didn't know what to do or where to go. They had spent their entire lives in the business since their release from World War II service.... Those few who retained their city real estate or managed property for other owners became known as "slumlords." Some earned this reputation, but most couldn't afford to provide the services expected by tenants, and others simply did not or could not leave the sinking ship. (Liebert, 1976, p. 102)

By 1975 the bottom had fallen out of the real estate market in many parts of St. Louis city. Paul Brune's auction of 94 properties held in September 1975 starkly revealed the extent of the disinvestment.[3] Brune, an investor and landlord for 55 years, offered most of his central city residential properties for sale in this well-publicized auction. About 150 people attended, a small number for those who remembered the large turnouts at similar events in the 1950s and 1960s. Most attendees were not buyers; many were retired investors and lenders who were friends of the seller. Others came to estimate the value of their real estate portfolios. It was not a happy occasion.

Brune's strategy was to sell everything if minimum bids were obtained. When a bid was too low, the building was made available to his son or daughter if either one wanted it at the bid price. Brune retained those buildings not taken by outsiders or family. He was shrewd to hold the auction at the bottom of the market, because when a bid was below the depreciated value, as it was in all but a few cases, the property could be transferred to his children at the depreciated value. Brune made no profit on the sale and hence had to pay no federal taxes on the sale.

Results of the auction showed the weakness of the market. Only 14 of the 94 parcels offered sold to outside bidders; Brune's children purchased 36 others after the sale, and Brune retained 44. After adjustment for inflation the median sales price on 14 outside sales amounted to just 26.5 percent of Brune's purchase price 20 years earlier. Family members paid even less, averaging 21 percent of the original purchase, while the bids on the no-sale buildings were only 9 percent. In no instance did Brune receive more than he paid for a building. Eroded real estate values were also apparent in the gross rent multipliers of the auction buildings. When city properties had been in demand, prices had been about five or six times annual gross rents. Data on the outside sales in the Brune auction showed a median gross rent multiplier of 1.68. Multipliers for the family and no-sale parcels were even lower at 1.10 and 0.76 respectively. These low rent multipliers indicated little expectation of future value and a desire only to derive maximum short-term income. In 1975 the city's weakest market was on the north side, which contained the most deteriorated housing and the heaviest concentrations of low-income and black populations. Although some neighborhoods, particularly the south side and west end, brought above-average prices at the auction, the general picture was bleak.

The fortunes of Brune and his family have improved unexpectedly since the auction.[4] Rents and sale prices have risen as young professionals have moved into south-side and central west-end neighborhoods; troublesome apartments in the west end have been sold to redevelopers at favorable prices, and even some north-side properties have been sold, with Brune taking back mortgages to complete the transactions. Between 1975 and 1978 outside investors bought 42 of the 80 buildings Brune and his family retained at the auction. Correcting for inflation, the average selling price during that period was 62 percent of the building's original purchase price, more than twice that of outside sales at the auction. Rejuvenation in St. Louis, however, has been limited primarily to south-side and west-end neighborhoods. The north side lost over one-third of its population in the last decade, and Brune created an artificial market in that area by selling buildings with small down payments and high loan-to-sale-price mortgages. If this type of financing had not been available, his north-side properties would have been virtually unsalable, for much of the north side remains desolate and abandoned.

Ultimately, central city revitalization depends on the accumulated choices of residential purchasers, and recent evidence indicates that most buyers still prefer the suburbs. The 27 percent decline in city population in the 1980 census confirmed a mid-1970s finding—between two and

Table 1. Housing Segregation in Selected Major Midwestern Central Cities

"How Many NonWhites
Would Have to Move?"[a]

City	1940 Percent	1950 Percent	1960 Percent	1970 Percent	1970 Rank[b]
Chicago	95.0	92.1	92.6	88.8	6
Cincinnati	90.6	91.2	89.0	83.1	3
Cleveland	92.0	91.5	91.3	89.0	7
Detroit	89.9	88.8	84.5	80.9	2
Indianapolis	90.4	91.4	91.6	88.3	5
Milwaukee	92.9	91.6	88.1	83.7	4
Minneapolis	88.0	86.0	79.3	67.9	1
St. Louis	92.6	92.9	90.5	89.3	8

[a] "How Many NonWhites Would Have to Move? This measures the difference between the actual distribution of households by race and a random distribution. It shows the percentage of nonwhite households which would have to move in order to achieve a random distribution of whites and nonwhites throughout the city" (Council on Municipal Performance, 1973, p. 17).
[b] Lowest rank (8) = most segregated.

three households moved out of the city for every one that moved in (U.S. Bureau of the Census, 1978). Of course, the back-to-the-city movement is not an unmixed blessing. As private entrepreneurs like Brune sell urban properties to incoming young professionals, low-income residents of these neighborhoods, many of whom are black, may be displaced to less desirable areas. Evidence from St. Louis and other midwestern cities indicates that gentrification has become a problem in certain neighborhoods and has created a dilemma for public officials who wish to encourage revitalization without creating hardship for the poor (Berndt, 1978).

Residential Segregation and Its Effects

No discussion of housing in St. Louis would be complete without reference to racial discrimination and its effect on housing patterns. St. Louis, like most large midwestern cities, has high levels of residential segregation. Block statistics indicate that St. Louis in 1970 had the dubious distinction of being the most segregated of all major midwestern central cities. As Table 1 shows, 89.3 percent of the city's nonwhites would have had to move in 1970 to achieve an even racial distribution throughout the city. Chicago, Cleveland, and Indianapolis followed

	Change in Percentage of NonWhites Who Would Have to Move			Percentage of SMSA Blacks out- side Central City	
1940–50 Percent	1950–60 Percent	1960–70 Percent	Rank^c	1970 Percent	Rank^d
-2.9	0.5	-3.6	4	10.4	5
0.6	-2.2	-5.9	2	17.9	2
-0.5	-0.2	-2.5	7	13.5	3
-1.1	-4.3	-3.6	4	13.2	4
1.0	0.2	-3.3	6	2.0	7
-1.3	-3.5	-4.4	3	1.3	8
-2.0	-6.7	-11.4	1	7.1^e	6
0.3	-2.4	-1.2	8	32.9	1

^{c} Lowest rank (8) = least change.
^{d} Lowest rank (8) = smallest percentage outside central city.
^{e} Includes city of St. Paul.

Sources: Format adapted in part from Council on Municipal Performance (1973, Table 11). Data on nonwhites who would have to move taken from Taeuber and Taeuber (1965), and personal correspondence, as reported in the *Municipal Performance Report*. Data on blacks outside central city computed from U.S. Bureau of the Census (1980, Table B).

close behind and only Minneapolis showed a residential segregation index lower than 70 percent.[5]

Along with Cleveland and Indianapolis, St. Louis showed the least change in racial housing patterns between 1940 and 1970. All major midwestern cities experienced some desegregation during this period, especially during the civil rights era of the 1960s. The table shows substantial desegregation of housing in Minneapolis but less impressive change elsewhere, with St. Louis exhibiting the lowest rate of change between 1960 and 1970.

Interestingly, St. Louis contains a higher percentage of black residents who live outside the central city than do the other major midwestern metropolitan areas. As the table shows, nearly one-third of all blacks in the St. Louis SMSA resided outside the central city in 1970. The unique history of St. Louis created this settlement pattern. After the city of St. Louis separated from surrounding St. Louis County in 1876, the region continued to grow, and population spilled out into the county. Because the city was unable to annex contiguous areas, the St. Louis SMSA developed substantial pockets of black population outside the central city. A few areas such as Kinloch, Missouri, were originally built as black suburbs, while others, such as East St. Louis, Illinois, became nearly all black through immigration and racial succession (Altes and Mendelson, 1980).

Most blacks who migrated to the St. Louis area originally settled on the city's near north side. Segregation increased with each wave of black immigration. Between 1910 and 1930 the segregation index rose from approximately 54 to 82 percent (Lieberson, 1963). With the massive outmigration of whites into St. Louis county shortly after World War II, blacks moved north and west into former white neighborhoods. Progressing along north-side radial boulevards, a substantial black population reached the city limits by the late 1950s. During the 1960s blacks continued their northwestward migration out of the city into the inner-ring suburbs of St. Louis County and then into the newer outlying suburban developments. This pattern of black residency outside the central city was not, however, accompanied by substantial desegregation of housing. Most black suburbanites still live in neighborhoods that are racially segregated or in the process of becoming so. Few areas in St. Louis have achieved long-term stability as integrated neighborhoods (Taeuber and Taeuber, 1965).

Initial data from the 1980 census for the St. Louis area indicate continued patterns of residential segregation.[6] After two decades of modest declines in segregation, the central city recorded virtually no change in the recent census. As in 1970, the 1980 block data showed that approximately 90.1 percent of all St. Louis blacks would have to move to create an even racial distribution throughout the city. St. Louis County also showed substantial segregation in the 1980 census; approximately 79 percent of county blacks would have to move to create an even distribution there. Segregation persists in the city of St. Louis even though the population of the largely black north side has declined by one-third since the 1970 census, and affluent whites have moved into a few predominantly black neighborhoods in the central west end and the near south side. South St. Louis, which lost people in the recent census but not as severely as the north side did, remains overwhelmingly white.

The durability of segregated residential arrangements in the St. Louis SMSA is no surprise to those familiar with the operation of housing markets in the region. As late as 1964 St. Louis newspapers carried separate housing ads for the "Colored," and *Jones vs. Mayer,* the 1968 Supreme Court case that struck down racial discrimination in privately financed housing, involved a suburban St. Louis developer (Leven et al., 1972). Overt racial discrimination in housing has almost disappeared in recent years because of litigation, the passage of fair housing legislation, and federal equal housing opportunity regulations. Nevertheless, informal practices that support segregation, such as racial steering by real estate brokers, remain a problem in some areas. Restrictive zoning, which excludes many blacks from suburban neighborhoods through its impact on housing prices and its strict limitation on the development of multifamily units, continues to be a major barrier to housing desegregation in the St. Louis area (Danielson, 1976).

Segregation in midwestern cities has cost blacks heavily. Historically blacks have been severely restricted in their choices of residential locations; they have most often been confined to inner city and older suburban neighborhoods that contain much of the region's dilapidated housing. One well-known study on housing markets and racial discrimination in St. Louis concluded that "blacks consume considerably smaller amounts of dwelling-unit quality and amenities and desirable neighborhood attributes. . . . black households face systematic restrictions in the housing supply available to them" (Kain and Quigley, 1975, p. 255). As a corollary, black households have experienced restricted opportunities for homeownership, even after their lower incomes and reduced purchasing power are taken into account. "While only 32 percent of black households in St. Louis [in 1967] were homeowners, 41 percent would have been homeowners if their housing-market behavior was the same as comparable white households" (Kain and Quigley, 1975, p. 295). With their reduced chances for homeownership, blacks have lost substantial income tax benefits and opportunities for capital accumulation.

Until the mid-1960s middle- and upper-income blacks were confined—with the black poor—to the north St. Louis ghetto. Black homeowners paid a heavy price for this restriction of movement. They typically experienced less appreciation of their property than did white homeowners, and many even lost equity in their homes. In some cases owners in severely blighted areas worked for years to buy their homes, only to discover, tragically, that their mortgage balances far exceeded the market value of their properties. As declining market values eroded equities, many black homeowners found themselves trapped, unable to resell their homes and escape from continuing financial losses. In extreme cases these homeowners simply stopped paying on their mortgages, believing that it made no sense to throw good money after bad (Mendelson, 1976).

Interestingly, the same forces that have depressed housing values in black neighborhoods also appear to have advantaged blacks in at least one respect. In a large-scale analysis of housing markets in 39 metropolitan areas, Follain and Malpezzi (1980) reported that blacks in the mid-1970s paid significantly less than whites for housing of substantially identical quality in all but eight of the markets examined. On average, black renters paid 6 percent less than whites, and black home buyers 15 percent less. Although blacks thus appear to have benefited from modest price differentials, it must be remembered that historically segregation has limited rather severely the range of quality levels available to them. On balance, the costs to blacks associated with racially segregated housing markets continue to outweigh the benefits.

Perhaps the most telling costs associated with the dual housing market are indirect and difficult to quantify. Substantial costs have been imposed on blacks because of their confinement to areas with high crime rates against both people and property. Vandalism is an especially serious problem, and increased costs of basic maintenance, repair, and property insurance are borne in varying degrees by homeowners, landlords, and renters (Quinn et al., 1980; Stegman, 1972). Ghetto confinement has also had an adverse effect on black quality of life by restricting choices for schooling and employment. Concerned north St. Louis parents filed suit in the early 1970s seeking citywide school desegregation; this has since been ordered by the court and expanded to include predominantly white St. Louis County. Black livelihood has also been harmed by the lack of employment in the ghetto, and by the difficulty of traveling to suburban jobs (Farley, 1981; Kain and Quigley, 1975).

Public Policy, Segregation, and Housing Dispersal Efforts

Residential segregation in American cities during the first half of this century has been attributed by one observer to "a powerful and persistent use of public power" (Orfield, 1974–75, p. 790). Working in harmony with local sentiment and private market forces until the early 1960s, when the situation began to change, federal housing policy promoted residential segregation. In a major program initiated in 1934 to encourage private construction, mortgage insurance underwritten by the FHA was refused to projects that did not conform to the segregationist guidelines against "inharmonious racial groups" set forth in its *Underwriting Manual* (Orfield, 1974–75, p. 786). The St. Louis County Real Estate Board formulated this requirement bluntly in a 1955 directive to its membership: "No member of our board may, directly, or indirectly, sell to Negroes or be a party to a sale to Negroes, or finance property for sale to or purchase by Negroes, in any block unless there are three separate and distinct buildings in such block already occupied by Negroes" (McEntire, 1960, p. 241). The practical effect of these guidelines kept blacks out of new suburban subdivisions well into the 1960s.

Federal policies for subsidized housing have usually respected local mores that restrict public housing for blacks to ghetto areas. As a result, the bulk of public housing is located in urban core areas; St. Louis is no exception. "In 1970, St. Louis had 10,000 units of public housing for its 622,000 residents, while suburban St. Louis County had 50 units for a population of 956,000" (Danielson, 1976, p. 102). By mid-1980 the situation in St. Louis County had improved, but the number of units still fell far short of the need. The county had 4,057 subsidized dwelling units, not including 1,500 privately owned units that received Section 8 rental assistance (Prost and Akos, 1980; *St. Louis Post-Dispatch*, 1979a).

Of the 4,057 subsidized rental units, approximately two-thirds contained one bedroom or less, and about one-half were designated exclusively for the elderly or handicapped. The bulk of the larger family units were located in substantially black, low-income areas. At the same time, approximately 15,000 renting households were in need of housing assistance, and vacancy rates for county apartments were very low (St. Louis County Department of Human Resources, 1979).

Suburban St. Louis has long been noted for its fierce resistance to construction of subsidized housing outside "impacted" areas. In probably the best known instance, a quiet suburban area in north St. Louis County incorporated itself in 1970 as the city of Black Jack in order to stop development, through zoning, of 210 units of subsidized rental housing for moderate-income families (Danielson, 1976). The Black Jack case wended its way slowly through the federal courts until 1979, when the Eighth Circuit Court of Appeals ordered Black Jack to provide sites for assisted units (Lhotka, 1979). Construction was underway in the late spring of 1981 when arsonists damaged several of the nearly completed units.

Subsidized housing remains unpopular in St. Louis County, even among many middle-income blacks who have moved to the suburbs since the Black Jack case began. Among both blacks and whites, talk of subsidized housing recalls images of Pruitt-Igoe, the ill-fated 2,870-unit public housing complex that was home to many black families on public assistance before it was demolished by the federal government in the wake of severe difficulties.[7] One black county resident revealed his fears in a 1979 interview: "I want the value of my home to increase. Hopefully, it will if we keep one class of people in the neighborhood" (Joiner, 1979a, p. 1A).

The brutal politics surrounding attempts to disperse subsidized housing are illustrated by two St. Louis cases. In the first the U.S. Department of Housing and Urban Development (HUD) threatened in mid-1979 to withhold St. Louis County's $9 million community development block grant unless it agreed to build 400 additional units of subsidized housing (Klotzer, 1979). HUD Secretary Patricia Harris sharply criticized the St.

Louis County supervisor: "If Mr. [Gene] McNary remains contuma-
cious. . . . and refuses to take care of the poor, we will decide what to do
with the [block grant] money" (Lucken, 1979, p. 1A). McNary replied in
kind: "For HUD to require obedience is an example of . . . bureaucratic
oppression. . . . Mrs. Harris' criticism points up the arrogance of this
federal bureaucracy. . . . Our battle is not with the poor—it's with HUD
and its arbitrary demands. . . . HUD's plan is a nightmare, with sociological objectives that will destroy the neighborhoods which in some cases
blacks and whites already are working together to preserve" (Lucken,
1979, p. 1A).

In the end, local mayors and most of the St. Louis area's congressional
delegation sided with McNary, and HUD backed down. McNary then
went after HUD's local supporters. He attacked a pro-HUD citizen-
based housing task force associated with the East-West Gateway Coordinating Council, the area's regional planning agency, and later abolished it along with the council's three other citizen task forces (*Focus
Midwest*, 1979). A "compromise" settlement was actually a defeat for
HUD; the county received block grant money in return for designating
an isolated spot on the Missouri River floodplain for subsidized development. HUD acquiesced, despite a public statement by McNary's chief
aide that the county would not seek a developer for the site (*St. Louis
Post-Dispatch*, 1979b, p. 1A).

During the same summer of 1979 East-West Gateway received a HUD
invitation to apply for a $100,000 Regional Housing Mobility Program
grant. A variant of an idea from Lyndon Johnson's Great Society era, the
program was designed to encourage selected regional planning organizations to increase the mobility of low-income persons. HUD would
facilitate mobility by offering additional Section 8 rental assistance
certificates for the St. Louis area, while Gateway was to work with local
communities to remove barriers to movement by offering housing counseling, referral, and provision of moving expenses. Gateway staff proceeded with the application, which was approved by the agency's board
of directors and submitted to HUD in November 1979.

Within two days of submission, Gateway's board of directors, under
pressure from a coalition of black residents from the city's north side,
moved to suspend their own application. The residents opposed the
mobility program as "a deceitful attempt to lull the poor and mis-
educated off north St. Louis' prime real estate into the least valuable
land in the metropolitan region" (Sutin, 1979, p. 10A). Another black
protester declared that the program was part of a nationwide conspiracy
"aimed at pushing blacks out of the cities. It would effectively damage
what little political power blacks have built up in inner cities" (Joiner,

1979b, p. 3B). In public hearings on the program after the board's suspension, Gateway's staff reported that HUD had assured them that the mobility program would be strictly voluntary; poor people would not be coerced into moving. Rather, the intent was to expand housing choices for the poor.

Staff comments did not calm the opposition, and on 30 January 1980 the Gateway board voted six to three to drop its application. One of the two metropolitan daily newspapers began its coverage with a tantalizing lead: "An unusual coalition of East St. Louis and suburban Illinois officials, who rarely see eye to eye on social issues, has stopped the East-West Gateway Coordinating Council from a controversial project aimed at helping poor people and subsidized housing throughout the region" (Sutin, 1980, p. 5A). In effect, the Illinois membership on Gateway's board agreed that poor people should be kept immobile. Under the ill-fated program East St. Louis blacks could have used Section 8 certificates in other communities, a possibility feared by local chief executives in nearby white working-class suburbs. East St. Louis's black mayor, who voted with his white counterparts, apparently did not wish to see his constituency dispersed.

These two cases point up the extreme difficulties that face those who would use public policies to make dispersed housing available to poor minorities. Affluent suburbanites, both white and black, have opposed this idea for some time, but they are now joined by inner city black leaders and politicians. The result is a formidable coalition against subsidized housing dispersal.

Implications for Public Policy

While this chapter has attempted to document its central theme—that housing patterns are influenced strongly by economic conditions, land use dispersion, and racial segregation—it has also touched on the problems of living in older midwestern metropolitan areas. Using categories ranging from affluence to atmosphere, prestigious research firms have characterized places like St. Louis as disasters, and have implied that the quality of life in such areas is inferior (Williams, 1973; Louis, 1975). Life is supposedly better in the growing regions of the South and West. From the perspective of many St. Louisians, this is not true—the selection criteria largely determine the conclusions. Often ignored are traits in which the area excels, such as housing costs, civility, architecture, and access to culture.

Of course, these advantages are not available to all residents; as in most American cities, the poor do not fare well in St. Louis. Twenty years ago it was argued that the problems of the poor and the blacks were interwoven, but that position has less validity today. Poverty damages the quality of life more than race does, and although many blacks are poor, those with money are not as restricted as they were two decades ago.

Public policy directed at reducing poverty still has a long way to go. Many "solutions" of the 1960s have been discredited, and such ideas as a guaranteed annual income, a federalized welfare system, and a government that serves as employer of last resort have little citizen support today. Messages from the current administration are little help to the poor, who are being told to "hang tough" and have faith that private market operations will somehow benefit them. At the same time this administration is reducing subsidy programs for the poor.

Against this background of reduced public support for the poor, a few recommendations might be made to policy makers concerned with the quality of life in midwestern central cities. First, the St. Louis case suggests that abandonment and wastage of housing and neighborhoods would be diminished if public policy favored conservation over new construction. Documentation of the public role in promoting suburban development is abundant and need not be repeated; it is enough to say that if less public money were made available for extending roads, bridges, parks, and sewers, builders would be discouraged from undertaking new projects. Building new housing in suburban fringe areas while abandoning serviceable structures in the urban core has been wasteful and has injured those forced to stay in or near decaying neighborhoods.

Where feasible, the use of public resources to rehabilitate housing should be favored over new construction. Public sector support for further dispersal of housing for the affluent should be terminated, and any new construction should concentrate on the unmet needs of low-income families. Because the market will not respond to the needs of the poor without substantial subsidies, public subsidies that promote continued suburbanization should be discontinued and these public resources should be applied to housing rehabilitation and construction in central cities and other low-income areas.

Additional subsidy dollars for housing the poor might be gained by reducing the indirect subsidies that homeowners receive in federal income tax writeoffs for mortgage interest and property tax payments. The lion's share of these benefits, which were estimated at $25.3 billion for interest deductions alone in fiscal year 1982, go to the relatively affluent (Minarik, 1981). By placing an upper limit on the amount of writeoff available to individual households, additional tax dollars could be generated from those who have little need for public subsidy, without harming the moderate-income homeowner. These additional tax dollars might then be used to help meet the housing needs of low-income households. This proposal could help alleviate the most pressing housing problems now facing older midwestern cities, but unhappily, the current American political climate makes its adoption in the near future unlikely.

Limited comfort can be taken from the fact that some revitalization has occurred in the urban Midwest and is likely to continue in parts of the region. Ironically, the relatively depressed economic conditions of older cities like St. Louis may actually encourage revival. Evidence is beginning to accumulate, for example, that companies—attracted by low housing costs, cultural amenities, central location, and ease of transportation—are again locating or expanding in the Midwest (*St. Louis Post-Dispatch*, 1981). It is not always easy to recruit corporate professionals to the coasts; recruitment often requires large housing subsidies from companies that are increasingly reluctant to provide them.

The problem with urban revitalization, as with the suburbanization that preceded it, is that it tends to benefit only the relatively affluent. In fact, the revitalization of older neighborhoods that contain substantial numbers of low-income households often results in involuntary displacement. Although this is not yet a major problem in St. Louis, the situation may change if the magnitude of redevelopment increases. Public officials should monitor the situation closely to ensure that hardships are not inflicted on the low- and moderate-income households that comprise much of the city's population.

Finally, although housing for blacks in the region is still highly segregated, progress has been made since the mid-1960s to expand housing opportunity for middle- and working-class blacks. It is hoped that public policy will continue to provide strong support for fair housing measures. Dispersal of subsidized housing, however, is another matter. As the case studies have shown, the coalition of inner city blacks and suburbanites, both white and black, has restricted new subsidized housing for poor families everywhere but in older core locations. Attempts to change this pattern seem almost futile. Until wealthy and powerful people accept subsidized housing in their neighborhoods, it is naive to expect that those with less money and mobility will do so. Theoretically, affluent districts are most capable of absorbing small numbers of poor people, but site selection battles over federally assisted housing have never been fought in those places. These struggles have been confined to middle- and working-class communities that have taken their cue from the wealthy and have resisted with tenacity. Given these realities, it seems likely that housing policy for poor families will have to rely increasingly on existing units in the private market.

Notes

1. Except as otherwise noted, population figures are taken from U.S. Bureau of the Census decennial census documents.

2. The employment figures for St. Louis include only the central city, while those for other midwestern central cities include some suburban employment from their central counties. Accordingly, the comparison on percentage decline in employment is probably somewhat overstated, although not by enough to alter St. Louis's position vis-à-vis other major central cities in the Midwest.

3. Much in this and the following two paragraphs draws heavily on Mendelson and Quinn (1977).

4. See Mendelson and Quinn (1980) for additional details on material presented in this and the following paragraph.

5. With Minneapolis being the most noteworthy exception. there is very little difference between percent nonwhite and percent black for the cities listed in the table. The U.S. Bureau of the Census did not begin to report percent black at the block level until 1970, so percent nonwhite is used in the table to allow for comparability with earlier years.

6. Data cited in this paragraph were furnished by the Center for Urban and Environmental Research and Services of Southern Illinois University at Edwardsville. The center is part of the Illinois State Data Center Cooperative and was established to facilitate user access to the results of the 1980 census.

7. Details on the Pruitt-Igoe case are contained in Roger Montgomery's chapter (11) in this book.

References

Altes, J. A., and R. E. Mendelson. 1980. East St. Louis: A persevering community. In D. M. Johnson and R. M. Veach, eds., *The middle-size cities of Illinois: Their people, politics, and quality of life*. Springfield, Ill.: Sangamon State University.

Berndt, H. E. 1978. *Displacement and relocation practices in five midwestern cities*. St. Louis: Metro Housing Resources for the U.S. Department of Housing and Urban Develoment. Unpublished report.

Burchell, R. W., and D. Listokin. 1981. *The adaptive reuse handbook*. Piscataway, N.J.: Rutgers University.

Council on Municipal Performance. 1973. City housing. *Municipal Performance Report* 1 (Nov.):3–36.

Danielson, M. N. 1976. *The politics of exclusion*. New York: Columbia University Press.

Drummond, M. C., and W. L. Eschbach. 1976. *Down by the Gravois*, St. Louis: Harland Bartholomew and Associates.

Evans Teeley, S. 1981. Resales average $100,900. *Washington Post*, 22 Aug., p. 1E.

Farley, J. E. 1981. Black male unemployment in U.S. metropolitan areas: The role of black central city segregation and job decentralization. Paper presented at the Annual Meeting of the Society for the Study of Social Problems, Toronto.

Ferguson, S. 1981. *River Bend Area Illinois: Patterns of growth.* Edwardsville: Southern Illinois University at Edwardsville, Center for Urban and Environmental Research and Services.

Focus Midwest. 1979. Editorial: Too Uppity? 13 (Dec.):5–6.

Follain, J. R., Jr., and S. Malpezzi. 1980. *Dissecting housing values and rent: Estimates of hedonic indexes for thirty-nine large SMSA's.* Washington, D.C.: Urban Institute.

Glazer, N., and D. P. Moynihan. 1963. *Beyond the melting pot: The Negroes, Puerto Ricans, Jews, Italians, and Irish of New York City.* Cambridge: MIT Press.

Joiner, R. L. 1979a. Black homeowners cool to subsidized housing. *St. Louis Post-Dispatch,* 22 July, p. 1A.

——— 1979b. Regional subsidized housing sought by council. *St. Louis Post-Dispatch,* 18 Nov., p. 1B.

Kain, J. R., and J. M. Quigley. 1975. *Housing markets and racial discriminations: A microeconomic analysis.* New York: National Bureau of Economic Research.

Kirschten, E. 1960. *Catfish and crystal.* Garden City, N.Y.: Doubleday.

Klotzer, C. L. 1979. The housing game. *Focus Midwest* 13 (Aug.):8–12.

Leven, C. L., et al. 1976. *Neighborhood change: Lessons in the dynamics of urban decay.* New York: Praeger.

Lhotka, W. C. 1979. Orders fair housing in Black Jack. *St. Louis Post-Dispatch,* 29 Aug., p. 1A.

Lieberson, S. 1963. *Ethnic patterns in American cities.* New York: Free Press.

Liebert, C. B. 1976. The role of the middleman in the housing market. In R. E. Mendelson and M. A. Quinn, eds., *The politics of housing in older urban areas.* New York: Praeger.

Long, N. E. What to do about St. Louis. St. Louis: University of Missouri at St. Louis. Unpublished manuscript.

Louis, A. M. 1975. The worst American city. *Harper's Magazine* 250 (Jan.):67–71.

Lucken, R. E. 1979. HUD millions in limbo. *St. Louis Globe-Democrat,* 6 July, p. 1A.

McEntire, D. 1960. *Residence and race.* Berkeley: University of California Press.

Mendelson, R. E. 1976. The more we build, the more we waste: Housing in older urban regions. In R. E. Mendelson and M. A. Quinn, eds., *The politics of housing in older urban areas.* New York: Praeger.

Mendelson, R. E., and M. A. Quinn. 1977. *The decline of an urban housing entrepreneur: Congratulations or condolences?* Edwardsville: Southern Illinois University at Edwardsville, Center for Urban and Environmental Research and Services.

———. 1980. Changing investment patterns in city neighborhoods: The St. Louis case. *Housing and Society* 7:80–90.

Metropolitan St. Louis Survey. 1957. *Path of progress for metropolitan St. Louis.* University City, Mo.

Minarik, J. J. 1981. Tax expenditures. In J.A. Pechman, ed., *Setting national priorities: The 1982 budget.* Washington, D.C.: Brookings Institution.

Orfield, G. 1974–75. Federal policy, local power, and metropolitan segregation. *Political Science Quarterly* 89 (Winter):777–802.

Prost, C., and C. Akos. 1980. *Regional subsidized rental housing directory.* St. Louis: East-West Gateway Coordinating Council.

Quinn, M. A. et al. 1980. Maintenance effort and the professional landlord: An empirical critique of theories of neighborhood decline. *Journal of the American Real Estate and Urban Economics Association* 8 (Winter):345–69.

St. Louis County Department of Human Resources. 1979. *St. Louis County community development block grant application: Fiscal year 1979–80.* Clayton, Mo.

St. Louis Post-Dispatch. 1972. Editorial: On halting urban decay. 30 Apr., p. 2D.

———. 1979a. Gephardt says county deserves housing chance. 2 July, p. 1A.

———. 1979b. Rezoning was sought for housing site. 24 Dec., p. 1A.

———. 1980. Population gains, losses by cities. 28 Nov., p. 14A.

———1981. Location, facilities make St. Louis attractive as headquarters site. 27 July, p. 8A.

Shirk, M. 1980. Rapport sour despite efforts. *St. Louis Post-Dispatch,* 31 Aug., p. 12A.

Stegman, M. A. 1972. *Housing investment in the inner city: The dynamics of decline, a study of Baltimore, Maryland, 1968–1970.* Cambridge: MIT Press.

Sutin, P. 1979. council suspends application for housing-program funds. *St. Louis Post-Dispatch,* 29 Nov., p. 1D.

———. 1980. Council rejects housing project. *St. Louis Post-Dispatch,* 31 Jan., p. 5A.

Taeuber, K. E., and A. F. Taeuber. 1965. *Negroes in cities: Residential segregation and neighborhood change.* Chicago: Aldine.

U.S. Bureau of the Census. 1978. Housing characteristics for selected metropolitan areas. St. Louis, Missouri-Illinois. *Annual housing survey: 1976.* Washington, D.C.: U.S. Government Printing Office, Current Housing Reports H–170–76–59.

———. 1980. *State and metropolitan area date book, 1979.* Washington, D.C.: U.S. Government Printing Office.

Wagman, P. 1981a: New vitality key to area recovery. *St. Louis Post-Dispatch,* 26 July, p. 1A.

———. 1981b. Impact of latest recession could be felt for years. *St. Louis Post-Dispatch,* 27 July, p. 1A.

———. 1981c. Obsolete equipment, labor costs blamed for closings. *St. Louis Post-Dispatch,* 27 July, p. 8A.

Williams, B. R. 1973. *St. Louis: A city and its suburbs.* Santa Monica, Calif.: RAND Corporation.

8

Community Development in the Metropolitan Midwest

HEYWOOD T. SANDERS

Since the New Deal local government efforts at urban renewal and revitalization have reflected the interests and financial incentives of the federal government. Midwestern cities, like those in other regions, have followed the lead from Washington, where concern has shifted from slum housing to downtown development and back to a focus on inner city social and physical revival. However, the Housing and Community Development Act of 1974 substantially altered this pattern of new federal program initiatives and local response. The act established a "block grant" approach to urban aid and changed both the intergovernmental relations game and the local practice of neighborhood improvement and downtown redevelopment. This chapter examines the community development block grant program and its impact on the metropolitan centers of the Midwest. It will also indicate some of the long-term prospects for urban revival and the potential impact of new federal agendas on the cities of the region.

Changing the Law Changes the Game

The conception of the 1974 community development legislation is generally dated to Richard Nixon's proposal in January 1971 for a group of special revenue-sharing programs, designed to combine a wide range of categorical grant programs. The three-year battle for passage of the community development legislation ranged over a number of fronts. Congress and the administration differed about the precise formula to be used to distribute funds, about the degree of federal involvement and supervision, and about the flexibility local officials should have to develop local projects. The conventional history of the 1974 act has been presented in a number of studies (Kettl, 1980; Nathan et al., 1977; Williams, 1980) and need not be repeated here. It is important to note, however, that the block grant proposal was not necessarily rooted in an approach to federalism that emphasized local discretion over federal involvement and a broad distribution of funds to replace rampant grantsmanship. Rather, the community development block grant initiative was a clear response to a failure of the existing categorical grant program, most notably urban renewal. The failure of renewal and its companion grant programs did not arise from an inability to deal with pressing needs or serious urban problems. Although urban renewal had been widely criticized for its disruption of neighborhoods and its forced removal of families, these did not prove to be the failings that induced the shift to block grants. The failure of urban grant programs was simply one of a lack of resources to meet the self-proclaimed needs of the cities.

When the Nixon administration took office in January 1969, the new administrators of the U.S. Department of Housing and Urban Development (HUD) faced a backlog of urban renewal applications that totaled over $1.9 billion. In spite of substantial efforts to reduce funding and limit new commitments, this backlog exceeded $2 billion in mid-1970. The final published figures on grant demand, dated 31 March 1971, indicate that applications for $2.996 billion were then awaiting HUD review and approval.[1]

The demand situation in urban renewal was by no means unique. Other HUD programs such as water and sewer grants, neighborhood facilities, and open space acquisition all elicited far greater levels of local interest than Washington was willing to support. The gap was simply largest and most immediate in the case of urban renewal, where the commitment to a long-term project—12 to 15 years was the norm—at a time of rising prices and land costs threatened to ensnare the Nixon administration in the obligations of its predecessors. The cost squeeze on existing projects indicated that the Republicans would be unable to aid new cities or initiate new programs. With four times more requested dollars than available funds, HUD also faced a budget problem. Congress was likely to press for an increase in overall levels of urban aid at a time when the administration was trying to free the domestic budget for other efforts. The complete elimination of the existing grant system appeared a reasonable solution to an intolerable situation of high grant demand and a limited budget.

The situation faced by the Nixon administration was paralleled by that of the local mayors and managers, who had been accustomed to getting substantially what they wanted in federal assistance. Many had built their careers on urban renewal and redevelopment aid. The increase in demand uniformly reduced the chances that any given city would receive Washington's dollars. During fiscal 1968 about 55 percent of all new renewal applications (in dollar terms) were funded. The proportion dropped to 35 percent for fiscal 1970, and to roughly 30 percent the following year. The federal largesse that had once seemed a sure thing became increasingly uncertain, and the reduced odds were accompanied by a series of shifts in program direction. The Nixon administration pressed cities to apply for the new Neighborhood Development program that replaced the 15-year federal obligation by an annual funding plan. Some cities found themselves overhauling project plans that had been waiting for review for two or three years, only to face another two-year wait. While a few cities successfully adapted to the new federal initiatives, others found that the new arrangement provided too little too late.

Block grants held out the promise of a solution for both the mayors and the president. The elimination of the categorical grant programs could wipe out the backlog of demand and provide the opportunity to rewrite the rules. The government could distribute funds more widely— to Republican, sunbelt cities—without facing continued pressures from those who waited in line. A reduction in federal review and oversight promised both a smaller federal work force and a change in the inner city orientation of HUD that dated from the Johnson administration.

The potential of the block grant approach to federal-local relations went beyond the removal of the grant backlog and the administrative heritage of eight years of Democratic direction. The adoption of block grants portended an enormous change in the budgetary pressures faced by the federal government. The demand for urban aid had provided both local officials and the Congress with the best possible argument for an increase in the size of HUD's grant budget. As new programs such as Model Cities had been drafted, there had been new pressures for more funds both to satisfy old constituencies and to gain new ones. This cycle of increasing demand followed by higher appropriations had brought urban renewal from a $200 million annual level under Eisenhower to a $1.4 billion annual level at the close of the Johnson years.

Block grant provisions solved the pressures of demand by eliminating demand altogether. Cities would no longer wait in line for a piece of the federal pie. Once the annual community development budget level had been set, their annual funding would be determined by formula. Although cities could still lobby for an increased appropriation, their benefit from a larger nationwide program would be tiny. In the absence of some measure of demand, there exists no index measure of "urban need" to support arguments for a greater share of total federal spending.

Table 1. Community Development Appropriations by Fiscal Year (in millions of dollars)

Fiscal Year	Actual Dollars	Constant 1975 Dollars
1975	$ 2,433	$ 2,433
1976	2,802	2,662
1977	3,248	2,915
1978	3,600	3,013
1979	3,722	2,872
1980	3,781	2,676
1981	3,695	2,369

The historical record suggests that the Nixon administration was following a well-trodden path in its efforts to resolve budgetary problems by changing the *form* of federal aid. The Eisenhower administration had faced a similar problem in the late 1950s with such urban assistance efforts as urban renewal and public housing. Partly in response to the spending proclivities of the Democratic Congress, the Bureau of the Budget drafted a proposal that was strikingly similar to the 1971 recommendations. Although the budget bureau invoked issues of grant narrowness, limited objectives, inadequate local applications, and excessive federal supervision, this earlier proposal was motivated by a concern with interest group pressures and program costs (U.S. Bureau of the Budget, 1958).

The success of the block grant approach in limiting expansion and budgetary growth is shown in Table 1. Following a growth spurt in its first years that resulted in part from the shift to Democratic control of the White House in 1977, the program has stabilized. The figures for appropriations in constant 1975 dollars indicate that community development funding has failed to grow beyond the rate of inflation. The cities of the Midwest now find themselves with no real increase in general levels of federal aid, despite continuing problems of housing deterioration, abandonment, and neighborhood decline.

The New Distribution of Federal Dollars

The provisions of the Housing and Community Development Act of 1974 altered the flow of federal assistance to both the Midwest and its constituent cities. Before 1974 categorical aid had been directed primar-

Table 2. Distribution of Urban Renewal and Community Development Funds by Federal Region

Federal Region (States)	Urban Renewal 1949–74	CDBG 1975	CDBG 1978	CDBG 1980
I (CT, MA, ME, NH, RI, VT)	12.1%	9.0%	7.1%	5.4%
II (NJ, NY)	18.3	14.8	17.6	17.8
III (DC, DE, MD, VA, WV, PA)	19.9	14.0	12.7	11.7
IV (AL, FL, GA, MS, NC, SC, TN)	12.1	15.3	13.7	14.3
V (IL, IN, MI, MN, OH, WI)	16.1	17.7	19.5	20.1
VI (AR, LA, NM, OK, TX)	6.0	10.0	9.6	9.8
VII (IA, KN, NB, MO)	4.4	5.2	4.7	4.7
VIII (CO, MT, ND, SD, UT, WY)	1.7	2.4	2.1	2.2
IX (AZ, CA, NV)	7.5	9.3	10.5	11.0
X (ID, OR, WA)	1.9	2.3	2.5	2.6

ily to the Northeast and Middle Atlantic regions. In the urban renewal program the big winners were Boston and New Haven, which received $547 and $1,318 dollars per capita respectively. Chicago, in contrast, managed to amass only $72 per person during the 25-year history of renewal assistance. Table 2 provides figures on the distribution of community development aid by federal region. Region V, including Illinois, Indiana, Ohio, Michigan, Wisconsin, and Minnesota, has seen its share of federal community development dollars grow from 16.1 percent in the categorical grant era to 20.1 percent in 1980. At the same time New England has declined from over 10 percent to about 5.4 percent in 1980. Although the share of federal dollars says little about funding in relation to actual urban needs, it suggests that the Midwest is faring relatively well under the new federal-local arrangements (Sanders, 1980).

The funding position of midwestern urban centers reveals two effects of the community development legislation. First, many older cities that failed to gain a major share of aid in the "grantsmanship" era have now improved their position. For example, Chicago, which received about $13 per capita on an annual basis before the block grant program, now receives roughly $38 per person per year. Similar increases have taken place in such notable examples of urban crisis as Detroit, Cleveland, and St. Louis. The formula for distributing funds, revised in 1977 to assist older cities with declining populations, had provided a substantial boost in current dollars to a number of central cities. Second, the provisions of the law that mandate assistance to all cities in metropolitan areas with populations of 50,000 or more have included a large number of cities that received little or no previous federal aid. Older suburbs such as Cleveland Heights, Evanston, and Oak Park, smaller central cities such as Muncie, Kalamazoo, and Kenosha, and newer suburban areas such as Skokie, Illinois, and Southfield, Michigan, have all received either their first federal revitalization aid or major dollar increases. As will be noted below, the inclusion in the community development program of a number of relatively high-income communities that contain substantial housing stocks has a number of troublesome implications. For the present it should be noted that the recent arrival of federal money has enabled a number of such locales to initiate housing improvement and stabilization programs of a kind that only a few years ago were locally derided as unwarranted and "socialistic" government intrusions into private affairs.

The new patterns of federal aid across cities are mirrored by new patterns *within* cities. Earlier categorical programs required the detailed planning of specific projects and project areas. An area that qualified both for the city's attention and Washington's largesse could receive a substantial infusion of capital and physical improvements. Yet outside the limited project bounds no federal dollars would be available and even local funds might dry up. It was not uncommon to see redeveloped areas that contained new schools, shopping, streets, and homes sprouting up incongruously in the midst of continuing decline and decay. The block grant effort largely removed this often artificial distinction and made assistance available to a wider range of neighborhoods that covered far larger geographic areas than in the past.

The Local Spending Game

The current system of relatively fixed annual entitlements for individual cities has brought with it a massive change in the local politics of neighborhood renewal. This change can best be characterized as a shift from the "politics of announcement" to the "politics of budgeting."

During the categorical grant era of the 1960s the acquisition of federal funds became both a major concern and a coveted accomplishment for city mayors and managers. Federal dollars reduced the need for new local revenues—although perhaps only in the short run—and made possible new programs and activities that had received little interest or support from the voting populace. Federal assistance also enhanced the images of local officials, who could claim credit for new monies without having to worry about the ultimate problems or costs of grant-aided projects.

This pattern of executive behavior was best demonstrated by the urban renewal and Model Cities programs. The initial project awards were invariably occasions for civic pride and self-promotion. The mayor's acquisition of millions of federal dollars was often seen as a testament to astute political leadership and bright urban future. Mayors and managers besieged by urban strife and political pressures could announce grants with the assurance that their successors would have to contend with the messy problems of whose house was to be demolished and which social service agency did not merit additional funding. This unique "advantage" was most apparent in the case of urban renewal. The mayor who unveiled a downtown model studded with new glass skyscrapers and retail stores was rarely in office later when the cleared sites were offered for sale and found no takers.

The block grant approach of annual funding has effectively eliminated the politics of announcement. Although the Urban Development Action Grant program still provides the opportunity for pride and promotion as in the old days, the larger dollar amounts of the community development program are greeted with little or no media attention or public interest. The grant-giving process has become so regularized and assured that there is scarce political hay to be made. Local concerns are now bounded by the annual cycle of application preparation and HUD review—a process that simply requires a list of projects and areas that adds up to the available federal dollars and satisfies HUD review requirements. The broad politics of community development now generally follows the politics of local budgeting, by making marginal adjustments to existing programs and projects to arrive at a total that matches available resources.

The position faced by many midwestern communities in 1975 was almost unprecedented in the annals of urban politics. These local governments now had to devise and allocate funds for an entirely new program, under few constraints from either federal officials or a largely uninterested public. Areas such as Detroit, Cleveland, and Milwaukee, which had been deeply involved in categorical programs and committed to activity in neighborhoods covered by Model Cities and urban renewal programs, might budget the majority of new federal funds in the first year or two of the block grant program to these prior commitments. But the problem facing these large urban centers differed in degree, not in kind, from that facing smaller cities with no history of community upgrading efforts. Both types of locality were forced to generate new programs, new projects, and new administrative arrangements in a limited time span and without a budgetary base.

Cities adopted a variety of strategies to deal with the new block grant program and create an acceptable local effort. A research study of 20 midwestern localities identified six broad strategies that had been used to generate annual community development programs. These strategies, either alone or in combination, determined the shape of local programs that reflected the unique political and organizational environment of each locale.[2]

The first strategy can be called "Doing your thing." Cities that had previous experience in community development and contained an organization with experienced personnel often continued to pursue prior activities. Chicago's Department of Human Resources and Department of Urban Renewal each sought to maintain its existence and operations in the first few years of the block grant program. The former sought to continue social services begun under the Model Cities program, while the latter began to expand its land redevelopment activities to include economic development. The fact that these categorical grant agencies existed as a regular part of city hall made them potent competitors for block grant dollars. In Peoria, Illinois, the local urban renewal agency assumed management of the block grant and continued a land clearance and housing development emphasis in the first years of the community development program. Efforts at housing rehabilitation were undertaken slowly and received little political support. An agency with a history of commitment to reshaping the urban landscape is unlikely to be enthusiastic about paying for street resurfacing. Many local officials, however, prefer living with the limited repertoire of such an agency to putting their energy into creating new organizations and programs. As a result, the community development block grant program contains few direct incentives for new initiatives; the tried and tested triumph.

The second strategy can be entitled "Help your friends." Where past local experience or existing organizational routines are insufficient to handle a full annual entitlement, city decision makers often look to those divisions of city hall with program ideas and experience. "Friendship" with other city departments can generate a number of benefits for local community development administrators. In the first place such alliances can enlarge the stock of potentially fundable (and often necessary) projects. Local public works agencies often have a backlog of street resurfacing and drainage projects; parks departments have plans for new recreation centers or mini-parks; fire departments often need new equipment. Regular city line departments can also increase the political support and visibility of community development. The endorsement of a popular city department such as the parks department may bolster the reputation of a community development official while shifting popular attention away from controversial renewal or housing efforts. Finally, some city departments are particularly valuable because of their ability to spend federal dollars rapidly. As federal pressures to increase spending rates mounted during 1978 and 1979, some communities increased their budgets for traditional public works activities such as sidewalk construction, street repaving, and new street trees in order to get the money out faster. A public works department that can rapidly perform or contract out construction jobs is an invaluable ally in improving program performance and providing visible results. More community development dollars may also spur better performance from city line departments.

The third strategy is best summarized as "Meet popular demands." The block grant regulations have always required citizen participation in program development and selection. The 1977 amendments to the Housing and Community Development Act expanded these to include provision for a written citizen participation plan, public hearings, participation by low- and moderate-income persons, and the submission of citizen comments. In spite of these formal requirements, the role of the public varies substantially from place to place. In many cities, especially the larger central cities, the citizen role is limited to watching from the sidelines as city staff and elected officials draft the program. Smaller suburban jurisdictions often allow for a much greater level of citizen involvement by delegating the authority to choose programs and allocate funds to local organizations. This strategy effectively shifts the burden and unpleasantness of choice outside city hall and allows organizations considerable freedom on their own turf. Increased involvement also broadens the search for new projects considerably. Evanston, Illinois, illustrates the first case (local autonomy), where a local community development corporation accounts for roughly one-quarter of the city's annual funding and operates a number of programs, including housing rehabilitation, within the only minority community in this largely white suburban city. Oak Park, Illinois, provides an example of the second instance (a broadened search for new projects). Faced with a large increase in federal funds ($1.7 million in 1978 compared with $562,000 in 1977), the city accepted ideas and proposals from many individuals and groups, in an effort to allocate the full entitlement amount.

The fourth strategy is to "Bank the money." If an annual grant exceeds a city's ability to generate new programs in order to spend it, one response is to "bank" the funds for future needs. Unlike other federal programs, community development funds are released by the treasury only as expenses are incurred. The "banking" of funds is thus connected with the processes of both budgeting and project selection. A city may allocate funds to a project planned for some time in the future and in this way save dollars for an expensive project over a period of years. This form of banking federal funds allows local officials to meet the needs or demands of a particular group without sacrificing projects with different constituencies. The idea of staging an expensive project over a period of years is not unique to community development, but the program's willingness to commit funds to projects of limited feasibility or potential for completion is unique. One suburban Chicago community "banked" funds to acquire sites for assisted housing. It was thus able to demonstrate an effort at providing subsidized housing to federal officials while deferring any real action on the project. Other cities have budgeted funds for projects of dubious value or legality, hoping that either local preferences would change or that HUD would intervene in order to kill them.

In addition to these cases where cities have budgeted money without intending to spend it, there are additional cases where cities have spent money for no clear purpose. Elgin, Illinois, devised a program of acquiring blighted areas near the downtown area without planning for new uses or redevelopment. The acquisition effort absorbed federal funds easily at a time when the city was not sure what kind of program it wanted to operate and allowed the city to recoup its investment when it sold the land.

The fifth strategy can be named "Spread it around." The block grant approach to federal assistance opened a large number of new geographic areas for local action. Rather than concentrating their efforts in particular renewal areas, cities could now provide a broad range of assistance to a wide variety of neighborhoods. The tendency to spread local activities across a wide geographic area is present in even the best-managed and most rational local governments and is motivated by the desire to demonstrate that the government cares about all parts of the city. The spreading tendency is nonetheless particularly notable in highly political cities and those with councils elected by ward. Cleveland's early efforts saw assistance (generally housing rehabilitation loans or public improvements) provided to 27 of the city's 33 wards, scattering the program over more than 60 percent of the city.

Chicago's 50-member city council exerts similar pressures for geographic spreading of benefits. However, where city staffs play a major role in decision making and rely on "rational" planning criteria, the spreading tendency is greatly reduced. For example, in both Peoria and Decatur, Illinois, the dominance of the community development staff and the at-large city council combined to allow a high degree of targeting even in the first years of the program.

The spreading phenomenon is not solely geographical. Communities also attempt to distribute funds across a number of projects in order to minimize the risks of program failure or slow progress and to benefit a maximum number of local organizations.

The final strategy can be called "Leave some for the politicians." Local community development efforts operate in a political environment and are subject to the review and oversight of elected officials. Some local administrators "trade" a portion of the annual budget for political purposes so that city council intervention in the larger program will be limited. Cleveland's council directly controls the allocation of roughly $2.5 million for public services by social service organizations and neighborhood groups; it selects projects largely independently of the city's staff. Springfield, Illinois, also provides a political cut that is equally divided by the city departments directed by each elected commissioner. Such political compromises are *not*, however, the rule in the program. Federal regulations on program benefit and targeting effective in early 1978 limited the ability of local decision makers to spread dollars around while it also provided a new tool for staff influence over allocation.

The common theme of these local strategies is the local search for projects to absorb the annual federal entitlement. The often "clean slate" of local urban revitalization programs forced cities to generate quickly a set of fundable and easily implemented projects. This process was repeated in 1978 when the congressional enactment of an alternative funding formula provided a fiscal bonus to most midwestern localities.

The last two years of program operation have seen an increasing formalization of local programs. Although the annual application process still allows for program flexibility, cities are now sticking to a relatively fixed agenda that allows only limited changes from year to year. The major exception to this pattern was directly caused by local political change. A new mayor in Cleveland supported a shift from some large sewer projects to the rehabilitation of 30 deteriorated bridges that required over $6 million. A new city manager in Cincinnati provided the impetus for a reduction in social services funding and an increase in the targeting of community development dollars. In the absence of such political currents, however, the community development program tends to operate with only modest variation in objectives and programs from year to year.

Local Activities and Results

The summary of community development allocations by entitlement cities presented in Table 3 reveals something of the character of the program in recent years. Public works and public facilities have

Table 3. Community Development Budget Allocations by Function for the United States and Region V, 1979 and 1980

	1979		1980	
	U.S.	Region V	U.S.	Region V
Public works and facilities				
Streets/walkways/parking	13.1%	12.5%	14.5%	13.6%
Water/sewer/drainage	5.7	4.0	5.4	2.5
Parks/playgrounds	4.2	3.2	4.0	3.6
Neighborhood and special centers	2.7	2.7	3.9	2.6
Other Public Improvements	1.3	1.8	1.0	2.0
Housing rehabilitation and preservation	26.4	26.3	26.8	26.4
Land acquisition and redevelopment	14.1	19.5	12.6	19.6
Economic Development (specially authorized)	2.1	1.7	2.1	1.1
Urban renewal project completion	2.3	0.2	2.0	0.1
Public services	7.9	10.7	5.4	5.2
Planning/administration	11.9	11.5	12.7	14.7
Other activities	8.3	5.9	9.6	8.6

Note: Federal Region V includes Illinois, Indiana, Michigan, Minnesota, Ohio, and Wisconsin.

accounted for a substantial share of local spending. Housing rehabilitation programs have occupied an equally important position in local efforts. Urban renewal—land acquisition, clearance, and relocation—has accounted for only a modest part of local budgets. The pattern for midwestern cities (including those in Illinois, Indiana, Michigan, Minnesota, Ohio, and Wisconsin) has been quite similar to that of the nation as a whole, with the most consistent difference showing up as a slightly greater emphasis on new urban renewal activities in the Midwest.

This broad characterization of program activities suggests little of the real content and impact of spending, although it does show that the resource allocation outcomes in the Midwest resemble those of the nation as a whole. A more detailed examination of specific activities can, however, suggest some of the linkages between community development and local politics of midwestern cities.

The primary public works emphasis in the Midwest has been on street improvements. This category, which includes street resurfacing, replacement of sidewalks, and new curbs and gutters, represents a traditional function of local government. Such public works activities provide a visible demonstration of local government concern for a particular neighborhood; they also alleviate problems of traffic, drainage, and physical deterioration. Community development program regulations have linked housing rehabilitation assistance to other physical improvements, such as streets, in the same general area. It might even be said that popularity of rehabilitation aid may have prompted spending on public works activities.

The financial needs of city departments may have also contributed to the high proportion of public works projects. While some cities contract for street resurfacing and sidewalk replacement, others perform it with city crews by funding personnel and material from the community development grant. Keeping federal dollars within city hall can aid in maintaining local staffs and payrolls during a period of fiscal constraint. Cleveland, for example, has been quite successful in supporting the bulk of its highway maintenance staff with block grant funds. St. Louis began such a pattern of direct city work on streets with funds in 1977. Although the block grant regulations prohibit maintenance and repair activities such as the "filling of pot holes in streets [and] repairing of cracks in sidewalks" (U.S. Department of Housing and Urban Development, 1980), cities have found it relatively easy to shift their efforts to necessarily more expensive resurfacing and replacement projects.

A final organizational rationale for the emphasis on streets was the need to develop eligible projects rapidly in 1975 and again in 1978. Public works activities could literally be pulled "off the shelf," because most cities have a backlog of paving projects that have been identified by engineers and maintenance personnel. In such suburban communities as Oak Park and Evanston, Illinois, street improvements proved to be an efficient and eligible consumer of a sudden glut of federal dollars.

The ease with which local governments can budget for and perform street improvements testifies to the magnitude of need for such work. Many midwestern cities, particularly suburban areas and small central cities, allowed new subdivisions to be built without curbs and sidewalks, and with poor-quality streets. This neglect reflected in part a limited civic concern with such neighborhood amenities and a general attitude that residents could pay for improvements that directly benefited them through special assessments. In some cases subdivisions were built outside city boundaries where city construction codes did not apply, only to be annexed later along with their problems. A governmental attitude that property owners should bear the responsibility for initial street improvements also limited maintenance to very modest levels over the years. The federal dollars under the community development program now allow cities to do what they were often unwilling to do in the past even when they had local financial resources available.

Housing rehabilitation has been the second major budgetary emphasis of midwestern community development programs. Rehabilitation aid takes a variety of forms, including low-cost loans to homeowners, direct grants for both general rehabilitation and specific purposes such as weatherization, and actual city purchase of and renovation of buildings. The widespread adoption of local housing rehabilitation programs is one of the major success stories of the block grant program. Although land clearance and public works were common local activities in the early 1970s, direct assistance to homeowners was highly uncommon. The federal government had made loans and grants available to residents of renewal and code enforcement areas, but their scale was modest and their administration largely in federal hands. The early years of the community development program saw almost uniform local adoption of some type of rehabilitation assistance program and the creation of entirely new organizations and staff. Cities effectively created a new local government function.

This pervasive response to the flexible provisions of the 1974 Housing and Community Development Act suggests that a common factor was at work in most cities across the country. Some evidence indicates that the very nature of rehabilitation assistance, in contrast to the acquisition and relocation emphases of urban renewal, prompted city hall initiative. Direct loans and grants provided an easy and popular way to upgrade neighborhoods and to benefit property owners directly. While the obvious political returns from giving money directly to owners may have supported its adoption, rehabilitation assistance finally provided local government with a housing improvement tool that made friends rather than enemies.

The successful development of local housing rehabilitation programs, praised by both neighborhood activists and preservationists, should not blind us to the limitations of such efforts in practice. Rehabilitation has consistently been provided for only one segment of the population—homeowners. Figures for the first five years of the community development program in midwestern cities show that over 80 percent of the aided units have been owner-occupied. Another 13 percent of the units are in public housing projects, largely in such metropolitan centers as Detroit and Chicago. Only about 5 percent of the total rehabilitation effort has gone to rental housing rehabilitation. The avoidance of rental housing aid is perhaps the outstanding failure of local rehabilitation programs. Although some cities have defended their approach on the grounds that it is too difficult or costly to implement rental unit rehabilitation and that such assistance enriches landlords at the expense of tenants, this policy nonetheless results in total lack of help for those families who suffer the most serious housing problems. HUD pressure has resulted in some modest movement toward increasing rental housing rehabilitation, but it is unlikely to alter the current trend.

The emphasis on rehabilitation of owner-occupied dwellings parallels local decisions on the selection of target areas for assistance. The distribution of limited federal dollars through local political means has led to public intervention in neighborhoods where many people own homes and where there are few signs of serious physical or social deterioration. This strategy of conserving viable neighborhoods at the expense of more needy areas may be debated. Even the implications and implementation of the conservation strategy itself are open to question. With few exceptions, midwestern cities have operated their rehabilitation program on a walk-in basis and thus provide assistance only to those who seek it. The result is often a scattershot pattern of improved dwellings that reflect personal initiative and social networks rather than actual housing needs.

This bias in selection is reinforced by a bias in the assistance standards, which generally include the elderly and handicapped in the category of "low and moderate income," making them eligible for the highest levels of financial assistance. The result has been that elderly homeowners receive a disproportionate share of rehabilitation aid. The elderly occupy over 40 percent of the community development–funded dwellings rehabilitated by the city of Cleveland in recent years. The percentage for Chicago is strikingly similar. In smaller metropolitan centers, such as Bloomington, Illinois, the proportion rises to over 50 percent. This singular concentration on elderly households suggests that local government may feel particularly constrained to aid only the "deserving poor" and those whom local bureaucrats find it easy to deal with.

The combination of self-selection for rehabilitation assistance and de facto favoritism toward elderly homeowners results in a distribution of benefits that favors the less needy segments of the population, despite regulatory requirements for aiding low- and moderate-income persons. The impact of this pattern of housing assistance is difficult to define over a short period of time. Impressionistic evidence from a number of city neighborhoods that receive funds suggests that revitalization efforts do not make these neighborhoods more desirable and do not foster increased market activity in housing. Rather, the result of rehabilitation programs has been to encourage existing residents to remain in older housing which they may otherwise have sold. Neighborhoods are thus "frozen" in terms of population and housing stock. For a number of midwestern communities, rehabilitation assistance has provided the first public tool for altering the traditional patterns of racial change and succession, largely by limiting housing turnover. The political advantages of stabilizing older ethnic neighborhoods are obvious to local officials, particularly those who represent wards or districts.

The effect of such an implicit policy choice on the city as a whole is not yet discernible. It is clear, however, that the framework of the block grant allows for local policy decisions that might raise a greater public outcry were they made more openly.

The distinctiveness of the Midwest appears most clearly in its emphasis on urban renewal activities, including land acquisition, clearance, and relocation. The 1980 community development budget figures show that midwestern cities have allocated about 20 percent of their annual funds for renewal efforts, compared with about 13 percent for the nation. The success of recent renewal in the Midwest has been made possible by a combination of local history and urban need. Because the region made only limited efforts at slum clearance during the 1950s and 1960s, it received relatively modest aid under the categorical programs. Renewal in the Midwest thus generally avoided the period of wholesale clearance that created massive public disapproval in other regions. At the same time midwestern cities that *did* initiate renewal programs generally operated them within city hall. Unlike many eastern localities, where independent authorities removed renewal programs from public scrutiny and debate, the location of renewal organizations enabled the public to assume a management role in community development functions. As a consequence, the rancorous battles over organizational authority and responsibility that occurred in many regions were rare in the heartland.

The continuing economic decline of the largest midwest urban centers caused projects for industrial and commercial redevelopment to absorb a large share of local renewal expenditures. Chicago's 1979 community development program contained about $24 million (19 percent of its annual budget for community development) for land acquisition and redevelopment, including a $9 million economic development program. About 47 percent of Detroit's 1979 community development program involved redevelopment, including some $12 million in downtown economic development projects. The Detroit effort includes such familiar responses to urban ills as the construction of a landscaped pedestrian mall in the downtown core.

Urban renewal efforts are also continuing in residential neighborhoods. In Chicago clearance is generally paired with rehabilitation programs in project areas. In smaller urban areas, such as Peoria, clearance remains the only possible approach to acres of cheaply built and structurally unsound dwellings that have been largely ignored by public agencies over the last 50 years. The ability of local governments to grapple with the problems of the worst urban housing is now limited by increasing inflation, by the leveling off of federal aid, and by the pressures to spread these funds to a wider variety of city neighborhoods.

Has the Game Really Changed?

The proponents of the block grant approach to federal aid promised that the removal of red tape from the grant process would bring great things. The shift in the flow of aid—from the Northeast to the rest of the country, from central cities to suburbs, and from the largest central cities to a number of smaller locales—represents a major change. There have also been changes of similar magnitude in the *process* of federal assistance. The great bulk of the 3 ½-inch thick *Urban Renewal Handbook* has been replaced by a volume of regulations about one-quarter its size. The formal application for aid, greatly reduced from the categorical era, saw an increase in size and scope during the Carter administration. But the 1981 amendments to the Housing and Community Development Act did away with the application entirely and replaced it with an annual statement of objectives and projected use of funds. HUD is no longer required to approve the application, and it need not be submitted to an areawide organization for review. These legislative steps, together with the Reagan administration's New Federalism, suggest an even greater increase in local discretion and flexibility and a much more modest level of federal regulation and oversight.

While the elimination of a formal application suggests a more limited federal role, it may mark the beginning of a period of intergovernmental conflict and uncertainty. HUD is still required by statute to review and audit the performance of grant recipients annually. Some communities may even find themselves subject to repayment of grant funds in cases where they have pursued ineligible activities or failed to carry out required procedures.

The results of the block grant shift can also be seen in the products of the program. Block grant aid was designed to be a local program, locally conceived and designed to address local needs rather than federal goals. Yet today cities pursue much the same kinds of programs they undertook in the last years of the categorical programs. The stress on neighborhood revitalization and housing rehabilitation is quite similar to the efforts under the Neighborhood Development program in the late 1960s and early 1970s. However, the substantial local investment in direct assistance for housing rehabilitation is a genuine change that institutionalizes an entirely new function for local governments. Indeed, the striking popularity of rehabilitation assistance across the country suggests that the idea that differing local needs require unique local responses is a myth. For most cities the fiscal and political incentives that support a mix of housing and local public works are clear and overwhelming. Local needs—an alcoholism program, a fair housing effort, the preservation of a landmark—affect the program only marginally.

The Midwest presents one of the few instances where local needs have generated some variance from national norms. For cities like Detroit, St. Louis, and Gary, community development represents a major new revenue source for strapped local governments, which have responded to this opportunity by initiating a variety of programs that are quite distinct from neighborhood upgrading. Cleveland, where the city's default eliminated its access to the bond market for capital improvement monies, has used the community development program as a general-purpose urban aid vehicle. Its earliest efforts included the funding of local police services that the city could no longer afford to provide. More recently, it has employed community development dollars to support critical sewer and bridge rehabilitation programs for which the city lacked the funds. The use of federal aid for such essential purposes may be the result that matches the intention of the legislation's drafters. It also, however, entails a notable cost in the other necessary programs the city fails to carry out. Community development dollars may keep Cleveland operating as a city a bit longer, but by being used for this purpose, they are unavailable for housing and neighborhood improvement efforts that affect the city's long-term future.

Federal Aid and the Future of the Midwestern City

The large central cities of the Midwest have suffered as a result of a number of long-term trends. The migration of people and firms, both to the suburban ring and to other regions, has sapped these cities of both economic vitality and taxable resources. The weakness of heavy industry, such as steel, automobiles, and capital machinery, has hurt such places as Detroit, Cleveland, and Chicago most severely. These communities might best be characterized as two distinct "cities within the city." In a large number of older residential neighborhoods the familiar pattern of decline and decay still prevails. Migration from the city and the abandonment of rental housing continue; for example, the city of Cleveland has demolished between 2,500 and 4,000 housing units per year since 1972. Community development aid is unlikely to alter this general pattern, especially where the exit of a neighborhood employer leads to a further population loss. Although recent private upgrading and gentrification are often cited as a hopeful sign for the future of these cities, these movements are unfortunately too limited in scale and location to promise much for most central city neighborhoods.

The bleak outlook for older residential areas is balanced by the relative strength of the downtown cores of many midwestern urban centers. After decades of loss in retail space and sales, these central business districts appear to be holding their own. Although they no longer function as the focal point of the larger metropolitan areas, downtowns are playing a substantial role as office centers, notably in banking, finance, insurance, and government. Central districts have also emerged as major centers of education and medical care, even as their role in retail sales and entertainment has declined.

Federal aid, almost regardless of its magnitude, will be unable to alter the migration and economic trends that affect the Midwest. Major public investments in housing rehabilitation and neighborhood facilities have acted to stabilize a small number of older residential areas. If community development assistance continues at a reasonable level, it appears possible, at the very least, to slow the rate of exodus from the central city. Economic development investments, especially in the downtown core, appear to have a greater impact, largely because they are "running with the tide" of basic economic strength. These projects have become more appealing of late because they have a substantial effect on a community's image and its tax base. The political appeal of large-scale redevelopment projects may well overwhelm a number of more modest neighborhood initiatives, especially as federal spending decreases.

The prognosis of more glittering downtown revitalizations paired with the abandonment of the city's older rental housing is not an encouraging one. Even this prospect, however, may be overly optimistic in light of recent efforts to reduce the general level of federal urban assistance. In late 1981 the Office of Management and Budget proposed a phaseout of the community development block grant program "because of the need to reduce Federal spending." The OMB proposal called for a decrease in budgetary authority to $2.15 billion in fiscal 1982, $1.1 billion the following year, and zero dollars in 1984. President Reagan saved the program from extinction, although there has been a real reduction in the level of aid. With little or no increase in community development aid, the cities of the Midwest may well find themselves limited to "placing the drop in the bucket" in order to stave off yet another fiscal crisis.

Notes

1. Figures on grant demand and processing during the categorical era are taken from unpublished internal reports of the U.S. Department of Housing and Urban Development. They are a part of a larger study in progress on the history of HUD's role in urban development.

2. The discussion of budgetary strategy and program choice is based on field research in more than a dozen cities in Illinois conducted by the author with assistance from the Institute of Government and Public Affairs, University of Illinois. This has been supplemented by fieldwork in other midwestern cities and examination of numerous local community development block grant applications and performance reports.

References

Kettl, D. F. 1980. *Managing community development in the new federalism.* New York: Praeger.

Nathan, R. P., et al. 1977. *Block grants for community development.* Washington, D.C.: U.S. Government Printing Office.

Sanders, H. T. 1980. Block grants and federal bucks. *Illinois Government Research* 50: Urbana: University of Illinois, Institute of Government and Public Affairs.

U.S. Bureau of the Budget. 1958. A reappraisal of federal aids for urban development. Washington, D.C. Unpublished staff study.

U.S. Department of Housing and Urban Development. 1980. *Consolidated community development block grant regulations.* Washington, D.C.: U.S. Government Printing Office.

Williams, W. 1980. *Government by agency.* New York: Academic Press.

9
Untapped Labor in the Midwest

DAVID BERRY and STEPHANIE WILSON

"Most jobs don't pay that much, so that it's not worth your time to take them, and that's why you don't go off welfare. Once I get my GED, and then maybe some school, I'll have a real chance of getting a decent job I can keep, something that I'll be satisfied with and that will take me off welfare."

"Do you know a job that can support a woman with two children? Some *men* can't even support two kids on the salaries they earn. I've tried everything I can to get into a school, and I can't do it without the help of somebody. If they want me to sit on welfare all this time when I'm ready to get up and do something, I will."

"I don't know. Maybe something to do with filing. Maybe I can brush up on my typing. I think I would like to work in an office, maybe as a receptionist. I guess I don't know. I've been tired, not feeling well, I guess I'm finally admitting to myself that I'm scared, scared to go out and work, scared of the world out there. I'm 45 years old and I don't have any skills. I'm afraid."

"I got good pay (at a paper factory), but it was terrible. It was really hot, and it smelled. People would faint all over. They had a back room where you could go if you were feeling bad, but the bosses didn't like it if you went there because it meant you'd be taking time off work."

"Practically speaking, you and I both know that you can't break in any place without a degree."

These comments by clients of a work training program in the Midwest make vivid the barriers to employment many Americans face.[1] A number of conditions alone or in concert can create these barriers: lack of skills or unfamiliarity with the labor market on the part of job seekers, race or sex discrimination, the industrial structure of a given region, and fluctuations and trends in the national economy.

This chapter analyzes three programs that have attempted to reduce both human capital and behavioral barriers to employment. Human capital refers to the stock of skills and labor market familiarity that workers bring to their job searches, while behavioral features of the market refer to the systemic slotting of minority or women workers into specific jobs simply because female or minority workers have traditionally performed such jobs.

Human capital and behavioral barriers to employment are deeply woven into the fabric of the midwestern economy. Workers who have limited skills and education or little familiarity with the labor market may cycle through multiple jobs and suffer long spells of unemployment. Many remain on welfare for extended periods of time, encouraged to do so in part because earnings from those jobs they can find may not exceed welfare benefits. Indeed, after two decades and the expenditure of over $64 billion nationally on job training and related programs, the American people have not yet found the means to overcome employment barriers for vast numbers of discouraged, unemployed, and marginal workers (Ginzberg, 1980).

Although employment barriers caused by labor market discrimination are still widespread, the Civil Rights Act of 1964 and, to a lesser extent, affirmative action programs have attacked many of them. By removing race-biased tests, by judging a firm's labor market performance relative to other firms, by allowing redress for victims of discrimination, and by forcing some companies to move quickly to eliminate the effects of past discrimination, civil rights and affirmative action programs have sought to break down behavioral barriers on many fronts. Blatant discrimination is now relatively rare, but subtle forms can still influence career choices and career progress. The Civil Rights Act and affirmative action programs are national, not just midwestern, in origin and scope, but they have had considerable influence in the Midwest, as our discussion will demonstrate.

Before turning to a detailed analysis of efforts to remove behavioral and human capital barriers, it would be useful to describe the economic and social structures in which they function. The Midwest suffers from a set of interrelated maladies that are discussed throughout this book. In the next few paragraphs we review these problems as they present and reflect structural barriers to employment, i.e., barriers rooted both in the industrial structure of the region and in economywide factors.

Structurally, the midwestern labor market retains vestiges of the late nineteenth-century industrial city. Its metropolitan areas, by and large, are more dependent on heavy manufacturing than are those in the rest of the nation. Consequently, the midwestern occupational distribution, in contrast to the national labor market, is characterized by larger percentages of workers employed in operative and craft occupations. Conversely, lower percentages of the region's work force are employed in professional, technical, managerial, administrative, sales, and clerical positions than in the United States as a whole (U.S. Bureau of the Census, 1979).

Manufacturing, however, is a comparatively weak sector in the American economy. As a point of reference, the number of people employed in manufacturing in the United States (22 percent of all employees in 1978) increased by only 700,000 between 1968 and 1978 while total employment grew by 18.5 million (Rones, 1980). The relative importance of manufacturing in the national economy is clearly declining.

In large part, then, the industrial and occupational mix of the Midwest may explain the recent migration out of the region. Between 1970 and 1979 there was a net outmigration of 1,619,000 persons from the North Central region (U.S. Bureau of the Census, 1980b). Although the data appear to fluctuate from year to year, the *Current Population Report* on geographical mobility from 1975 to 1979 indicates a trend in outmigration from the North Central region: all major occupational categories except operatives and transport equipment operatives experienced net outmigration in the late 1970s (U.S. Bureau of the Census, 1980b).

Structural barriers to employment can be overcome by continued outmigration or possibly by state or local efforts to retain existing economic activities and to stimulate new action in growing sectors of the economy. These approaches are discussed elsewhere and will not be addressed further here.

The Minnesota Work Equity Project

The first program to be examined in this chapter, the Minnesota Work Equity Project, has several features that make it appropriate for analysis. It is, obviously, a midwestern project; more important, perhaps, it has recently generated detailed data about human capital barriers to employment among program participants. Moreover, this project is fairly typical of other efforts to overcome human capital obstacles in labor markets. Thus it provides a comprehensive view of skill and labor market familiarity problems and the proposed solutions to these problems.

The Work Equity Project was a two-year demonstration employment and training program that began in 1978 and operated in the city of St. Paul and several counties in central Minnesota. Participation in the project was mandatory for clients in selected welfare programs (Aid to Families with Dependent Children in St. Paul and AFDC, General Assistance, and Food Stamps in the other program areas) who were determined to be employable according to statutory criteria. Because the project was designed to place its clients in suitable jobs that would reduce their dependence on welfare,[2] it stressed the development of community work projects in order to guarantee jobs for *all* clients. It also sought to motivate clients to participate actively in the program.

The Work Equity Project was an employment and training program, as distinct from an income maintenance program; it therefore sought to make clients employable by focusing on job skills and job placement. In contrast, income maintenance strategies provide grants to low-income families in amounts that decrease as income is earned. Although welfare programs deal with problems of poverty and income inequality, they do not train the disadvantaged to achieve economic independence. Thus the Work Equity Project attempted to address the employment barriers of low-income persons more directly than income maintenance programs do.

The Work Equity Project has only recently ended, so that outcomes cannot be measured with confidence until assessment of the follow-up interviews is completed. It is possible, however, to make tentative inferences about employment barriers in Minnesota based on the preliminary findings of the program. These suggest that sample clients can be classified into three groups: women who have little previous work experience, women with substantial work experience, and men who experience difficulties in the labor market (Wilson, Steinberg, and Kulik, 1980). The chief employment barriers among women with little work experience are unfamiliarity with the labor market, absence of marketable skills, and low earnings potential. For women who have work experience, preliminary project findings show that career counseling and training, coupled with subsidized jobs, may help them attain earnings potentials sufficient to reduce or end their dependence on public assistance. As for men, no conclusions are yet possible, because there appears to be little relationship between human capital and wages earned for these program clients.

A review of the employment histories of Work Equity Project clients (see Table 1) shows that a woman's age, level of education, and the presence of children aged 6 to 17 in the household are the more significant indicators of her full-time employment pattern over the previous five years. Women who have only school age children, who are older, or who are relatively well educated are more likely to have held a full-time job than are childless, young, or more poorly educated women. These results are consistent with the findings of other analyses of female labor

Table 1. Minnesota Work Equity Project: Determinants of Full-Time Work Experience for Males and Females (Signs of Regression Coefficients)

	Males	Females
Years of education	+	+
Age	+	+
Married	0	0
Never married	-	0
Black	0	0
Other race	0	0
Presence of preschool age children	0	0
Presence of school age children	0	+
Presence of children older than age 17 only	0	-
Presence of preschool *and* school age children	+	0

Source: Steinberg et al. (1980).

Notes: The signs of the regression coefficients were determined by regression of the dependent dummy variable, "employed full-time in all five previous years," on the independent variables indicated.

A "+" indicates a positive significant coefficient, a "-" indicates a negative significant coefficient, and a "0" indicates no effect.

supply, which have shown that women with school age children, controlling for other demographic influences, are most likely to enter the labor force as full-time workers (Cogan, 1975).

Among men in the Work Equity Project, those who are older and better educated tend to have more full-time work experience. Men who have children of all ages in the home are also more likely to have worked full-time in the past. Single men are significantly less apt to have worked, controlling for other variables such as race, age, and presence of dependent children, a finding that suggests that single men may need increased support from the program both to obtain and to hold jobs (Steinberg, et al., 1980).

Because the Work Equity Project seeks to remove impediments to employment through its various training and job components, it concentrates on human capital and behavioral barriers to employment. But it does so in the context of the structural configuration of the local labor market. For example, under conditions of structural unemployment, it is more effective to emphasize classroom and on-the-job training than to stress job search, because most unskilled clients entering a poor job market have slim chances of finding and retaining jobs unless they can obtain extensive training.

Given the large number of female AFDC clients and the better employment opportunities for educated women, a major issue for the Work Equity Project is whether to encourage female welfare recipients without high school diplomas to take unskilled jobs or to enter classroom training instead. These women may take unskilled jobs and experience short-term rises in earnings followed by declines as industrial demand shifts. If, on the other hand, these women are directed into classroom training, they may acquire skills that would make them relatively immune to structural employment barriers. Effective training can lead to successful job placement of program clients, especially women, in service industries. The catch is that service jobs generally do not pay well, so that these individuals may still remain at least partially dependent on welfare.

The Minnesota experience should not, however, be assumed to be typical of the Midwest. Minnesota has, in general, escaped the strong structural declines felt by the rest of the region. Even so, the tentative preliminary findings from this project do not appear to differ significantly from the findings of programs conducted elsewhere (Ginzberg, 1980).

Reducing the Effects of Discrimination in Metropolitan Labor Markets

Race and sex discrimination pervades the labor market in such a way that minorities and women are often channeled into certain kinds of jobs. Actual employment discrimination, the socialization of minority youngsters and of girls toward traditional types of jobs, and the limited educational opportunities available to minorities and women all conspire to create this pattern. In addition, racial segregation in housing, which limits access to suburban jobs far from central city minority areas, contributes to employment discrimination. Socioeconomic differences between whites and blacks and occupational differences between blacks and whites and men and women are partially summarized in Table 2 for eight large metropolitan areas in the Midwest.

Although there is great intermetropolitan variation, the table shows a clear pattern of black-white differences in educational levels, residential location, public school enrollment, and occupational distribution. Blacks tend to be more poorly educated than whites; they are concentrated in the central city public schools; and they hold relatively fewer jobs in craft, professional, technical, managerial, sales, and sometimes clerical occupations.[3] Women also show strong differences in occupational distribution from men. This is due to the concentration of women in traditional "women's jobs" such as clerical and service occupations

Table 2. Black-White and Male-Female Differences in Eight Large Midwestern Metropolitan Areas

Metropolitan Area	Percentage of Persons 25 and Older with High School Education, March 1979[a]		Index of Concentration of Blacks in Central Cities[b]	Index of Concentration of Blacks in Central City Public Schools[c]	Index of Occupational Dissimilarity, 1978	
	White	Black			White vs. Black[d]	Males vs. Females[d]
Chicago	70.7	53.6	1.9	1.83	16.6	38.4
Detroit	70.7	65.0	2.5	1.81	20.8	47.0
Minneapolis– St. Paul[e]	81.0	n/a	2.5	$\begin{cases}3.41 \\ 2.57\end{cases}$	n/a	39.0
St. Louis	70.5	55.7	5.8	1.76	24.9	44.9
Cleveland	72.3	51.7	2.4	1.51	23.0	45.4
Cincinnati	n/a	n/a	2.5	1.92	21.6	43.0
Kansas City	n/a	n/a	1.9	2.81	30.1	45.9
Indianapolis	n/a	n/a	1.4	2.72	27.7	42.6

[a] U.S. Bureau of the Census (1980a, Table 9).

[b] Percentage of population black in central city divided by percentage of population black in SMSA, 1970. A value greater than 1.0 indicates concentration of blacks in the central city (U.S. Bureau of the Census, 1978).

[c] Percent 1976–77 black enrollment in central city public schools divided by percent black population in central city in 1970. A value greater than 1.0 indicates a concentration of blacks in public schools (U.S. Bureau of the Census, 1978; U.S. Department of Health, Education, and Welfare, 1979).

[d] Index computed as $\frac{1}{2} \sum_j |W_j - B_j|$ where W_j is percentage of employed whites in occupation j and B_j is percentage of employed blacks in occupation j, based on nine major occupational categories. Similar formula for males-females. A higher value of the index indicates greater dissimilarity (U.S. Department of Labor, 1979, Table 13).

[e] Minneapolis and St. Paul shown separately for central city statistics, Minneapolis first.

Note: n/a indicates that the information is not available.

and in some professional occupations such as nursing and teaching. Conversely, women are underrepresented as managers and administrators, as craftworkers, as transport equipment operatives, and as laborers.

In the next two sections we examine the two major programs designed to reduce employment discrimination, Title VII of the Civil Rights Act of 1964 and affirmative action. Although the Civil Rights Act pertains to many aspects of discrimination, we shall focus here only upon direct employment discrimination. The following discussion does not, therefore, address changes in schooling, housing, or individual career attitudes, even though these changes are known to affect employment discrimination patterns.

Civil Rights Act of 1964

Title VII of the Civil Rights Act of 1964, as amended, is the centerpiece of federal legislation to remove barriers to employment caused by discrimination:

It shall be unlawful employment practice for an employer
1) to fail or refuse to hire or to discharge any individual or otherwise to discriminate against any individual with respect to his compensation, terms, conditions, or privileges of employment, because of such individual's race, color, religion, sex, or national origin; or,
2) to limit, segregate, or classify his employees or applicants for employment in any way which would deprive any individual of employment opportunities or otherwise adversely affect his status as an employee, because of such individual's race, color, religion, sex, or national origin. (U.S. Code Annotated, Title 42, Ch. 21, Sec. 2000e–2)

The Civil Rights Act provides the necessary catalyst for change. Persons adversely affected by the discriminatory practices of employers can sue either directly or through the Equal Employment Opportunity Commission to eliminate these practices. They can also seek relief by such means as suing for back pay to compensate for losses suffered because of discrimination.

On the basis of the Civil Rights Act of 1964, the courts have played an active role in eliminating barriers to equal employment opportunity. Many cases from the Midwest testify to the effectiveness of such litigation. For example, in *Donnell v. General Motors Corp.* (17 FEP 712) a major issue was the discriminatory effect of the policy of a General Motors plant in St. Louis to admit only persons with a high school education into a skilled trades training program. Donnell argued that the education requirement was an employment barrier to blacks because a significantly smaller proportion of blacks completed high school than whites. Census data for the St. Louis SMSA supported this contention. General Motors was called to justify the educational requirement in the face of the Supreme Court's earlier conclusion that "if an employment practice which operates to exclude Negroes cannot be shown to be related to job performance, the practice is prohibited" (*Griggs v. Duke Power Co.*, 401 US 431). The court rejected General Motors's argument that a high school diploma was necessary for effective functioning in the training program and on the job. In fact, General Motors changed its requirements for admittance into the training program prior to the final resolution of the case. This example of judicial intervention shows how obstacles to employment opportunities can be eroded.

In St. Paul the Minnesota Mining and Manufacturing Company agreed, in a 1981 out-of-court settlement, to undertake "steps to insure the continuance of education and training programs for plant employees and to further encourage the upward mobility of women in plant locations" (*Wall Street Journal*, 1981, p. 20). This kind of action, if actually carried out, breaks down systemic employment barriers. As part of the agreement, subject to review by the court, Minnesota Mining will pay $2.1 million in back pay to 2,000-3,000 women hourly workers who faced sex-related employment barriers in the past. The Minnesota Mining case is further evidence that the Civil Rights Act of 1964, through the intervention of the Equal Employment Opportunity Commission and the federal courts, has influenced the metropolitan Midwest.

On another front, the courts have come to accept the geographic and occupational characteristics of the labor market in which an employer operates as one standard of evidence for discrimination by that employer. In *Hazelwood School District v. U.S.* (15 FEP 1) the central issue was whether the city of St. Louis's policy of maintaining a 50 percent black teacher corps increased the availability of black teachers in the labor market of Hazelwood, a suburb of St. Louis. If St. Louis were determined to be in the Hazelwood labor market, then the standard of comparison, as measured by the relative availability of blacks, would be far higher (and the statistical evidence for discrimination by the Hazelwood School District would be much stronger) than if St. Louis were determined to lie outside the Hazelwood labor market. The Supreme Court remanded the case to the district court with instructions to clarify the geography of the labor market and the effect of St. Louis's hiring policies on suburban school districts. In giving these instructions, the Supreme Court placed its authority behind the principle that the proportion of minority members or women in a given labor market is a relevant determinant for the existence of discrimination.

Has the Civil Rights Act been influential only in isolated cases such as these, or has it had a widespread effect on job opportunities for minorities and women in the Midwest? A study by Freeman (1974) suggests that the civil rights legislation has had an economywide effect. Taking time series data for the period 1955 to 1972, Freeman used regression analysis to explain statistically the percentage of nonwhite workers in each of 11 broad occupational categories. As explanatory variables he used time to represent changes in attitudes, expenditures per nonwhite worker by the Equal Employment Opportunity Commission to represent enforcement of the law, and the cyclical deviations of the Gross National Product from its trend level to represent recessions or recovery periods. The principal conclusions from this analysis, when controlling for time and cyclical effects, are: (1) the Civil Rights Act has improved the employment opportunities of nonwhite men in managerial and clerical work; (2) it has not improved employment opportunities for nonwhite men in professional, craft, and sales occupations; and (3) it has improved the employment opportunities of nonwhite women in clerical, sales, operative, and managerial occupations. One shortcoming of this analysis, however, is the difficulty of isolating the effects of civil rights legislation from the effects of other simultaneous factors, such as changes in social attitudes, that may influence job opportunities.

In a study of wages and total income rather than of occupational distributions, Burstein (1979) conducted a time series analysis of minority and female earnings (and income) as a percentage of white male earnings (and income). This study took into account influences other than the enforcement of the Civil Rights Act more thoroughly than Freeman's study did. Burstein's clearest results are for nonwhite male earnings; he found that civil rights activities have significantly improved the earnings of male minority workers, whether these activities are measured in cumulative EEOC expenditures per covered worker, cumulative number of court cases favoring minorities, or number of actionable charges based on race processed annually by EEOC. This effect is evident when unemployment rates, educational levels of nonwhite males relative to white males, and social attitudes toward minorities are controlled for statistically.[4] Moreover, the magnitude of the effects is greatest when marginal workers (i.e., those not working full time year round) are included, suggesting that civil rights legislation has helped this group considerably.

Affirmative Action

Affirmative action is usually interpreted to mean personnel actions that seek to eliminate the effects of past discrimination more quickly than would otherwise occur, even if the Civil Rights Act of 1964 were fully enforced. Under affirmative action an employer goes beyond nondiscriminatory action to hire or promote minorities or women in ways to enhance their employment opportunities. Many public and private employers have undertaken such actions, but the magnitude, nature, and effects of affirmative action in practice are largely unknown.

Affirmative action has been codified for one class of employers, however, those who have large contracts with the federal government, the so-called "contractors." Bureaucratic interpretations of Executive Order 11246, issued by President Johnson in 1965 and entitled "Equal Employment Opportunity," have created regulations that require each contractor to prepare and implement an affirmative action plan. The Office of Federal Contract Compliance Programs monitors and enforces these plans, and the regulations of this office shed some light on what constitutes affirmative action, not only by the contractors for whom they are intended but also by other employers as well.

Affirmative action by contractors consists of two basic parts: (1) an underutilization component that is intended to bring federal contractors up to current availability levels, that is, up to the current average level of utilization of minorities and women in the labor market for each relevant occupational category; and, (2) an enhancement component that obligates a contractor to go beyond the elimination of underutilization and to improve the employment opportunities of minorities and women by applying exceptional personnel practices.

In practice, the two-component nature of affirmative action has proven difficult to implement, in large part because of the way the regulations are written. These require that employers consider eight determinants for the availability of minorities or women. But these eight factors are applied both to set a standard of comparison to measure underutilization of minorities and women in a particular job relative to the firm's labor market, and to encourage efforts to increase the availability of minorities and women. Consequently, the factors confuse in a single index the currently available qualified work force in a given labor market on the one hand, and the potentially qualified and available work force—that is, those who could acquire skills and could live in a given labor market—on the other. In effect, the regulations mix together the utilization requirement, which measures current availability of minorities and women, and the enhancement requirement, which measures potential availability.

On the basis of this compound index, OFCCP typically found contractors not in compliance because their current utilization of minorities and women fell short of current plus potential future availability. This approach is illogical. If the twin goals of affirmative action were implemented as two separate processes—one requiring that contractors eliminate underutilization and the other requiring them to undertake exceptional enhancement efforts by, for example, offering subsidies for moving and commuting costs or expanding their recruitment and training programs—more concerted action could take place.

Affirmative action is further hampered by the fact that no clear guidelines have been set for the enforcement of enhancement efforts. A criterion is needed for each occupation in each labor market to define the ultimate goal of affirmative action and the maximum time period allowed to reach this goal. Because both the goals and the rates for their achievement are politically and statistically difficult to establish, they remain nebulous and subject to ad hoc interpretations.

In spite of these difficulties, enhancement is clearly the distinguishing feature of affirmative action. Enhancement can and should increase employment opportunities for minorities and women in higher-status jobs than they are routinely offered; this is true especially in expanding areas within a company. A firm's enhancement efforts can include the payment of commuting or moving costs to bring minorities and women into a labor market, the maintenance of employment offices in minority communities, the active recruitment of women and minorities into training programs, the establishment of day care programs, and the initiation of new skill development programs. These efforts may be costly, and their effectiveness will vary according to the jobs involved and the target populations addressed. Hence, a uniform approach would not be effective.

The Detroit Police Department offers an example of successful affirmative action through enhancement efforts. This department instituted a policy to modify traditional criteria for promotion to sergeant so that black patrolmen could be promoted more rapidly. The implicit goal of these actions was apparently to create a racial composition at all levels in the police force that matched the racial composition of the population served, that is, the population of Detroit (*Detroit Police Officers Association v. Young*, 20 FEP 1728).[5]

In spite of such successes, however, affirmative action goals remain vague. This indeterminacy seems to have contributed to the outcome of *Timken v. Vaughn* (413 F. Supp 1183). At the time this case was initiated, various federal agencies administered their own affirmative action contract compliance programs. In this instance the Defense Supply Agency of the Department of Defense debarred the Timken Co. of Bucyrus, Ohio, because its affirmative action plan had not made the city of Mansfield part of its labor market. Timken had apparently used commuting patterns to set its labor market boundaries, and this empirical standard excluded the city of Mansfield, 25 miles from Bucyrus. The

Defense Supply Agency, taking an enhancement view of availability, argued that Mansfield should be in the firm's labor market, an inclusion that would slightly increase the availability of blacks to the firm. The government case, however, made no mention of a specific enhancement plan to recruit and employ this potential target population of black workers in Mansfield, so that the ultimate purpose of Mansfield's inclusion in an expanded labor market area was not explicit. The U.S. District Court for the Northern District of Ohio ruled in favor of Timken, making its determination on the basis of current availability alone. It excluded Mansfield from the labor market on the grounds that few workers at any firm actually commuted from Mansfield to Bucyrus or would be likely to do so under normal labor market conditions.

Going from this micro-view of particular cases to marketwide impacts, what effect has affimative action had on the employment opportunities of minorities and women? Statistical evidence about the Midwest is slim, but one study, based on a comparison of contractors and noncontractors in Chicago and surrounding areas for the period 1970 to 1973, suggests that affirmative action, as it operated in firms with federal contracts, concentrated on black males during those years (Heckman and Wolpin, 1976). In an analysis of all employees in 3,610 establishments for the year 1973, Heckman and Wolpin found that contractors employed more black males as a percentage of all employees than noncontractors did. When white-collar employees alone are tabulated, the same pattern emerges, with the added feature that contractors increased their hiring rates of black males more rapidly than noncontractors did.

Conclusion

The three programs discussed in this chapter are intended to weaken behavioral and human capital barriers to employment, but they have little influence on structural barriers. Yet the metropolitan Midwest suffers from serious structural problems that are currently solved by outmigration. Given these economic conditions, how have the discouraged workers, the displaced homemakers, the unemployed and underemployed workers, and the occupationally segregated minorities and women of the region fared? Our review has not covered all the evidence compiled in the last few years and, indeed, much remains uncertain. Yet several conclusions seem warranted.

The Work Equity Project and similar programs can remove some human capital and behavioral barriers by providing labor market experience and job training. However, many employment barriers are difficult to overcome. It is essential to identify the potential, hard-core unemployed and welfare-dependent populations before they become chronically unemployed or capable of working only at low wages. If this were done, additional progress could be made to remove employment barriers that arise from lack of labor market familiarity, lack of career objectives, and lack of education and training.

The Civil Rights Act of 1964 has been effective in promoting the employment opportunities of minorities, especially black males. In large part this success can be attributed to the act's systemic character. It applies to minorities and women in all jobs and in access to all jobs. By taking such a comprehensive approach, the Civil Rights Act attacks discrimination across the board and consequently is more successful than if it focused only upon limited aspects of labor market participation or individual career patterns.

Except in some important instances, affirmative action has apparently been less successful in enhancing employment opportunities than the Civil Rights Act has been in overcoming current discrimination. It attempts to accelerate the rate of improvement in employment opportunities beyond what the Civil Rights Act and the slow changes in education and attitude would achieve. Affirmative action, however, runs into limitations imposed by the rate at which target populations can improve their skills through education and training. These difficulties are aggravated for government contractors by the confusing enforcement of Executive Order 11246.

What is the future of the metropolitan Midwest? Several issues are likely to dominate in the 1980s. First, the problem of eliminating human capital barriers remains. At the beginning of his administration President Reagan announced two proposed solutions to this issue. One is to increase the role of state and local governments and to reduce the constraints imposed by the federal government. The other is to emphasize programs that improve the training and job search skills of workers in order to achieve a high level of placement in private sector jobs. The opportunities for workers whose employment barriers can be removed by such training programs will probably continue as in recent years, although there may be state-to-state variations.

Second, no solution to the problems of the hard-core unemployed seems imminent. Short-term projects geared to eliminate the chronic problems of these individuals have been disappointing. The Reagan administration, aware of these shortcomings, has shifted from short-term "demonstration" projects to long-term "forced work" plans in order to remove employment barriers. The administration has lifted many of the incentives used previously to motivate clients to work while remaining on welfare. Programs such as public sector employment (PSE) and the Comprehensive Employment and Training Act (CETA) have been drastically reduced or eliminated. President Reagan has replaced the incentive approach to work by the workfare approach.

In some states clients are required to work off their welfare benefits. In addition, the Reagan policy of shifting control of the welfare system from the federal government to the states promises more discretionary and restrictive spending in many states. The "stay in school" solution to youth unemployment and youth welfare enrollment may also be jeopardized by school cutbacks and teacher lay-offs, for reduced spending in the schools will eliminate many of the training and special education programs that have catered to significant portions of the low-income population and have served as an inducement for longer school tenure. It is clear that future government plans to eliminate welfare-generated barriers will reduce the welfare opportunity cost to work so as to drive all but the most needy individuals off the welfare rolls. This policy requires that those employable welfare clients who were previously given alternatives to full-time private sector employment now work *and* their welfare receipts are reduced by 100 percent of their earned income after four months on welfare. The reduced tax rate on earned income of welfare recipients would be eliminated. Those who cannot find work may be made to provide direct labor in proportion to welfare benefits received.

The Reagan administration obviously sees the substitution of the stick for the carrot as an immediate means to remove employment barriers. This approach may, however, aggravate employment problems, as it drives large numbers of low-income persons who have no opportunity for training and skill improvement to vie for temporary dead-end jobs in order to stay out of a harsh welfare system. Reagan's policy will undoubtedly reduce the welfare rolls and may even foster improved work habits in certain segments of the welfare population. However, many marginally employed persons may find themselves in the bottom half of a dual labor market among the low-income and unskilled population who stand at the end of job queues and receive only the lowest paid and most unattractive jobs, with little hope of advancement. This dual labor market may persist for a long time.

Third, antidiscrimination efforts are likely to have unintended consequences. In slack economic periods with widespread lay-offs of workers, attempts to protect the gains of minorities and women, who are likely to have the least seniority in higher-status jobs, will be met with charges of reverse discrimination. This is a politically charged issue that will be highly visible in the short-term future.

It is uncertain what the future commitment of the American people will be toward enforcement of antidiscrimination programs. Many minorities and women worry that tenuous gains made since the mid-1960s might slip away if not strengthened by continued rigorous enforcement of the Civil Rights Act of 1964 and of affirmative action requirements. Yet all the signs indicate that federal agencies intend to level off their monitoring and enforcement in the 1980s.

Finally, continued industrial decline will exacerbate the barriers to employment in the Midwest. As a consequence of structural barriers, outmigration of workers will continue, and if the outmigration process proves selective, it may leave an increased concentration of hard-core unemployed in midwestern cities. The future does not appear promising.

Notes

1. We are indebted to Joe Frees for making these quotations available. We also wish to acknowledge the assistance of Chris Ostrow and the helpful comments of Ralph Jones, Michael Phillips, and Susan Wood.

2. The project replaced WIN in those counties where Work Equity operated and drew from the WIN and CETA programs for legislative authority and certain operating procedures.

3. LaGory and Magnani (1979) compared 50 large metropolitan areas using the index of occupational dissimilarity in Table 2. They found the best employment opportunities for black workers to be in large metropolitan areas that have rather low percentages of black population and well-integrated school systems.

4. There seems to be a complicating relationship between EEOC activities and educational levels when just year-round full-time workers are considered such that EEOC activities are not statistically significant when educational level is introduced into the model.

5. Such actions often engender resentment by whites, leading to cases like *Detroit Police Officers Association v. Young* (20 FEP 1728).

References

Burstein, P. 1979. Equal employment opportunity legislation and the income of women and nonwhites. *American Sociological Review* 44:367–91.

Cogan, J. 1975. Labor supply and the value of the housewife's time. Santa Monica, Calif.: RAND Corporation, Report R–1461.

Freeman, R. 1974. Alternative theories of labor market discrimination: Individual and collective behavior. In G. von Furstenberg, A. Horowitz, and B.

Harrison, eds., *Patterns of racial discrimination*, vol. 2. Lexington, Mass.: Lexington Books.

Ginzberg, E. 1980. Overview: The $64 billion innovation. In E. Ginzberg, ed., *Employing the unemployed*. New York: Basic Books.

Heckman, J., and K. Wolpin. 1976. Does the contract compliance program work? *Industrial and Labor Relations Review* 29:544–64.

LaGory, M., and R. Magnani. 1979. Structural correlates of black-white occupational differentiation: Will U.S. regional differences in status remain? *Social Problems* 27:157–69.

Rones, P. 1980. Moving to the sun: Regional job growth, 1968 to 1978. *Monthly Labor Review*, Mar., pp. 12–19.

Steinberg, D., et al. 1980. *The Work Equity Project study sample: Client profile and labor market history*. Cambridge, Mass.: Abt Associates.

U.S. Bureau of the Census. 1978. *County and city data book, 1977*. Washington, D.C.: U.S. Government Printing Office.

———. 1979. Demographic, social, and economic profile of states: Spring 1976. *Current population reports*. Washington, D.C.: U.S. Government Printing Office, Series P-20, No. 334.

———. 1980a. Educational attainment in the U.S.: March 1979 and 1978. *Current population survey*. Washington, D.C.: U.S. Government Printing Office, Series P-20, No. 356.

———. 1980b. Geographical mobility: March 1975 to March 1979. *Current population reports*. Washington, D.C.: U.S. Government Printing Office, Series P-20, No. 353.

U.S. Department of Health, Education and Welfare, Office for Civil Rights. 1979. *Directory of elementary and secondary school districts, and schools in selected school districts: School year 1976-77*. Washington, D.C.

U.S. Department of Labor, Bureau of Labor Statistics. 1979. *Geographic profile of employment and unemployment: States, 1978: Metropolitan areas, 1977-78*. Washington, D.C., Report 571.

Wall Street Journal. 1981. Minnesota Mining says it will pay $2.1 million to settle sex bias suits. 19 May, p. 20.

Wilson, S., D. Steinberg, and J. Kulik. 1980. Guaranteed employment, work incentives, and welfare reform: Insight from the Work Equity Project. *American Economic Review* 70:132–37.

▐▌▐ Planning and Politics

10

Urban Transportation Equity in Cleveland

NORMAN KRUMHOLZ and JANICE COGGER

Ours is a private automotive society. In the 12 years following the end of World War II the number of automobiles in use in the United States more than doubled to over 50 million, and the figures have continued to rise steadily. In spite of the energy crisis and the rapid inflation in the prices of motor vehicles, gasoline, and maintenance, the number of motor vehicles in use has accelerated. From 1950 to 1975 the proportion of American households owning at least one car rose from 52 to 83 percent, the proportion of households owning two or more cars rose from 7 to 33 percent, and the percentage of adult Americans licensed to drive increased from 43 to 83 percent (Motor Vehicle Manufacturer's Association, 1953, 1978).

Although most Americans enjoy the freedom of movement conferred by automobiles, those without access to automobiles have found their mobility reduced in both relative and absolute terms. Indeed, the rise of the private automotive society has contributed to the decline of the public mass transit systems on which many people in cities depend for mobility. As most people began driving between home and work, public transit ridership dropped, fares increased, and service declined. For the transit-dependent rider each passing year has brought fewer destination options, longer waits, and higher costs. The Cleveland Transit System (CTS) ran 14.9 million fewer vehicle-miles per year in 1974 than in 1960 and at almost triple the fare (Cleveland Transit System and Regional Transit Authority, n.d.). From 1950 to 1970 vehicle-miles of transit service declined nationally by 37 percent. In addition to these reductions in transit mileage, the scattered patterns of new development in metropolitan areas make many destinations virtually inaccessible to those without a car.

This might be a relatively unimportant problem except for the fact that those who are transit-dependent—the poor, the elderly, the young, the sick, and the infirm—make up a substantial group in most central cities. In Cleveland an estimated 32 percent of all households did not own a car in 1970; of the 46,000 Cleveland families with annual incomes under $5,000 a year, 46 percent owned no car; 48 percent of all households headed by persons over 65 had no car (Cleveland City Planning Commission, 1975). In a very real sense these transit-dependent households have been injured by the private automotive society. It follows that they are entitled to some redress through transportation measures directed specifically at their welfare.

For most city planners, however, the issues arising from transit dependency have not been paramount. Planners have traditionally defined urban transportation problems in terms of automobile access and traffic congestion. During the 1950s and early 1960s planners and highway engineers united to call for the expansion of arterial systems and highways. As highway construction met increasing opposition in urban areas and as energy, air pollution, and environmental issues became popular, planners shifted their emphasis from the automobile to mass transit. Implicit in this turn to mass transit was a commitment to make transit service more accessible and attractive to those with automobiles—not necessarily to those who were transit-dependent.

In the early 1970s the Cleveland City Planning Commission and its staff developed a different planning orientation, and questioned the relevance and utility of traditional planning approaches to urban problems. Cleveland has little need for elaborate plans to control new development, for the city was declining, not growing, and demand for land was weak. Its problems were less physical in nature than social, economic, and political, and they bore most heavily and most unfairly on the poor, elderly, and black persons.

Traditional city planning, which has focused around narrow land use and physical design issues, seemed inappropriate for Cleveland's situation. Cleveland planners decided that planning should instead be user- and problem-oriented and that it should be redistributive in nature and activist in style. With the support of the Planning Commission and the mayor, planners sought to serve one simple, overriding goal—to promote a wider range of choices for those Cleveland residents who had few choices or none at all (Cleveland City Planning Commission, 1975; Krumholz, Cogger, and Linner, 1975). In planning literature this approach is sometimes called "advocacy planning."

This goal led planners to define Cleveland's highest transit priority as the restoration of some of the mobility lost by the poor and elderly when the nation (and the city) turned to automobiles. The aim was not to seek general support for transit subsidies to be used for purposes unrelated to equity or even to transportation, but instead to deliberately improve the equity of the distribution of transit subsidies and alleviate extreme transit deprivation.

This chapter describes a case study of a struggle to restore equity to urban transportation. It documents the fight by planners of the Cleveland City Planning Commission to provide for the needs of the transit-dependent population and to bring more equity to transit decision making in Cleveland. It traces the involvement in the areas of the Five County Transit Study, then in the negotiations leading to the establishment of the Regional Transit Authority (RTA), and finally in the specific terms and conditions controlling the transfer of CTS to RTA. It is based on the first-hand experiences of the authors, participant-observers in the events described.[1]

The Five-County Transit Study and Plan

In 1969 officials of the Urban Mass Transit Administration (UMTA) of the U.S. Department of Transportation advised Cleveland officials that for CTS to qualify for the federal funds it desired, a regional transit plan would be required. Cleveland owned the CTS, which carried over 85 percent of the transit trips made within Cuyahoga County, and which also extended into two adjoining counties. At the time, however, CTS was operating exclusively from fare-box revenues and was rapidly approaching financial disaster.

When CTS pointed out that because of its three-county service area it was already a regional transit system and would be pleased to prepare the required plan itself, UMTA informed the agency that a broader, regional planning framework was necessary. City and county officials then prepared a joint application for planning funds which UMTA again rejected as too narrow in scope. Prodded by UMTA, CTS finally agreed to join a five-county planning effort directed by a 22-member transit task force operating under the Northeast Ohio Areawide Coordinating Agency (NOACA), the regional planning agency. This was awkward, since the city was at that time suing NOACA in federal court for additional representation on the NOACA board (Krumholz, 1972). Nonetheless, the price of obtaining access to federal transit funds was clearly participation in the broader planning effort, and it was a price CTS was prepared to pay.

What followed was a two-year, $750,000, five-county study for which UMTA provided two-thirds of the funds, leaving $250,000 as the local share. Cuyahoga County furnished $100,000 and, because of the city's chronic fiscal crisis, the local chamber of commerce, the Greater Cleveland Growth Association, provided $150,000. It seems likely that the Growth Association volunteered to provide the city's share because members of the Cleveland business community viewed the transit issue as significant.

The Cleveland City Planning Commission participated in this planning effort from its inception, as the transit task force representative first for Mayor Carl Stokes and then for Mayor Ralph Perk.[2] As a part of the task force's executive and consultants screening committees, our goals were simple and frequently stated: to increase the mobility of the transit-dependent population and to bring greater equity to the allocation of transit subsidies. The task force agreed with the first goal and declared that one of the study's two overriding objectives was "to provide mobility to those persons in the area . . . who do not have reasonable access to alternative forms of transportation—the transit-dependent population. . . ." These views prevailed in the selection of a prime contractor that appeared from both its presentation and its reputation to be sensitive to socioeconomic considerations. These views also influenced the designation of a systems design subcontractor with a similar reputation for a study of the transit-dependent population and in earmarking adequate funds for that study.

But these victories were fleeting. The prime contractor's team and the project management set about responding to—or even anticipating—political pressures from the executive committee. The staff essentially disregarded the work done by the systems design subcontractor on the needs of the transit-dependent. The final long-range plan placed major emphasis in its recommendations not on improved equity but on a massive rail construction program.

Cleveland City Planning Commission staff members prepared a critique of the draft plan. The plan included both a five-year and a ten-year transit development program. The five-year program focused upon fare reductions, service coordination and expansion, capital improvements to upgrade existing service, and Community Responsive Transit (CRT).[3] The ten-year program called for the investment of $1.6 billion for rail development. The underlying rationale for this proposal appeared to be a mix of civic pride and political trade-offs. If Atlanta, Baltimore, Washington, Buffalo, and San Francisco were to have rail systems, then Cleveland must also have one—especially since the largest share of costs would be borne by the federal government.

Planning staff members had minor reservations about the short-term program. We were concerned because the fare structure contained apparent inequities and the funding for CRT within Cleveland was sharply below the level recommended by the consultants. But we were opposed to the entire rail expansion program, since it seemed counterproductive to our goals to provide mobility for the transit-dependent and to improve equity in transit subsidies allocation (Cleveland City Planning Commission, 1974a, b).

We sought to document our objectives. We tended to believe that most sophisticated, quantitative analyses are elegant techniques that are at least partially designed to obscure the value biases of their creators, although concepts like "model" or "paradigm" had generally intimidated us. Luckily, one of our staff members had an engineering and operations research background and was not easily awed by the quantitative mystique. Working with him, we discovered that by asking the obvious questions, by identifying assumptions and tracing their quantification, and by ferreting out the differences between what numbers were claimed to prove and what they actually indicated, we could effectively criticize the consultants' sophisticated analyses.

We knew from the outset that the cost-benefit analysis was vulnerable. We were present when it was first presented to the executive committee of the task force. A lawyer representing Ohio's largest bond counsel, who was the Growth Association's representative at this time, was disturbed to find that the cost-benefit ratio was only slightly in excess of 1.000. With skepticism based on experience, we proposed that something around 1.624 might be more acceptable to the task force and more salable to the public. Two weeks later, without making a single change in the plan, the consultants dutifully returned with a ratio of 1.721.

We found the "level of service" model, which was intended to provide a basis to compare and evaluate alternative transit proposals and which underpinned all of the patronage projections, to be equally meaningless. Work opportunity data were obsolete, differences in the proximity of residential zones to various employment centers were inadequately spelled out, and the list of regional educational, cultural, and social centers reflected elite tastes. The critical employment data were not only ten years out of date but had been imperfectly collected in the first place. There were methodological problems as well as data problems—for example, trip preferences were weighed only in terms of destinations and not in terms of origins. These errors tended to invalidate the entire study.

It seemed obvious to us that much of the scientific technical work done as part of the planning process was nothing more than window dressing designed to justify the prior preferences of task force members. Observations at meetings confirmed this as the case. For example, when a suburban county commissioner, who also was president of NOACA and a task force member, demanded that a rail extension originally proposed for termination in an eastern suburb continue 18 miles farther through very low-density development to a city in his county, it was done. When a suburban mayor, who also was a NOACA and task force member, demanded a rail extension toward his city but stopping at its boundary (to avoid displacement of his constituents), it was done. Only our planning staff raised questions about the technical justification for either proposal.

The consultants did even more than comply with the wishes of the policy makers; they frequently anticipated them. The five-county transit planning process offered several examples of what one analyst has termed "the premature imposition of constraints" (Kain, 1972, p. 336). For instance, when the consultants began to develop proposals for major transit corridor improvements, they realized that because of Cleveland's freeway pattern, the west side might be adequately served by busways while the east side might require rail improvements. Sensing that the politicians who represented west-side constituencies would find such a proposal unacceptable (because bus travel is "lower class" than rail travel), the consultants recommended rail development for all corridors. In one case, the southeast corridor, they stated that the costs were not greatly different for the busway and rapid transit alternatives. A more careful examination revealed that this difference amounted to $432 million!

The Community Responsive Transit proposal provides another example of the premature imposition of constraints. The system design subcontractor analyzed the needs of the transit-dependent and recommended that CRT be subsidized at $5 per capita within Cleveland and at $3 per capita throughout the rest of the region. But although this firm included that recommendation in its preliminary reports, the subcontractor never presented it to the task force. Instead, the task force staff recommended that CRT be funded at the $3 figure throughout the region, including Cleveland. We ourselves analyzed this proposal and concluded that whoever developed the technical justification for the recommendation confused round trips with rides, because there was a 100 percent discrepancy between the stated assumptions on ridership and the implied assumptions in the revenue projection.

Our critique of the ten-year transit development program discussed all of these points in detail (Cleveland City Planning Commission, 1974b). Our official position on the five-county plan reflected the criticisms raised in that evaluation (Cleveland City Planning Commission, 1974a). We sent our critique to UMTA officials in Washington. Several months later the Secretary of Transportation advised NOACA that no federal funds would be made available for rail development in the Cleveland area until an exhaustive analysis of less capital-intensive alternatives had been undertaken. We hoped (with little confidence) that someone in Washington had read our critique, and we assumed that the response to NOACA was a reflection of growing federal disenchantment with large-scale rail development. Whereas UMTA officials has authorized the Bay Area Rapid Transit and the Washington, D.C., Metro for 77- and 98-mile systems from the start, they authorized more recent rail proposals in Buffalo, Atlanta, and Baltimore for much shorter distances: 6-, 14-, and 8-mile first stages. In Cleveland, however, events were moving from the development of the transit plan to its implementation.

Establishing the Regional Transit Authority

One assumption underlying Cleveland's transit planning process was that a regional transit authority, with the ability to generate local tax support and capture state and federal subsidies, would be formed to carry out the five-county transit plan. Early in 1974 the Growth Association wrote and the Ohio General Assembly passed legislation that provided for the formation of such an authority in Cuyahoga County. Early negotiations between the city and county over composition of the authority's board broke down repeatedly. Cleveland's charismatic city council president used the meetings as an occasion to demand that Cleveland be given absolute control of the RTA board. The county commissioners played out their own political agendas. Cleveland's mayor, who was making a run for the U.S. Senate, issued press release after press release extolling his leadership on the transit issue.

However, Growth Association strategies had established a deadline. The state enabling legislation provided that unless a regional transit authority were formed before 1 January 1975, the power to create such an authority would lapse, and all participants would have to begin the process again from scratch.

More important, the Cleveland Transit System's financial crisis was worsening. The CTS was the only major transit system in the nation to be financed exclusively from fare-box revenues. Through cash reserves accumulated during the early 1960s and a loan from Cleveland in 1969, CTS had managed to limp along with periodic fare increases and service reductions. However, in November 1974 CTS had reached its limits. CTS management announced that cash reserves would soon be exhausted and the system would be able to provide only peak-hour service at approximately $1 a ride. The availability of federal subsidies promised to postpone this deadline by a few months and thus make it coincide with the city's 1975 November elections. The political pressure was on, for no local official wanted his opponent to blame him for cutting transit service and raising fares.

In December 1974, 15 days before the legislative deadline, Cleveland officials began the serious business of forming a regional transit authority. There were two major issues: the composition of the transit board, and the conditions governing the transfer of CTS to the regional authority. The type of tax to be levied was not an issue. Although the state enabling legislation drafted by the Growth Association provided two choices, sales taxes or property taxes, there was no political support for a property tax proposal.

The first issue was handled at meetings that included the mayor, the city council president, the county commissioners, and representatives of the suburban Mayors and Managers Association. The formula decided upon was: that the city appoint four city residents; that the suburban mayors and managers appoint three suburban residents; and that the county commissioner appoint three members, at least one of whom must be a city resident. While area elected officials placed great emphasis on this phase of the negotiations, we ourselves had learned from experience that it makes very little difference who appoints whom when policy decisions that could benefit the deprived sectors of our society are being made. City representatives, whether they actually live in the city or not—and usually they do not—are just as likely as anyone else to ignore the interests of poor and working-class residents and to use their power instead to feather their own nests.

The second issue was more vexing for city representatives. They had little notion of what to demand in return for the transfer of CTS to the regional authority. While some city council members favored a cash settlement, the county commissioners were adamant that the city should receive no more than the $11 million it had loaned CTS in 1969, thus writing off to zero a system with a book value approaching $80 million. The question of cash compensation was settled quickly; the county commissioners won. The commissioners were equally adamant that the city should retain no special powers over the regional system's decision-making process. The idea that the city should demand the right to veto certain types of decisions was also quickly dismissed. It was clear that the city of Cleveland should demand fare and service guarantees, but the politicians were unclear about what those guarantees should be.

Although our planning staff was more knowledgeable about the transit issue than others in city government, we were not asked to participate in the early negotiations. We considered a mass resignation in protest but rejected the idea. Instead, we decided to force our way into the negotiations, reasoning that we were long-term players in the issue whose presence was appropriate and necessary. In one memorable session in the mayor's office to which we were not invited, planning staff walked in with a graph and flip-chart presentation and confidently laid out the city's position, much to the mayor's surprise (and pleasure). Since no one knew we had not been invited, everyone assumed that we, in fact, represented the mayor. From that day we spoke for the mayor on this issue.

We based our general strategy in the negotiations on findings from a number of transit-related studies conducted by the City Planning Commission in the early 1970s, as well as on our analysis of the transit development plan. We knew that the transit-dependent relied heavily on public transportation for nonwork purposes and thus traveled largely at off-peak hours. We knew that because of their location they were already relatively well served to downtown locations by the existing radial configuration of the system, but that they needed generally more diverse destinations and a system that was attuned to their health and social needs. We knew that physical infirmity might make it impossible for many transit-dependent individuals to use a fixed-route system even if they lived only a few blocks from a regular stop.

We also knew that the city's poor relied on buses rather than rapid transit or commuter railroads for an overwhelming number of their trips, and that per-trip subsidies were much heavier to commuter railroads and rapid transit than to buses. In fact, we had concluded that because of flat fare structure and regulatory policies that favor users farthest from the central business district, the main beneficiaries of present transit subsidies were the more affluent riders. In New York, Boston, and Philadelphia the most heavily subsidized riders are the users of commuter railroads. In Cleveland 50 cents is the fare for a 16-mile ride from affluent Shaker Heights to the airport, just as it is the fare for the 2-mile ride from the East 55th ghetto to downtown.

Our package, which was based on these findings and on our principles, was easily understandable, if not original. We resurrected much of the short-term program of the five-county plan, modified it to serve our strategic objectives, and translated it into terms that the decision makers could understand. We believed that the Community Responsive Transit element of the plan offered the greatest potential benefits to the transit-dependent population, and recommended that the city demand a substantial commitment to CRT as one of its highest priorities, that the elderly ride free 24 hours a day, that off-peak fares be substantially lower than peak fares, and that funds earmarked for rail system expansion be diverted to improved bus service.

Ours was the only detailed proposal brought to the bargaining table. Until it was presented, the only guarantees that had been discussed had stated that "50 to 60 percent of the service improvements should be located within the city of Cleveland" and that "the base fare should initially be established at 25 cents." Our proposal spelled out the specific service improvements that Cleveland should demand and pointed to the need to define more than the "base" fare, for longer than "initially."

On 31 December 1974, the last day possible under the state enabling act, legislation was passed that established the RTA. Although the only guarantees included in the legislation were those that dealt with 50 to 60 percent of the service improvements and the initial base fare, provision was made for a more detailed delineation of that city's guarantees in a subsequent memorandum of understanding. The legislation also included a provision forbidding the RTA to construct, engineer, plan, or otherwise contemplate a downtown distribution system during its first five years in operation. We had drafted this provision and included it in the legislation because we knew that the downtown distribution system was key to an expanded rail system and hoped that the provision might slow RTA down.

Negotiating the Terms of Transfer

Almost five months of bargaining followed. At issue was the nature of the city's guarantees to be contained in the memorandum of understanding. The controversy continued to be one of flexibility for the RTA as opposed to firm guarantees for the city. Those allied on the side of unlimited flexibility for the RTA included the county commissioners, the suburban representatives, the Growth Association, NOACA staff, and, ironically, the management of the CTS. Thwarted in their initial effort to transfer CTS without guarantee to the RTA, this coalition fought to ensure that the fare and service guarantees provided to city residents be kept as meaningless as possible.

Why did this coalition come together? What were their interests? The county commissioners and suburban politicians apparently wanted the major share of service and improvements to go to suburban areas, because almost two-thirds of the total county population is located outside the city. NOACA, the regional planning agency, supported the interests of a majority of its board, which is heavily dominated by out-of-city and out-of-county representatives. The Growth Association, representing major corporations, law firms, and property owners in downtown Cleveland, supported fixed rail systems as a means to stimulate regional economic growth, raise downtown property values, and make downtown more accessible. Major law firms were interested in the expensive bond issues required for construction because they provide fees for the bond counsel who attests to the legality of the bonds. RTA management was devoted to rail lines because of the cost and prestige associated with such systems and because an unstinting devotion to rapid trains is apparently written in stone in the American Transit Association guidebook for general managers.

There are, of course, many other reasons why a transit system might prefer broad, general, and unencumbered subsidies rather than earmarked subsidies directed toward the transit-dependent. Broad-ranged transit subsidies can be used to benefit a wide number of other people besides transit patrons. For example, a well-subsidized transit agency can improve the relative accessibility of downtown, thus benefiting downtown property owners and businesses through higher rents, land prices, and sales volumes. It can raise salaries for transit management, who are, incidentally, already among the highest paid of all public employees, and for other employees who are also very well paid. It can also provide lucrative contracts for consultants, planners, lawyers, contractors, and others. It can open up land not otherwise accessible and thus benefit property owners and developers. Finally, general transit subsidies can also be used to benefit high-income transit riders without having to bother too much about the less vocal transit-dependent or low-income riders.

The city's advocates were divided over the subissue of whether to place priority upon fare guarantees or service guarantees. Early in the negotiations council leadership committed itself totally, and almost exclusively, to a 25-cent fare.

Since the fare structure proposed in the five-county plan and supported by the anti-city planning forces (a 25-cent base plus both express and peak-hour surcharges) would cost the transit-dependent little more than a 25-cent flat fare and would provide funds for substantially more service, we too supported this particular point. We decided to focus our efforts on obtaining strong service guarantees, particularly guarantees of Community Responsive Transit service. The only modification in the fare structure that we were prepared to fight for was reduced fares for the elderly. Our ally in this was the new law director of the city.

An important element of the negotiations was a series of technical meetings at which representatives from the city, county, NOACA, Growth Association, and CTS met to discuss economic feasibility. The first few meetings were intended to establish a common vocabulary and to ascertain current CTS costs and ridership, past county sales tax receipts, federal operating subsidies available to the Cleveland urbanized area, and other economic matters. After that the agenda was a matter of technical bargaining.

This was not an assembly of unbiased technicians. Each representative had a definite interest to serve. We wanted to justify strong service guarantees for the city; the other participants wanted to justify no guarantees. The technical representatives from all other jurisdictions accused us of estimating revenues high and costs low; we accused them of the reverse. The key to the game was instant sensitivity analysis. When they offered us a million additional riders in return for reducing the increase on the sales tax by 1 percent, we rejected the offer. We proposed instead that we leave the ridership figure alone and reduce the rate of increase on operating costs by 2 percent. Efforts to reach consensus generally stopped at the point where our yielding a few more dollars would cost us our case, and their yielding a few more would give it to us.

These meetings served two functions: they established a framework for other facets of the negotiations, and they discredited "our transit experts at CTS" in the eyes of Cleveland's law director. These meetings taught him that in discussions of this sort there are no truths; there are only different objectives. His new understanding of "expert" testimony was crucial to our obtaining his sustained support so that we would have free rein to fight.

A second aspect of the negotiations was the Thursday policy meetings at which technical experts presented their cases to elected officials. Although these meetings accomplished some education of officials, they served primarily to keep the transit issue in the news. One of the more memorable meetings opened with a Cleveland councilman stating his pro-city interests while most of the suburban officials nodded contemptuously. As the meeting progressed, some officials suggested that the elderly might maintain their dignity if they were to "pay their way." We argued that if the elderly were given free fares by the system but wanted to pay, no one would stop them. Anti-city forces characterized trips to day care centers, neighborhood shopping facilities, and doctor's offices as "frills," but rail extensions to low-density exurbs were "essential." Revealed in all this was the tendency of politicians and technical functionaries to mistake their private interests for truth.

Cleveland's 33 council members, each of whom is elected on a ward basis, have been well educated by the media about their "provincialism" and lack of "statesmanship." On the other hand, suburban officials who directly serve the needs of their constituents are not "provincial" but are engaged in the "democratic political process." Businessmen who pass taxes and costs off to others while maximizing their own profit and convenience are just "doing business," a form of behavior that is above reproach.

Throughout the negotiations there were bids and counterbids. Under Cleveland Planning Commission direction, the Law Department developed a memorandum of understanding based upon the fare guarantees that we had proposed. Council members rejected it, calling the proposed peak-hour surcharge a "rush-hour rip-off." It made great headlines but little sense for many council constituents. County representatives took this opportunity to propose a 25-cent fare for two years. Council members demanded that this fare be guaranteed for four years. And so the bargaining went.

A senior citizens' coalition recruited some of its members to attend every public hearing on transit, and had significant impact on the final outcome. Though efforts to charge standard fares to the elderly continued for some time, anti-city forces reluctantly granted free fares for the elderly at off-peak hours (20 hours per day) and half-fares at peak hours.

Cleveland officials have never developed effective strategies to deal with citizen participation. While the City Planning Commission has not been known for its efforts to encourage citizen input in the planning process, we have found ways to facilitate it in the political process. The planning staff had, for example, worked closely for years with the senior citizens' coalition on housing and transit issues, and we had been responsible for putting together the city's first Dial-a-Bus project for the elderly. Over the years a symbiotic relationship had developed; the senior coalition had learned to trust us, and we had learned to use their manpower toward common objectives. Calls to the senior citizens' coalition to inform them of transit meetings, to lay out the issues, to advise them on strategy, and to coordinate their transportation to meetings are undoubtedly worth more in Cleveland than invitations to Planning Commission meetings and discussions of unfocused objectives.

The Thursday policy meetings also reached agreement on such service guarantees as those that covered headways and route spacing. By the final stages of the negotiations only two issues remained: fares and Community Responsive Transit.

A last-ditch technical meeting was called by the president of the Growth Association, who also was managing partner of a prestigious Cleveland law firm. Although the stated purpose was to develop consensus among the technicians on anticipated costs and revenues, the not-so-hidden agenda was to whip the city's planners into line on a proposal for a three-year fare guarantee and *no* Community Responsive Transit. When we refused to give up CRT, we were ordered to leave the meeting.

We complied, wondering at that moment if we had lost the whole game, not only on transit but also our advocacy efforts in all other areas as well. We could not have chosen a more powerful adversary; it often appears that the Growth Association president personally constitutes a third branch of government in Cleveland.

On the evening of this meeting the mayor asked the planning staff to "make a deal" lest CTS be hung around his neck like an albatross in the upcoming election. We reassured the mayor that a few more days of negotiation would make him "look like an angel." As it turned out, this was correct. The ax did not fall. If anything, the Growth Association president's tactics strengthened our alliance with the law director. The final round of negotiations began and ended during two days of council meetings in May when the stage was set for agreement on a three-year, 25-cent fare guarantee. The only issue that remained was CRT, and our allies were few.

The representatives of the senior citizens' coalition were still in the audience. Having benefited from a Dial-a-Ride program funded by a federal demonstration grant that the Cleveland Planning Commission had helped obtain, the elderly had no doubts about the value of CRT. We had also convinced some members of council to fight for CRT, but we had not succeeded in convincing council leadership. Only Councilman Dennis J. Kucinich, who later would serve a term as mayor, understood, shared, and fought for our objectives. His support was an important part of the final, generally positive agreement.

On the evening between the first and second days of meetings our morale was low. The game was almost over, and we had no aces in the hole. We visited the law director for a last-minute strategy discussion, and he confided, "It's not a wonder that you haven't won; it's a wonder that there is still a fight."

The next morning an editorial appeared in the *Cleveland Plain Dealer,* the largest newspaper in Ohio, advising the city to give up on CRT. A similar editorial appeared in the afternoon *Cleveland Press.* Clearly, the powers aligned against CRT were powerful enough to call forth the thunder, let alone editorials.

Until this final day we had demanded that the city's CRT guarantee be expressed in terms of an annual per capita subsidy. The opposition argued that the funds available for service improvements might be less than we projected, that fulfilling the CRT guarantee might cause more than 50 to 60 percent of the service improvements to be located within the city, and that the suburbs might be denied their fair share of increased service. On the final day we reluctantly changed our strategy.

We agreed to take our chances and express the CRT guarantees as a percentage of the city's 50 to 60 percent share of service improvements. By noon an agreement had been reached. The anti-city forces agreed to a CRT guarantee; we agreed to a radical reduction in the level of the guarantee. We felt that we had no other choice. That afternoon the city council ratified the agreement at a meeting in the council president's office. The meeting was open to the press and open to the technicians; it was closed only (by order of the council president) to the two dozen people sitting in the council committee room to monitor the meeting for the senior citizens' coalition.

We declared the CRT decision a victory. We had achieved several fairly significant service guarantees: the elderly would ride at substantially reduced fares, and although the commitment to CRT was not enough, it did represent a new departure. It was a step in the right direction. In the final agreement Cleveland was guaranteed that a 25-cent fare would be maintained for at least three years; that senior citizens and the handicapped would ride free during nonpeak periods (20 hours daily) and pay only half-fare at peak; that service frequencies and route coverage within the city would be improved; and that Community Responsive Transit would be initiated.

Today Community Responsive Transit is still in place. Ironically, now that CRT has been tried and has developed a strong constituency, the Regional Transit Authority's ads boast devotion to the service. CRT has been expanded from the city to the entire county and provides free-fare, door-to-door, intraneighborhood service to all elderly and handicapped. Its 1980 budget was $2.3 million, about 2 percent of the RTA operating budget. Fares for general ridership were held at 25 cents for three years as promised, then raised to 50 cents where they remain at this writing, although another fare hike is in the offing. Fares for the elderly and handicapped have held firm. The RTA elderly and handicapped fare policy enables the elderly and handicapped to ride the fixed route system for one-half of the regular adult fare during weekday rush hours and at no fare during all other hours.

But in the area of capital improvements RTA has yielded to its strong bias in favor of rail systems, so that its distribution of subsidy has been unusually inequitable. Of its first $120 million capital improvement program, RTA spent $100 million completely renovating the Shaker Rapid suburban line, which carries 4 percent of the system's ridership—not surprisingly, the most affluent, influential, and vocal 4 percent. RTA is planning an extension of one of the Shaker Rapid suburban lines that will cost more than $50 million; it has supported an automated downtown people-mover; and it has budgeted $694 million in its 1982–86 transportation improvement program for a four-mile subway from downtown to University Circle. All of these capital improvements benefit Cleveland elites. None provides significant benefits to the transit-dependent population.

Toward Greater Equity in Transit Planning

The highest priority of transit subsidy should be to restore to the transit-dependent population some of the mobility they lost when the United States became an automotive society. As noted previously in this chapter, the transit-dependent tend to be disproportionately poor and elderly, to travel at off-peak hours, and to use transit for nonwork-related trips. Major capital improvements appear to be inversely correlated to benefits accruing to this population. Yet major capital improvements continue to be the prime focus of transit plans across the country. In the Cleveland metropolitan region, for example, the approved areawide transportation plan calls for 664 miles of new high-facility highways and 81 miles of new rapid rail lines in spite of a regional population decline of 3.3 percent between 1970 and 1975 (Northeast Ohio Areawide Coordinating Agency, 1969).

As we have seen, a powerful lobby of politicians, lawyers, bureaucrats, property owners, construction unions, and vendors enjoys the benefits of new construction. So long as federal subsidies to transit authorities make up 80 percent of the cost of new construction, it is difficult to be optimistic about a transformation in the emphasis of transit planning. But given a commitment to the goal of greater equity, changes in national policy can reshape the transit development process.

Federal funding for mass transit is now available under sections of the Urban Mass Transportation Act of 1964. Some funds are discretionary and available to operators for existing and new rail systems. Others provide for operating subsidies as well as capital grants. Operating subsidies fund up to 50 percent of eligible operating deficits, while capital grants fund up to 80 percent of project cost. This system of federal inducements obviously favors new construction and must change if equity is to be achieved. In order to reduce emphasis on new capital construction, federal subsidies for such construction should be reduced. A community that still wanted to build new rail systems would then get less "free" federal money and would confront the necessity of raising more of its own money.

A new system of transit subsidies should be developed that focuses not broadly, on entire transit systems, but narrowly, on those transit users least able to use an automobile. This system might entail issuing identification cards to the poor or very young to entitle them to reduced fares, much as RTA now handles reductions for the elderly and handicapped. Welfare objectives might also be met by reducing fares for trips that begin or end in defined poverty zones where it can be assumed that transit dependency is high.

Cities should relax regulations governing the entry of individuals and companies into the public transit, taxi, or jitney business. The taxi business in most cities is rigidly controlled; one or two vendors usually provide all service and city councils set fare schedules. Relaxation or total elimination of restrictions on competition (subject to simple safety and insurance tests) would go far toward providing the off-peak, non-work trips most needed by the transit-dependent. The emergence of a nonregulated transit industry made up of buses, jitneys, and taxis would offer not only greater mobility and security to the transit-dependent but also direct employment to some of the unemployed residents of the city. Among the few skills possessed by many of the unemployed are the ability to drive a car and knowledge of the local street system. If some new jitney or taxi licenses could be sequestered for this disadvantaged group, the employment and income benefits might be extensive (Cleveland City Planning Commission, 1972).

Federal funds should be provided to encourage transit innovation and brokering. A transit broker identifies transportation resources and mobility needs and brings them together. Brokers would mix data collection, needs analysis, marketing, and transit operation. If we could "make a market" out of transit-dependent riders, both equity and marketing objectives might be well served. In short, we can expect to improve the equity of transit planning not with large, unfocused transit subsidies but with innovative subsidies that carefully target welfare objectives.

Notes

1. The authors were director and senior staff member of the Cleveland City Planning Commission.

2. The senior author, as director of the Planning Commission, represented the mayors on the task force committees.

3. Community Responsive Transit is a system that aims to augment the main-line system with para-transit type services providing short trips within and among neighborhoods.

References

Cleveland City Planning Commission. 1975. *Policy planning report.* Cleveland.

———. 1974a. *Staff report ont he Five-County Trȧnsit Study.* Cleveland.

———. 1974b. *Staff report on the ten-year develoment program.* Cleveland.

———. 1972. *Toward equitable transportation opportunities for Cleveland's elderly and poor: Two proposals and an analysis of taxi problems.* Cleveland.

Cleveland Transit System and Regional Transit Authority. N.d. *Files on vehicle mileage and fare structure.* Cleveland: Regional Transit Authority.

Kain, J. 1972. How to improve urban transportation at practically no cost. *Public Policy* 20 (Summer):335–58.

Krumholz, N. 1972. Cleveland's fight for a fair share of the region. *Planning* 38 (Nov.):275–78.

Krumholz, N., J. M. Cogger, and J. H. Linner. 1975. The Cleveland policy planning report. *Journal of the American Institute of Planners* 41 (Sept.):248–304.

Motor Vehicles Manufacturer's Association. 1953. *Motor vehicles facts and figures.* Detroit.

———. 1978. *Motor vehicles facts and figures.* Detroit.

Northeast Ohio Areawide Coordinating Council. 1969. *Framework for action.* Cleveland.

11
Pruitt-Igoe: Policy Failure or Societal Symptom

ROGER MONTGOMERY

"Pruitt-Igoe, the outstanding failure of public housing, has been a stigma on public housing for many years ... the stigma of Pruitt-Igoe must be removed."
U.S. Department of Housing and Urban Development (1974, p. 25)

"It was perfect, the nicest place I'd ever had."
Frankie Mae Raglin, first Pruitt-Igoe resident (*New York Times*, 1973, p. 72)

"It's been home to a lot of people and leaving hurts some real bad."
Lillian Townes, last Pruitt-Igoe resident (Canfield, 1974, p. 1)

Pruitt-Igoe, the infamous public housing project in St. Louis, has become a vivid symbol of the failure of American social policy. Again and again the demolition photograph confronts us, showing one of its 33 identical high-rise structures crumbling as the government-approved dynamite charges explode. Popular media and scholarly publications continue to cite this symbol of imputed failure. Public housing antagonists and policy experts routinely refer to it as a shorthand for the presumed failure of big city public housing in the United States. Often the connotations of the symbol go beyond public housing to include much or all of the apparatus of social welfare. Simply reprinting the famous photograph is enough to trigger these connotations.

From the day St. Louis politicians and Washington bureaucrats decided to build Pruitt-Igoe, it had problems. Some problems were internal to the project. At a general level the project suffered from crippling flaws that were built into public housing through legislation and public policy. In its specific local realization, faulty physical design and construction flawed it. It was flawed by venality and wrong-doing; many people seem to have had their hands in the till. Faulty policy, design, construction, and architecture, even some of the probable graft have received considerable attention from analysts seeking to explain the recent history of public housing in St. Louis. This attention includes most notably the work of Eugene Meehan, whose books and papers provide an unmatched resource. He examines in great detail the internal forces that contributed to Pruitt-Igoe's destruction and explores the implications of the St. Louis experience for national housing policy (Meehan, 1975, 1977, 1979).

External forces also hurt the project in ways that, with the clarity of hindsight, contained from the start the seeds of the project's destruction. In all probability these forces would have doomed it even in the absence of the internal factors. The first goal of this retrospective, revisionist inquiry is to uncover some of these exogenous or contextual forces. A second goal is not to deal with Pruitt-Igoe per se but to raise a question concerning the growth of a symbolic Pruitt-Igoe that connotes public policy failure and the perverse intractability of poverty in America. To what degree does Pruitt-Igoe represent an internal programmed failure and to what extent an external or societal one? To what extent does its symbolic meaning divert attention from inherent contradictions in its social, political and economic context toward convenient, and doubtless partially at fault, scapegoats?

The Record

Pruitt-Igoe was conceived as part of St. Louis's response to the public housing program, born in the Depression and reborn in the U.S. Housing Act of 1949. It also was conceived as part of the city's attack on urban blight, a postwar struggle shared with other, older, large central cities. Before World War II city planning engineer Harland Bartholomew analyzed St. Louis and marked a ring of slums around the central business district for clearance and redevelopment (St. Louis City Plan Commission, 1936). Plans were drawn at that time, but work had only just begun when war came. Two small slum clearance and public housing projects were completed in 1942. Table 1 provides a simplified chronological review of these and later events in the history of Pruitt-Igoe. In the postwar period the federal dollars necessary for slum clearance, public housing, and redevelopment became available under

Table 1. Pruitt-Igoe: Chronological Highlights

1936 Bartholomew ring plan published calling for redevelopment of slum belt around St. Louis central business district.

1942 First public housing in St. Louis begun under U.S. Housing Act of 1937, located in Bartholomew ring, divided according to racial segregation principles, black project on north side, white on south, first units occupied in 1943.

1950 St. Louis requests 12,000 units and receives federal commitment for 5,800 units of public housing under U.S. Housing Act of 1949, first project begun.

1951 Bulldozing begins for Pruitt-Igoe, the second postwar project. Architectural magazine acclaims design, housing authority proclaims it model for the rest of the country. A total of 2,700 apartments in 33 11-story buildings were to be built on 57 acres for $50 million, roughly equal to the then current price for an equal number of three-bedroom ranch houses in suburban St. Louis. Pruitt-Igoe was actually two projects located near a prewar black project, Pruitt for the blacks, Igoe for the whites.

1954 Pruitt's first tenant, Frankie Mae Raglin, moves in. She later would recall: "It was perfect, the nicest place I'd ever had. Back in Mississippi I'd had a house, but it was an old house. I'd never seen any place—as nice as Pruitt."

1955 First recorded accidents as two girls fall, one from seventh, one from ninth floor, firemen rescue children from stalled elevator.

1956 First manager resigns over rent arrearage, first signs of Housing Authority fiscal crisis.

1958 Occupancy rates start to slip.

1961 Pruitt-Igoe selected for U.S. Department of Health, Education, and Welfare "concerted services program" designed to coordinate all federal activities at a public housing project, $4 million special grant. Occupancy averages only 82 percent. Crime rate highest of all city projects.

1962 State opens special Pruitt-Igoe welfare office with 45 additional caseworkers, two-thirds of households on welfare. Person falls to death from tenth floor.

1963 Washington University Pruitt-Igoe project begins, team of live-in participant-observers, directed at various times by sociologists Gouldner, Shapiro, Pitman, and Rainwater, $750,000 grant. Rainwater (1970) reports findings that poverty is responsible for social problems.

1964 Federal program launched to repair damage and create four- and five-bedroom apartments out of the smaller, unoccupied Pruitt-Igoe units, $5 million new grant. Northside Team Ministry ecumenical Protestant project and St. Bridget's Roman Catholic parish do missionary work in Pruitt-Igoe.

1965 Office of Economic Opportunity (OEO) grants money to the Urban League Neighborhood Stations project to organize Pruitt-Igoe residents and hire 76 of them as researchers to "determine their needs" as part of the War on Poverty.

1966 Power failures become commonplace. Gas explosion, several central heating system breakdowns damage buildings and tenants' possessions, water supply freezes, pipes burst.

1967 OEO and the Department of Housing and Urban Development (HUD) enter joint program of physical rejuvenation and site improvement at Pruitt-Igoe along with social program to plan and develop ways of transforming large housing projects from institutions into communities.

1968 Housing Authority director requests federal takeover or abandonment because of fiscal crisis. Massive rent increases force some occupants to pay three-fourths of income for rent.

1969 Pruitt-Igoe tenants join with other public housing tenants in nation's longest public housing rent strike—nine months. At one time 28 of 34 elevators were inoperable, other systems were in comparable states. Organized vandalism. Vacancies concentrated in Pruitt-Igoe as part of strike-resolving policy.

1970 Sixty-five percent of Pruitt-Igoe units *unoccupied*. Deliverymen, messengers, and maintenance personnel refuse to enter the project without guards. Rape, robbery, and assault rates soar, murders and accidents increase. St. Louis Housing Authority (SLHA) temporarily improves security by concentrating occupied units. Citing an expected $400,000 operating deficit and dwindling demand, SLHA announces intention of closing down many buildings.

1971 HUD concurs with closing plans. Remaining tenants moved to 11 buildings.

1972 Demolition experiment 16 March with controlled dynamite charges level three buildings in middle of project, $500,000 federal demonstration grant. Architect-planner team draws rehabilitation plans, $200,000 federal grant.

1973 Meehan begins analysis of fiscal crisis interpretation of Pruitt-Igoe destruction. St. Louis Housing Authority decides in June to cease operating Pruitt-Igoe. HUD announces in August the decision to demolish Pruitt-Igoe.

1974 Last tenant moves out in May. Mrs. Lillian Townes, 18 years in Pruitt-Igoe where she raised ten children: "It was beautiful, real beautiful, when it opened. . . . It's been home to a lot of people and leaving hurts some real bad." Jeff-Vander-Lou, a neighborhood community development corporation, tries to buy four buildings to rehabilitate and operate, HUD refuses.

1976 Final razing completed, $3.5 million HUD grant pays the wreckers.

1981 Rubble-covered, cyclone-fenced former site still vacant.

Sources: Coverage by *St. Louis Post-Dispatch* (1950–76); Meehan (1975, 1979); and author's notes. Compiled by author and Louise McCorkle Adams.

the 1949 Housing Act. This legislation gave St. Louis decision makers their first real chance to act on the Bartholomew plan.[1]

The plan and the Pruitt-Igoe project were grounded in a conceptualization Bartholomew had developed over several years. Shortly after his arrival in St. Louis following World War I, Bartholomew identified signs of central city population decline relative both to its earlier growth and to the then expanding suburbs. He predicted declines in employment, retail trade, commerce, and economic and civic vitality. For the next 30 years Bartholomew and his staff both documented the decline and proposed remedies to reverse it. These remedies took the form of extensive slum clearance in the inner ring followed by redevelopment into ideal neighborhoods with services and amenities necessary to compete with the suburbs. Bartholomew advocated public policies to advance these slum clearance and new neighborhood programs, public housing among them.[2]

Though the Bartholomew plan generally echoed contemporary ideas among urban policy experts, certain aspects of his analysis and proposals were particularly noteworthy. First, his analysis identified central city decline as an emergent problem in St. Louis before it was recognized in other old, northeastern and north central metropolitan areas.[3] Second, his plan followed a population strategy and used a housing-focused response rather than the more common real estate response of redevelopment to a "higher and better use."[4] His analysis and strategy received careful articulation in a series of publications culminating in the adoption of a new general plan in 1948. The public housing built in St. Louis during the 1940s and 1950s was conceived as part of an implementation strategy to concentrate clearance in the worst inner ring slums and use the cleared sites for housing at higher densities. The plan showed housing developed in comprehensively designed neighborhood units complete with generous public facilities, churches and other private institutions, recreation space, and commercial facilities. Public housing built with federal aid permitted none of these facilities and

Pruitt-Igoe housing project, built in 1954 and demolished 20 years later (photos courtesy of U.S. Department of Housing and Urban Development).

services, thus creating a gap between the plan and its realization. The plan was essentially silent on the question of race in this deeply segregated city, although some of the earlier analyses had clearly distinguished racial occupancy. Since St. Louis policy segregated public housing, when construction began, a rough parity of black and white projects was established with the black ones on the north side of the central business district at the approximate apex of the historic black ghetto, and the white projects on the south side. Initial planning designated Pruitt as black and Igoe as white, although they occupied adjoining sites in the apex of the black belt. From the start, however, Igoe was overwhelmingly black with only 12 percent nonblack heads of households the first year and less than 1 percent nonblack after 1960.

The planning of Pruitt-Igoe raises a number of political questions. No comprehensive understanding of the record can take place without answers to these questions, but unfortunately they lie outside the scope of the present inquiry. Why did Bartholomew's ideas dominate early political decision making? Whose interests were served both by the parts of the implemented plan and by other aspects of public housing such as the postwar shift to high-rise construction, the sharp increase in overall densities, the initial pattern of racial segregation and its relationship to the segregated private housing markets of St. Louis? Meehan explores some of these questions, particularly the role of organized labor and the construction trades. For the most part, however, the local political history of St. Louis public housing has yet to be written.

In any event, a massive public housing program began in the early 1940s and expanded during the 1950s to construct nearly 7,000 units of low-rent housing. In the process, the population holding capacities of some specific slum sites were quintupled. Site clearance and evictions of hundreds of tenant slum dwellers took place without relocation assistance. This occurred in a period of housing shortage, when St. Louis was passing its all-time peak in population. Accelerating federal highway and urban renewal programs exacerbated the situation by destroying thousands of units of low-rent slum housing and forcing poor people, most of them black, to relocate. Little evidence exists that the disruptive and destabilizing effects of such concentrated, forced relocation during a period of acute shortage were understood or taken into account. Slum clearance, public housing, highways, and renewal programs in St. Louis failed to consider the possibility that acute short-term effects would undermine ultimate goals.

At the same time these disruptive inner city programs proceeded, three external processes convulsed the St. Louis metropolitan area in ways that defeated the population strategy underlying public housing. The

Table 2. Pruitt-Igoe Housing Market Context, 1940–80

Population[a]

Year	St. Louis Metro Area[b]	Change	Black or Non white[c]	St. Louis City	Change	Black or Non white[c]	City as % of Metro Area
1940	1,368	—	11%	816	—	13%	60%
1950	1,681	22%	13	857	5%	13	51
1960	2,105	25	15	750	-12	29	36
1970	2,363	12	16	622	-17	41	26
1980	2,355	0[d]	17	453	-27	46	19

[a] In thousands.
[b] Definition of census metropolitan area varies.
[c] Census definitions differ for various years.
[d] Between 1970 and 1980 the St. Louis SMSA lost 0.3 percent of its population.
[e] First year completely open for occupancy.

effects of these processes are depicted in Table 2. Metropolitan population in the St. Louis area grew rather slowly in relation to the national average (164 percent in the 40 years from 1940 to 1980 compared with a national average of 244 percent). In the same period a massive migration of southern blacks came into the area via the central city ghetto. Finally a high rate of suburban home building produced new units faster than the aggregate population grew. Net new housing outside the central city of St. Louis expanded fivefold in the 40 years before 1980, while the population less than doubled.

These three metropolitan processes—slow growth, black influx, and overproduction of dwellings—combined to produce catastrophic effects on the inner city housing market. Table 2 shows this also. Within the city limits population tumbled by half over the 30 years following 1950. During this period city population changed from about one-eighth to one-half black. In the 40 years following 1940 more than half a million whites fled to the suburbs while net black growth amounted to less than 100,000.

The first postwar wave of public housing opened for occupancy just as the impact of these external processes began to be felt. While the site clearance had occurred earlier (when it actually had the effect of worsening the situation in the crowded ghetto area), by the time Pruitt-Igoe opened for occupancy, the need for public housing had abated. Low-income blacks by the late 1950s began to find space in formerly white

Housing Units[a]				Vacancy Rates			
St. Louis Metro Area[b]	Change	St. Louis City	Change	St. Louis Metro Area[b]	St. Louis City	1942 Low-Rise Project	Pruitt-Igoe
410	—	252	—	6%	7%	4% (1944)	not built
507	24%	263	5%	3	2	1	9% (1957)[e]
661	30	263	0	5	5	3	16
785	19	238	− 9	4	10	8	65
899	15	202	−15	n.a.	n.a.	n.a.	demolished

Sources: U.S. Bureau of the Census (1940a, pt. 3, Table 1, p. 869, Table 4, p. 871; 1940b, pt. 4, Table B–35, p. 455, Table B–44, p. 467; 1950a, pt. 25, Table 10, pp. 25–43 and 25–45; 1950b, pt. 25, Table 10, pp. 25–43 and 25–45; 1960a, pt. 1, Table 15, pp. 1–58 and 1–70; 1960b, p. 27, Table 13, pp. 27–39; 1970a, pt. 1, Table 15, pp. 1–73 and 1–88; 1970b, pt. 1, sec. 1, Table 67, pp. 1–316 and 1–332; 1980, Table 1, p. 38); Meehan (1975, Table 4–2, p. 54).

neighborhoods that were becoming increasingly vacant. Private market rents sank to public housing levels or below.

Though urban renewal, highways, and public housing sites cleared several square miles of low-rent housing, the market softened at an even faster rate. The vacancy data in Table 2 show this change as well. In 1950 both city and metropolitan areas had very tight housing markets (2 percent and 3 percent vacancy rates respectively). By 1960 both had eased to the 5 percent level that indicates a normal market situation. However, the rates in public housing told a different story. The two pre–World War II low-rise projects continued to be impacted, while even at the beginning Pruitt-Igoe's 9 percent rate indicated a weaker demand for housing in the new high-rise projects. This worsened. By 1960 a 16 percent rate in Pruitt-Igoe was a sure harbinger of trouble. Over the next decade the metropolitan area continued to show normal vacancy rates while vacancies in the city hit a depressed 10 percent level. Though the relatively older low-rent public housing projects continued to do better than the city average, Pruitt-Igoe reached a 65 percent vacancy rate by 1970, indicating that both tenants and housing officials had essentially abandoned it (Meehan, 1975).

Meehan's studies of St. Louis public housing make clear that in the immediate sense, local fiscal crisis forced the closing and destruction of Pruitt-Igoe. His exhaustive analysis of St. Louis Housing Authority records demonstrates convincingly that contradictions built into federal public housing policy put enormous, if not fatal, fiscal demands on the big St. Louis projects. In a period of rising costs, diminishing demand, and failing city services, the authority was forced to operate the projects out of declining rent incomes. Meehan argues: "The fundamental inadequacy of the fiscal arrangements was revealed starkly and rapidly . . . in the late 1940's. Tenant incomes dropped (as underemployed blacks replaced higher income war workers); Authority costs rose; Authority income fell" (1979, p. 61). This happened just before Congress passed the Housing Act of 1949 under which Pruitt-Igoe was to be built.

Within the projects themselves, especially within the increasingly derelict Pruitt-Igoe, the quality of life plummeted as the center city housing market emptied out and the Housing Authority's fiscal crisis deepened. A picture of this world comes through in a contemporary account by resident poverty program workers:

> When one drives or walks into Pruitt-Igoe, he is confronted by a dismal sight. Glass, rubble and debris litter the streets, the accumulation is astonishing . . . abandoned automobiles have been left in parking areas; glass is omnipresent; tin cans are strewn throughout, paper has been rained on and stuck in the cracked, hardened mud. Pruitt-Igoe from without looks like a disaster area. Broken windows are apparent in every building. Street lights are inoperative. . . . As the visitor nears the entrance to a building, the filth and debris intensify. Abandoned rooms under the building are receptacles for all matter of waste. Mice, roaches, and other vermin thrive in these open areas. . . .
>
> The infamous skip-stop elevator is a revelation even for those considering themselves prepared for anything. Paint has peeled from the elevator walls. The stench of urine is overwhelming; ventilation in the elevators is nonexistent.... When the visitor emerges from the dark, stench-filled elevator on to one of the building's gallery floors, he enters a grey concrete caricature of an insane asylum. Institutional grey walls give way to institutional grey floors. Rusty institutional-type screens cover windows in which no glass exists. Radiators once used to heat those public galleries have been, in many buildings, stripped from the walls. Incinerators, too small to accommodate the quantity to refuse placed into them, have spilled over—trash and garbage are heaped on the floors. Lightbulbs and fixtures are out; bare hot wire often dangles from malfunctioning light sockets. (Pruitt-Igoe Neighborhood Corporation, 1966)

In less than a decade an ambitious and expensive housing project had become a slum. How had this happened?

Scholars, politicians, and professionals ranging from architects to social workers began to direct their attention toward this question in the mid-1960s. Yet as people studied it, the project and life in it grew continuously more desperate. By 1967 the acting St. Louis housing director publicly called for either federal takeover or abandonment and demolition. More than five years passed before the first dynamite charges in 1972 began the long demolition process that took five more dreary years to complete. The long delay did permit the final actions to happen at splendidly symbolic moments. The dynamiting of 1972, and the attendant world wide media coverage, coincided beautifully with the Nixon administration campaign against public housing that culminated in the January 1973 moratorium on subsidized housing production. And the heavy work of finishing the demolition by conventional wrecking technology provided a unique Bicentennial celebration for St. Louis's hot summer of 1976.

Interpretations

Substantial research and interpretation have been devoted to the questions involved in the demise of Pruitt-Igoe. The failure of environmentally deterministic architecture is the most widespread interpretation. Literally hundreds of citations link the end of Pruitt-Igoe to faulty architecture. Chief among these is the thesis put forward by architect-researcher Oscar Newman (1972).[5] Newman cites Pruitt-Igoe in his "defensible space" argument that the architectural design and site layout of housing projects have a deterministic influence on behavior and especially on violent crime and vandalism. Though Newman does not assert a direct connection with the abandonment and demolition of Pruitt-Igoe, the dust jacket designers made the connection by reproducing the famous demolition photograph and asserting that the book provides an alternative to this "final remedy." A great many architects and architectural critics have adopted this implied causal connection between architectural design and the demolition of Pruitt-Igoe as revealed truth. Today the phrase "Pruitt-Igoe" widely symbolizes the imputed impossibility of serving social objectives through architecture.[6]

Eugene Meehan's view, that flawed federal policy created the local fiscal crisis which necessitated demolishing Pruitt-Igoe, stands sharply against the environmental determinist interpretation erected on Newman's work. Meehan argues: "After 1960, neither of the two white elephants [meaning Pruitt and Igoe] managed to cover operating costs from rental incomes. In fact, after depleting their own small reserves, Pruitt and Igoe absorbed the lion's share of the reserves that had accumulated from the other developments" (1979, p. 76). Later, after federal policy changed to provide some, albeit irregular, operating subsidies,

Pruitt-Igoe absorbed as much as three-quarters of all the St. Louis Authority's allotment of rehabilitation subsidy funds. Meehan concludes: "Until the complex was closed and demolished, it was literally impossible for the Authority to put its financial house in order" (p. 105).

The third interpretation of the Pruitt-Igoe episode, and the most ambitious in terms of research funding and staff, concerned social life in the housing development. Alvin Gouldner, Lee Rainwater, and a succession of sociologists and live-in, participant-observer graduate students produced a rich set of ethnographic materials on daily life in Pruitt-Igoe. Rainwater (1970) reports on these materials but hardly touches the question of Pruitt-Igoe as a physical setting. What little is said tends to be at odds with the Meehan and Newman interpretations. Rainwater asserts most Pruitt-Igoe residents "liked their apartments very much" (1970, p. 11). According to Rainwater, it was the larger surrounding environment and their neighbors that frightened them and led them to leave Pruitt-Igoe. And it was the problem of coping with poverty in America that led them to violence, vandalism, and welfare dependency.

In summary, a Rashomon-like story emerges: behind the demise of Pruitt-Igoe Newman sees a failure of architecture, Meehan a fatally flawed public policy-making process, and Rainwater by implication a symptom of a defective society, unable or unwilling to deal with the structural poverty and unemployment of lower-class blacks. By standing outside of their three professional worlds of architecture, policy analysis, and sociology respectively, one can see each view neatly nesting into that of the next, more general interpretation.

Meehan helps draw these interpretations together. He fails to develop any empirical case at the contextual level to show how the structural facts of poverty and racism determine the local failure of public housing policy, but he does spot a critical note in Rainwater's interpretation that effectively incorporates the architectural argument. He focuses his analytical attention on the local housing authority operation, and he shows that similar populations, with heavy representation of large, female-headed, black, welfare families, in other St. Louis projects did not lead to similar levels of vacancy and subsequent abandonment. Meehan finds that "Carr Square [one of the low-rise, pre–World War II projects], for example, was entirely populated by blacks from the beginning, and most of the tenants living there were receiving public assistance, yet it remained the most orderly and easily managed complex in St. Louis" (1979, p. 86). By implication Meehan characterizes Rainwater's analysis as a "culture of poverty" argument and dashes it by showing that the same people in the other projects produced a different story. In doing so he makes a measured case for Newman's position, distinct though these two interpretations may seem. Meehan writes of the situation in 1976 and observes, "Despite age and long neglect, Carr Square and Clinton Peabody [the two 1942 projects] were once again operating at capacity— a fitting tribute to good design and sound construction. Pruitt and Igoe were in their death throes, only some part buildings still awaiting the headache ball—an equally fitting tribute to bad design and poor construction" (1976, p. 132). Thus the three interpretations nest one in the other. Given an explanation of St. Louis's extreme position, Newman's architectural rationale provides a plausible reason why Pruitt-Igoe rather than Carr Square became the first U.S. public housing project to be officially abandoned. Similarly, Meehan's careful analysis of the St. Louis Housing Authority's finances suggests—neither he nor Rainwater offer much to fill in the gaps—how a society's de facto commitment to maintain poverty and racism produces dysfunctional social policy with respect to official goals.

To thus orchestrate the results of the remarkable attention scholars have given Pruitt-Igoe ironically answers no questions, only generates a more pressing set of unanswered problems. Why was the project built in the first place? Who won, who lost? What was the evolving political and economic context during Pruitt-Igoe's brief 20-year life? Perhaps most troubling of all: Why the decision to use such a dramatic means of demolition, one so sure to invoke maximum media coverage and to ensure it would become a symbol?

These questions only begin the inquiry. Why did Pruitt-Igoe come mainly to signify the failure of social architecture, public housing, and social welfare policy? Why instead did it not become a symbol of the racial and social class contradictions afflicting American urban society?

Notes

1. The history of public housing in St. Louis is examined in Meehan (1975, 1977, 1979).

2. The documents that present Bartholomew's work on St. Louis include Harland Bartholomew and Associates (1947) and St. Louis City Plan Commission (1920, 1936).

3. Bartholomew measured center city decline in terms of declining shares of the metropolitan totals in such areas as population, building permits, and retail trade, but this could be seen as a statistical artifact derived from the political subdivision of the area. St. Louis's city limits, drawn in 1876, were fixed by virtue of its secession from its parent county; thus by the 1920s little metropolitan expansion could occur within the city limits, ensuring that the city's share of growth would decline while its share of aging and obsolete plants would increase.

4. The leading contemporary approach to urban decline was epitomized in the Urban Land Institute's advocacy of urban redevelopment. This approach emphasized business district expansion and the replacement of inner ring slum housing with commercial or industrial uses. See Weiss (1980).

5. Earlier references to the environmental determinism interpretation include a semiofficial mea culpa by Bailey (1965) and a number of articles in the *St. Louis Post-Dispatch* (1965; Lindecke, 1965a, b) in which Charles Ferris, the housing director in charge of constructing and managing Pruitt-Igoe, is quoted as blaming architectural design for problems in the project.

6. Jencks makes explicit the connection between Pruitt-Igoe and architectural failure: "[Pruitt-Igoe] had been vandalized, mutilated and defaced by its black inhabitants, and although millions of dollars were pumped back, trying to keep it alive ... it was finally put out of its misery. Boom, boom, boom ... the ruins should be kept ... so that we have a live memory of this failure in planning and architecture" (1977, p. 9).

References

Bailey, J. 1965. The case history of a failure. *Architectural Forum* 135 (Dec.):22–25.

Canfield, M. 1974. The silence at Pruitt-Igoe. *St. Louis Globe-Democrat*, 22 Apr., p. 1.

Harland Bartholomew and Associates. 1947. *Comprehensive plan for St. Louis.* St. Louis.

Jencks, C. 1977. *The language of post-modern architecture.* New York: Rizzoli.

Lindecke, R. W. 1965a. PHA approved $7,000,000 plan to mend flaws at Pruitt-Igoe. *St. Louis Post-Dispatch*, 3 Oct., pp. 1, 26.

——. 1965b. $7,000,000 Pruitt-Igoe plan to eliminate "gauntlet areas." *St. Louis Post-Dispatch*, 4 Oct., pp. 1, 16.

Meehan, E. 1975. *Public housing policy: Convention versus reality.* New Brunswick, N.J.: Rutgers University, Center for Urban Policy Research.

——. 1977. The rise and fall of public housing. In D. Phares, ed., *A decent environment: Housing urban America.* Cambridge: Ballinger.

——. 1979. *The quality of federal policy making: Programmed failure in public housing.* Columbia: University of Missouri Press.

Newman, O. 1972. *Defensible space: Crime prevention through urban design.* New York: Macmillan.

New York Times. 1973. City life: St. Louis housing project razing points up public housing woes. 16 Dec., p. 72.

Pruitt-Igoe Neighborhood Corporation. 1966. *A dream deferred.* St. Louis.

Rainwater, L. 1970. *Behind ghetto walls: Black life in a federal slum.* Chicago: Aldine.

St. Louis City Plan Commission. 1920. *The housing problem in St. Louis.* St. Louis.

———. 1936. *Urban land policy*. St. Louis

St. Louis Post-Dispatch. 1965. Editorial. 2 Apr., p. 2.

U.S. Bureau of the Census. 1940a. Missouri. *Housing: 1940. Vol. 2*. Washington, D.C.: U.S. Government Printing Office.

———. 1940b. Missouri. *Population: 1940. Vol. 2*. Washington, D.C.: U.S. Government Printing Office.

———. 1950a. *Census of housing. 1950. Vol. 2*. Washington, D.C.: U.S. Government Printing Office.

———. 1950b. *Census of population: 1950. Vol. 2*. Washington, D.C.: U.S. Government Printing Office.

———. 1960a. *Census of housing: 1960. Vol. 1*. Washington, D.C.: U.S. Government Printing Office.

———. 1960b. *Census of population: 1960. Vol. 1*. Washington, D.C.: U.S. Government Printing Office.

———. 1970a. *Census of housing: 1970. Vol. 1*. Washington, D.C.: U.S. Government Printing Office.

———. 1970b. *Census of population: 1970. Vol. 1*. Washington, D.C.: U.S. Government Printing Office.

———. 1980. Standard metropolitan statistical areas. *Census of population: 1980*. Supplementary Report. Washington, D.C.: U.S. Government Printing Office.

U.S. Department of Housing and Urban Development. 1974. Final environmental impact statement. St. Louis: Area Office, September.

Weiss, M. 1980. The origins and legacy of urban renewal. In P. Clavel, J. Forester, and W. Goldsmith, eds. *Urban and regional planning in an age of austerity*. New York: Pergamon Press.

12

Revitalizing an Urban Neighborhood: A St. Louis Case Study

BARRY CHECKOWAY

St. Louis is a midwestern city in decline. From 1950 to 1980 its population decreased almost 50 percent, from 857,000 to 453,000, the largest
percentage decline of any major U.S. city. More than 300 manufacturing
firms closed or moved away during the 1970s, with a loss of about 58,000
jobs. Although many people and jobs moved to the suburbs or elsewhere
within the metropolitan area, others left altogether. Since 1950 St. Louis
has lost more than 60,000 housing units, or about one-fourth of its
housing stock, many of these destroyed under a municipal policy of
tearing down abandoned units. Brick-strewn or weed-covered vacant
lots whose structures have been demolished cover several areas of the
city. Once the largest city in the region and the fourth largest in the
nation, St. Louis today is known as "the nation's most distressed big
city" (Maier, 1981; McGrath, 1981; Sawyer, 1981; Schmandt et al., 1979).

Low-income neighborhoods of the city suffer the most intense
decline. Analysts estimate that the heaviest population losses have been
from the poorest neighborhoods, predominantly those in the black
north side. Between 1970 and 1980 black north-side areas lost consistently higher proportions of their residents—between 28 to 60 percent in
some locations—than white neighborhoods in the south side. One analyst describes a pattern of "class skimming" in which certain neighborhoods have been left with a core of young unemployed, elderly, and
other poor people who depend on government aid (McGrath, 1981).
Housing in many such neighborhoods is poorly maintained or abandoned. Demolition and disinvestment have resulted in more than 5,000
vacant lots, 98 percent of these in the poorest neighborhoods (Leven and
Weidenbaum, 1972; Leven et al., 1976; Mendelson and Quinn, 1976;
Sawyer, 1981).

Despite these conditions, some low-income residents have organized to overcome decline and rebuild their neighborhoods. One major effort centers around Jeff-Vander-Lou (JVL), a neighborhood organization working in the predominantly black, low-income area of the city. The JVL neighborhood is a 500-square-block area in St. Louis's near north side within 12 blocks of the downtown business district. Since 1966 JVL has built and renovated housing, operated a range of social services, attracted new industry and jobs, and developed plans for local commercial development. This paper describes and analyzes the case of Jeff-Vander-Lou.[1]

Awakening the Community

In the mid 1960s a door-to-door survey in the heart of the Jeff-Vander-Lou neighborhood found that 50 percent of the housing was substandard, 70 percent without complete plumbing, and nearly all poorly maintained (Jeff-Vander-Lou, 1967). City officials estimated that three-quarters of the housing was "unfit for human habitation" under city codes (Watson, 1977). A national survey of "crisis ghettos" found more abandoned housing in this area than in comparable sections of other cities (Center for Community Change and National Urban League, 1971). Residents were for the most part either unemployed or dependent on welfare, with 67 percent unemployed and 71 percent receiving income below the poverty level (Human Development Corporation, 1968, 1972). A neighborhood fact sheet documented the worst health conditions, highest crime rates, and "the most unattractive and over-crowded living and working conditions anywhere in the city" (Jeff-Vander-Lou, 1967).

Conditions were exacerbated by the nearby Pruitt-Igoe public housing project. First occupied in 1954, Pruitt-Igoe housed 13,000 people in 2,700 apartments in 33 11-story slab-shaped buildings. Conditions at Pruitt-Igoe had declined by the early 1960s, resulting in physical deterioration, high crime rates, skyrocketing vacancies, tenant anxieties, and a "tangle of pathologies" (Meehan, 1972; Moore, 1969; Newman, 1972; Pruitt-Igoe Neighborhood Corporation, 1966; Rainwater, 1970). In Chapter 11 of this volume Roger Montgomery describes the Pruitt-Igoe environment: broken windows, abandoned rooms, urine stench, mice and roaches, filthy grounds, shattered glass, rusty cans, garbage and litter, broken sidewalks, dirty streets, and abandoned automobiles. Nearby residents perceived their housing as worse than in Pruitt-Igoe and their neighborhood as among the least desirable in the city (Stromberg, 1967).

Neighborhood decline resulted from a variety of factors. One survey (Center for Community Change and National Urban League, 1971) described a pattern of private and public disinvestment. This study showed that financial institutions "redlined" the area by refusing to consider conventional mortgages or home-repair loans and by directing the flow of funds into other areas. Public agencies also disinvested, refused to enforce housing codes, and reduced the level and quality of public services. They also threatened the area with urban renewal and highway projects. Residents themselves deferred housing maintenance, refused to pay property taxes, defaulted on mortgages, or abandoned the neighborhood altogether. A local advocate (Sporleder, 1971, 1972) described a process in which private and public officials together discouraged homeowners from making needed repairs, and thus contributed to neighborhood deterioration. By the mid-1960s less than 20 percent of the housing was owner-occupied, and 85 percent was owned or controlled by 13 absentee landlords (Jeff-Vander-Lou, 1967).

Despite declining conditions, some residents wanted to remain in the neighborhood. A core of homeowners held stable employment and resided in structurally sound housing. Some had lived in the neighborhood for years, while others had moved there as "urban renewal refugees." This latter group had been displaced two or three times before and now sought a stable community. Thus a core group wanted to stay where they were (Watson, 1977).

A series of crises provided a vehicle for community organization and leadership to develop (Lee, 1978; Smith, 1978; Snipes, 1978; Watson, 1977). In the spring of 1964 community residents mobilized in response to the school-yard shooting of a local youth by a police officer. Leading the protest was Macler Shepard, owner of a local upholstery store. He had been displaced twice before by urban renewal projects, and his home and store had been demolished to build Pruitt-Igoe. Shepard mobilized 8,000 people to march through Pruitt-Igoe to police headquarters, where he served as spokesman in meetings with officials to demand action. The wide publicity for the march brought the neighborhood to the attention of city officials and identified Shepard as a community leader.

Shepard, along with Hubert Schwartzentrubber, a white Mennonite minister, and Aritha Spotts, a long-time resident and retired school teacher, were selected by the mayor of St. Louis to lead the Nineteenth Ward Beautification Committee, which was formed to coordinate neighborhood clean-up through a new national program. Shepard, Schwartzentrubber, and Spotts viewed the committee as a vehicle for housing and community development, but city officials oriented the program around street and alley sweeps, trash pickups, tree planting, and fence and building painting. Despite their unsuccessful efforts to redirect city officials from cosmetic beautification to more pressing issues, the committee was successful in bringing local leaders together to discuss community problems. Schwartzentrubber opened a coffee house where residents and others met to discuss issues affecting low-income, black people.

During this period neighborhood leaders met with Urban League organizers hired to coordinate federal antipoverty program efforts in the community. The Urban League had hired these organizers to form a neighborhood advisory council to direct activities and resources through the Office of Economic Opportunity (OEO). Organizers had become frustrated that the advisory council did not effectively represent the community and that the agenda was largely predetermined by city and federal officials. The organizers, in their search for other groups to represent the community, joined forces with beautification committee leaders and formed a neighborhood action coalition. Neighborhood leaders sought to influence the use of OEO resources and won control of the advisory council in its election. But city officials threatened the organizers with dismissal, called for a new election, defeated local leaders in the election, and then directed the antipoverty funds outside the area.

Organizing took another step forward in 1966 when community leaders and organizers rallied opposition to a proposed $79 million city bond issue that promised "neighborhood improvements" through the city but excluded JVL. A neighborhood delegation met with city officials to protest their exclusion, but officials refused to alter the bond issue and convinced many residents that the area was scheduled for "urban renewal" in the form of further abandonment, massive demolition, and withdrawal of public services. In response, local leaders and Urban League organizers led a campaign to defeat the proposed bond issue. They organized meetings across the city, formed coalitions with white neighborhoods, conducted a vigorous publicity campaign, and defeated the bond issue by a sizable margin. This campaign provided the neighborhood with a major victory.

Organizing continued when residents confronted the building commissioner to force landlords to improve conditions through housing inspection and code enforcement. The commissioner responded that buildings in "slum areas" would be inspected only on a specific-complaint rather than on a communitywide basis. Neighborhood leaders then collected and filed 1,200 individual complaints against 12 absentee landlords. The commissioner countered that three-quarters of the housing was "unfit for human occupancy" and began to evict local families. The leaders returned the families to their houses, threatened to set up "refugee camps" in local churches and community centers, and solicited beds and emergency supplies from the Red Cross. City officials, fearing violence, then ordered the building commissioner to halt the evictions and negotiate a settlement. Local leaders demanded clarification of the city's plans for JVL and exacted a promise that the city would schedule no urban renewal for the neighborhood. Landlords, faced with massive housing complaints and the loss of potential profits from urban renewal, sold out or abandoned their properties altogether. Admitting that the city was unable to solve neighborhood problems, the mayor challenged local leaders to develop their own plan for revitalization.

Together these crises provided a means for residents to recognize common problems, develop community organization and leadership, and establish themselves as a political force. The confrontations with local government and efforts to influence "outside" agendas brought residents together and awakened the community. The next challenge was to develop an independent agenda.

Forming an Organization

In 1966 neighborhood residents incorporated as an independent organization, determined their boundaries, and gave themselves a name, Jeff-Vander-Lou.[2] Their organizational objectives emphasized housing, community development, education, social services, and efforts "to renew the physical and moral structures of the community." They adopted bylaws that provided for community participation, representation, and leadership in the new organization (Jeff-Vander-Lou, 1966). All area residents could participate as members in monthly meetings and elect representatives to a governing board that would set policy and elect officers. Macler Shepard was elected president to lead Jeff-Vander-Lou by implementing policy and directing staff. At its incorporation JVL had no established funding sources; membership dues were voluntary for those willing and able to pay. In adopting articles of incorporation, residents tacitly recognized their rights to form an organization, develop a governing structure and representative council, and make decisions on their own behalf.

JVL leaders recognized the need for a neighborhood plan. They enlisted a team of planners to join residents to survey conditions in a central target area. Both JVL leaders and residents participated in a simulation game designed to familiarize them with community planning priorities. They did a mock plan for the neighborhood, using styrofoam blocks and corrugated boxes to represent buildings, and constructed a hypothetical community that would best suit their needs.

According to Macler Shepard, the game taught residents that redevelopment, not demolition, was the top priority.

In the written proposals and plans that JVL leaders then prepared, the emphasis was on housing, but the program was designed to serve physical, economic, and social development needs as well (Jeff-Vander-Lou, 1967). The leaders proposed to acquire and rehabilitate old housing in the heart of the neighborhood, and they also proposed programs for job training, community education, tenant training, family health, and child care. With travel provided by a local businessmen's association, Macler Shepard took the proposals to Washington to seek federal funding. Officials expressed limited interest but stated they would not consider funding until JVL developed experience in handling funds and in housing rehabilitation.

Unable to obtain government funding, JVL leaders initiated their own program. They decided to acquire abandoned or deteriorated houses that were still structurally sound, rehabilitate them with voluntary donations and private resources, and sell them to residents. The program began with a single run-down house. Money for the project was raised through membership dues, grass-roots fund-raising projects, a local bank loan, and contributions from businessmen and residents. Volunteer architects and builders examined the house and made estimates. Volunteers stripped the house to the studs, fumigated it, and furnished it with dry wall and new floor tile. Black contractors and union men installed plumbing, heating, wiring, windows, and kitchen appliances. The house, which was completed at a cost of only $18,000, received wide publicity throughout the city. At a Sunday open house more than 5,000 people came to see the first JVL house.

After this initial success JVL leaders challenged local churches to support neighborhood revitalization (Groves, 1971). The Mennonites, who had formed congregations in JVL and other black neighborhoods throughout the country, were the first to respond. SHARE, Inc., a nonprofit group established by Mennonites who had visited JVL, made an interest-free loan for housing rehabilitation and donated funds to hire a construction supervisor. The Mennonite Disaster Service, identifying JVL as an area requiring emergency services, sent skilled craftsmen to rehabilitate houses. At the same time the Illinois Mennonite Youth Fellowship raised funds to purchase and rehabilitate a house, and fellowship members spent a summer working on the house under the supervision of the contractors.

The rehabilitation projects came to the attention of a successful St. Louis businessman whose family had once lived in the neighborhood. When he learned of the organization's plans, he contacted JVL leaders to discuss restoration of his family's old home. Because the original house was not available, Shepard asked this businessman to pick an alternative. He did, hired a contractor from the area, rehabilitated the house, and turned it over to JVL at no cost. Impressed by JVL plans, he subsequently financed additional housing units and provided the organization with office space and staff salaries. He also formed the Arrowhead Foundation to solicit and manage the private contributions to JVL, which amounted to more than $1 million in grants and interest-free loans. In order to accomplish this, the businessman served as an advocate for neighborhood projects in the St. Louis business community. As a consequence, the city's business leaders came to view JVL as a legitimate social cause and later served as an instrumental force in several JVL projects. The businessman who made all this possible called the private resources "tools" made available to community "craftsmen."

One of the Arrowhead Foundation's first projects was to assist in the completion of Opportunity House, a temporary relocation and home management training center. Opportunity House, three two-story row houses rehabilitated into six temporary living units, provided a refuge for temporarily displaced residents and offered basic instruction and education on how to manage and live in houses. The program included training in home maintenance and repair, consumer problems and practices, the use of community services and resources, and community participation. JVL staff also monitored family finances, found jobs for those who were unemployed, and assisted residents to establish savings for home repairs and to negotiate loans from local banks. Opportunity House thus not only dealt with displacement but also helped residents develop resources and skills to become homeowners and maintain their housing (Arrowhead Newsletter, 1968; Jeff-Vander-Lou, 1967).

In addition, the Arrowhead Foundation arranged a series of meetings in which JVL leaders helped persuade Brown Group, a St. Louis–based shoe manufacturer, to build a shoe factory in the neighborhood (Pratter, 1975). JVL leaders functioned as a chamber of commerce by expressing the need for economic development through employment and formulating a specific proposal for cooperative effort. Company officials accepted the proposal and agreed to relocate people displaced by the new factory, open a training school, and allow JVL to screen, test, and counsel applicants for jobs. JVL continues to perform these functions today, thus establishing JVL as a major employment vehicle in the neighborhood. The plant has provided JVL with both a continuing source of jobs—300-500 people employed when operating at full capacity—and the recognition that it could attract industry without depending on charity or government assistance. The factory was publicized as one of the first in an inner city black neighborhood in the nation.

The Arrowhead Foundation also helped improve neighborhood care. Jeff-Vander-Lou had no medical facilities, few doctor's offices, and the worst health indices in the city. In cooperation with Arrowhead, anonymous donors rehabilitated a large building into a medical center, and prominent doctors and assistants formed a medical group for diagnostic and emergency treatment. Patients paid a nominal fee for services. As a result, JVL attracted other health clinics and facilities, and some residents today continue to receive care from prominent St. Louis doctors.

In this stage, then, JVL established an independent organization and initiated its own projects. The organization drafted proposals and plans, made program decisions, enlisted private assistance, and began building a track record. They privately rehabilitated a number of houses, sold them to residents, and took steps related to employment and health care. Although these were relatively small steps, they laid the foundation for later projects.

Building Capacity

Following private rehabilitation of a number of houses, JVL leaders again sought federal funding for housing on a larger scale. This time federal officials agreed to insure mortgages and subsidize interest on a project if JVL could first acquire and complete the houses. JVL raised initial private capital to purchase and rehabilitate a "package" of five houses that subsequently received federal funding under the 221H housing program, the first such assistance to a neighborhood organization. As part of this project JVL persuaded a major contracting firm to hire black subcontractors and train unemployed neighborhood residents for construction; they also convinced a union contractor to open to black membership. This project also resulted in the formation of Pantheon Corporation, a new contracting company that has since handled most JVL housing construction and has earned a reputation as one of the leading inner city developers in the nation (Riesenberger, 1977). JVL continued its program with ten more 221H packages, for a total of 75 units rehabilitated and sold by 1970.

Neighborhood leaders in that year formed the JVL Housing Corporation to expand its services to include subsidized rental housing. JVL had developed the capacity to rehabilitate houses for ownership, but many families remained unable to make a down payment or pay the price of purchase and maintenance. Neighborhood houses that had sold for $9,500 in 1968 cost $17,000 two years later. JVL proposed to develop federally assisted rental housing, but HUD officials again questioned the adequacy of local experience and insisted on a co-sponsor. The new JVL Housing Corporation thus joined forces with the Elijah Parish Lovejoy Presbytery as a co-sponsor to develop housing units under federal programs and rent them to people in the area. The housing corporation paid JVL to hire staff to manage the properties and consequently became a major source of JVL staff expansion.

The first rental housing project under federal funding was the Aritha Spotts Apartments, a complex consisting of 74 one- to four-bedroom units arranged around three landscaped courtyards. Despite warnings that rentals in the area would be in low demand, over 100 applications came in on opening day. The project included a central building to house the expanding JVL offices, laundry rooms, employment facilities, day care centers, and meeting rooms. Aritha Spotts Apartments became the new neighborhood center (Marshall, 1972; Miers, 1972).

As part of its housing program JVL attempted to secure and rehabilitate four Pruitt-Igoe buildings (Starrels, 1975). By the mid-1970s Pruitt-Igoe had become a notorious public housing failure. Federal officials had commissioned several studies of project conditions, authorized funds to repair damages and provide new facilities, hired residents to study tenant needs, established a neighborhood corporation, and finally barricaded empty buildings and made demolition plans. JVL, which had built support among downtown business interests, submitted plans to purchase four buildings and sought federal guarantees and rent subsidies for the proposed project. But federal officials opposed rehabilitation and had the Pruitt-Igoe buildings demolished.

Although JVL lost on Pruitt-Igoe, their housing corporation and Spotts Apartments were landmarks in local history. They demonstrated JVL's capacity to complete projects with federal partners and allowed them to expand staff, widen their networks, and work with others. Most important, they led to a succession of housing and community development projects supported by government funding. By 1980 JVL had added more than 800 housing units and $21 million of capital improvements in the neighborhood. According to Macler Shepard, it was not until the new housing projects emerged as tangible signs of JVL's effectiveness that other programs gathered support to succeed.

Diversifying the Program

As neighborhood development increased, JVL recognized the need for additional social services, especially those related to senior citizens, child care, and community education. JVL leaders had identified these needs earlier, but only with expansion in resources, capacity, and community support were they able to diversify their program.

Senior Citizens

Senior citizens comprised a significant proportion of the neighborhood population. They experienced not only the general problems of the neighborhoods but also the special access problems of the elderly. With initial assistance from Washington University and funding from the Model Cities program, residents formed an outreach team to provide services for the elderly. The team began by supplying meals on wheels for the most needy and continued by developing plans for a senior citizens' center. Officials from the local Area Agency on Aging went back on a promise of funding, but JVL leaders organized protests and received a hearing from the governor, who ordered that the center be funded through the Older Americans Act. By 1977 the center served close to 250 clients with a wide range of activities.

Neighborhood leaders also sought to provide housing for elderly residents. While many senior homeowners wanted alternative housing that suited their incomes and special needs, there was a short supply of well-maintained and reasonably priced rental units. JVL leaders recognized that the construction of housing for the elderly would provide structurally sound houses not only for senior citizens but also for new families. JVL leaders thus developed plans for 100 units of elderly and handicapped housing that included multipurpose facilities for common meals, meetings, and social events. In 1977 federal officials approved plans for a $2.9 million project through the Section 202 program, and the buildings were completed and occupied by 1980.

Child Care

Early studies of JVL had shown that the area needed child care services because it contained a relatively high number of preschool children, many households in which both parents worked, and a large number of single-parent households in which the mother was employed (Jeff-Vander-Lou, 1967). Completion of the new factory and apartments intensified the need by putting many mothers to work and providing housing and employment for new families with young children. As the need increased, however, adequate facilities were difficult to locate. The neighborhood had no licensed centers, and facilities in adjacent areas were inaccessible to those who lacked transportation.

In 1973 JVL opened a child care center in the Aritha Spotts Apartments under a Title VII HEW grant in conjunction with the Early Child Care Development Corporation. The center stressed education to develop skills and promote interaction, provided meals and transportation for children, and encouraged parents to participate in curriculum development and classroom activities. JVL staff sought "to join the home, community and classroom into a link to promote complete development of the child with his family" (Smith, 1978). In 1975 JVL opened a second center in a local church basement. Together these centers serve 64 children, employ 25 staff, and involve volunteer senior citizens from the neighborhood. JVL staff keep careful records of "their" children as they pass from the centers through the public schools and beyond.

Community Education

JVL leaders formed an education committee to analyze major problems and alternatives in neighborhood schools (Short, 1980; Smith, 1978). They documented overcrowded classrooms, dilapidated buildings, poor teaching, and outdated curricula that rarely referred to the neighborhood or encouraged community problem solving. Graduating students typically left the area, "taking with them the education, energy, creativity, and resources the community needs to survive" (Jeff-Vander-Lou, 1977). JVL leaders sought to improve local education through public meetings, school board elections, direct contacts with teachers and school officials, and other traditional channels, but these produced little change. They then considered possibilities for an alternative school system but found no resources or support. They finally decided to pursue cooperative educational programs in the community.

Cooperation began with the city-sponsored Summer Youth Program. Local high school students had complained that this program had given them summer work that offered little employment training, skill development, or productive accomplishment. JVL leaders approached school officials and proposed to bring youth to neighborhood projects "to show them that their community was a place of opportunity, that things could be changed and improved" (Jeff-Vander-Lou, 1977). School officials approved the program and provided resources for young people to analyze community medical needs, publish a community newspaper, produce architectural designs for abandoned buildings, and develop secretarial, proposal-writing, and administrative skills.

In 1976 the program focused on communications, an area in which schools were especially lacking. Proud, Inc., publishers of a regional black magazine, had moved to Jeff-Vander-Lou and volunteered to help increase circulation of the community newspaper and expand the program to other communications media. Students and parents showed enthusiasm, and school officials agreed to provide academic credit for experiential learning. This support motivated JVL to develop a full-time communications program in cooperation with local schools.

JVL proposed the idea to the Stuart Mott Foundation, which provided resources to create the JVL Communications Center. Completed in 1978, the center includes television and film studios, newspaper facilities, and a radio station for live broadcasts to the neighborhood. The center provides career training, employment skills, and a production facility and dissemination center for community programs. Students consult residents regarding their informational needs, document problems of local concern, and produce programs about JVL projects.

Toward Local Commercial Development

As housing and social services have expanded, neighborhood leaders are turning to the local economy. Until the early 1960s the neighborhood business district included more than 100 establishments. Over time, however, businesses have withdrawn, threatened by urban renewal and the demolition of Pruitt-Igoe, by private and public disinvestment, and by population loss, crime, and physical decay. Despite JVL efforts to use Model Cities funding for physical improvements, business conditions have continued to decline (Kinerk et al., 1981). A Washington University study found that only 35 commercial establishments remained in 1975, so that residents have to purchase most goods and services outside the area (Meier, 1975). Thus the dollars that come into the neighborhood through wages and transfer payments go out again almost immediately when residents go shopping. St. Louis officials have concluded that the JVL business district has "widespread deterioration, obsolescence, and underutilized land. The general environment along the street is a serious economic and cultural liability to the neighborhood and the entire city" (St. Louis Community Development Agency, 1976).

JVL today is formulating plans for local commercial development. In 1976 they received Model Cities funding to commission a market study of the central JVL business district (Ochsner and Associates, 1977). The study assessed neighborhood population movements, market patterns, and consumer behavior, and found that market area income had risen, crime had decreased, and commercial reinvestment was desirable and warranted.

In 1980 JVL formed an Economic Development Consortium with Washington University and Monsanto Corporation to revitalize the neighborhood business district (Kirkland, n.d.). The focus is on a pedestrian shopping mall at the site of the original district. Early plans would rehabilitate some existing facilities, demolish those that are beyond repair, construct new buildings for lease from JVL, and develop an entertainment and cultural center. JVL, as principal owner, would reinvest money from property and services into the community.

Neighborhood leaders view this project as a step toward locally controlled commercial development. They seek to establish the conditions for reinvestment, stimulate local ownership and employment, halt the flow of dollars out of the neighborhood, and bring goods and services closer to home. They also recognize that previous programs relied increasingly on outside funding and "soft money," and view such reliance as a means to increase independence and control. Like others elsewhere (Carnoy and Shearer, 1980), they consider this control instrumental in local development.

Lessons Learned

Because each case is different, the St. Louis project described above may be unique in many respects. The following analysis of the major lessons learned in Jeff-Vander-Lou is nevertheless offered in the hope that others may be helped to analyze their own community problems and to find solutions for them.

Community organization is central for individuals seeking to participate in neighborhood planning. Neighborhood planning operates in an imbalanced political arena (Ahlbrandt and Brophy, 1975; Boyer, 1973; Cassidy, 1980; Downie, 1974; Gans, 1962; Hartman, 1974; Marciniak, 1977; National Commission on Neighborhoods, 1979; National Training and Information Center, 1976; Stone, 1976). Outside economic interests— including some landlords, real estate agents, financial institutions, commercial establishments, and city governments—are narrow and concentrated enough to facilitate intervention and to make the effort required to influence local planning. These powerful groups are more likely to pay the costs of participation than are unorganized neighborhood interests. Individual residents tend to face their neighborhood alone and know little about discrepancies in the delivery of services or about the neighborhood as a planning unit. Residents also hesitate to "intrude" in areas that involve concentrated power, and they come together intermittently and without community organization. In the absence of special circumstances, outside interests can be expected to produce the most powerful inputs and therefore to dominate planning decisions.

JVL demonstrates the importance of community organization in neighborhood planning. Organization served to mobilize individuals, to develop a common program, and to generate power to carry out that program. By organizing, JVL residents not only determined their boundaries and gave themselves a name but also came to view their neighborhood as a political unit. The organization provided a vehicle for residents to participate in planning, develop leadership and confidence, and eventually to improve the scope and quality of housing and services. It was only after individuals organized that they developed programs to meet neighborhood needs.

Most neighborhood studies do not focus on community organization as a factor in neighborhood change. Previous studies have examined the impact of ecological forces (Park et al., 1925), social preferences (Hoyt, 1939), cultural traditions (Firey, 1945), social organizations (Shevky and Williams, 1949), demographic variables (Hawley, 1950), and community attachments (Bell and Boalt, 1957). Others have applied ethnography to analyze the importance of slum conditions (Whyte, 1943), social class and ethnic ties (Gans, 1962; Liebow, 1967), shared values (Suttles, 1968, 1972), historic and symbolic meanings (Hunter, 1974), and subcultures (Fischer, 1976). Recent studies recognize that community organizations formed to deal with neighborhood problems have increased in number and capacity (Boyte, 1980; Goering, 1979; Perlman, 1979) and that some have grown to a stage where they develop plans of their own (National Commission on Neighborhoods, 1979; U.S. Office of Consumer Affairs, 1980). But most neighborhood planning studies focus on "subarea planning" in which central planning agencies deconcentrate facilities or functions to subunits (Rohe and Gates, 1981; Werth and Bryant, 1979). Only exceptional studies focus on "neighborhood planning" in which self-starting community organizations develop plans and exercise power over neighborhood decisions (Cassidy, 1980; Urban Systems Research and Engineering, 1980; Mayer and Blake, 1980).

Voluntary action is instrumental to develop support and build organization. Participation in JVL began with citizen protest, continued with informal meetings to discuss common problems, and led to the formation of a community organization to develop neighborhood plans. Participation continues today, through regular community meetings, elected representatives, community information and media programs, and personal contact among leaders and residents. Such participation increases awareness and builds organizational strength.

The quality of voluntary participation contrasts sharply with official participation programs mandated by the government. These mandates have proliferated in recent years as part of most federal domestic programs and city governments. For example, the neighborhood advisory council of the federal antipoverty program and the Nineteenth Ward Beautification Committee established by the mayor of St. Louis were two official programs in which neighborhood residents were expected to participate. However, official participation programs are characterized by marked contradictions between stated aims and actual practice. Many such programs contain citizen demands and serve administrative ends without transfer of power to citizens (Arnstein, 1969; Checkoway, 1981; Checkoway and Van Til, 1978). It is no wonder that JVL leaders found that the advisory council did not represent their area and was unreceptive to resident initiatives, or that the beautification committee was blind to local priorities and would not alter its pre-set agenda. Given these responses, JVL was undoubtedly wise to withdraw from these programs to form its own organization. The frustrating efforts to influence official programs brought citizens together and gave them their start, for in this process they learned that voluntary action and community organization were the best ways for them to bring about local self-determination.

Leadership can expand organizational capacity and mobilize resources for change. Early studies of social movements emphasized cases in which widespread grievances gave rise to organizations that selected leaders to carry out ameliorative actions (Leites and Wolf, 1970). More recent studies emphasize cases in which public and private institutions provide resources for leaders who build organizational capacity and expand awareness of needed change (McCarthy and Zald, 1973; Zald and Berger, 1978). In contrast, JVL originated in reaction to crises that awakened the community and produced leaders who helped form an organization to bring ordinary people into planning. A businessman, a minister, and a retired school teacher took the initial lead with subsequent support from private and public institutions.

JVL leadership today reflects a "web approach" in which community participation and leadership are closely related (Snipes, 1978). Monthly meetings provide a setting for residents to discuss local problems and issues. Elected board members not only represent community interests and identify issues but also make policy decisions. The JVL president chairs meetings, leads discussions, and develops action proposals. In addition, he informs and consults with residents and directs staff to administer the core programs that build on community services to serve expressed neighborhood needs. Residents in turn attend meetings, provide organizational support, and advocate neighborhood interests. The president's authority is based on his capacity to deliver services in accordance with needs.

Macler Shepard has been president of JVL since its formation. He emerged spontaneously as a leader and developed experience through trial and error. He has worked to identify issues and to build an organization that can bring about change. In doing so, he has developed relationships with funding sources, convinced outsiders of local capacity, and moved many projects toward completion. Residents and outsiders see him as a charismatic leader who understands and mobilizes neighborhood sentiments and embodies the ideals of the Jeff-Vander-Lou organization (Cooper, 1979; Curry, 1973; Jackson, 1972; Schweitzer, 1977).

Staff skills contribute to project planning and implementation. JVL began with a loose leadership and small staff that shared responsibilities without specialization. With increases in resources and activities, leadership and staff have become more differentiated. Board members serve as a communication channel between residents and staff; they also make some policy decisions and work to generate support for them. Staff implement policy, develop and administer programs, and apply technical knowledge and skills. "Core staff" prepare proposals that follow required formats, make presentations to funding and review bodies, lobby for projects on a person-to-person basis, help assess the priorities of residents, and complete the steps in project planning and implementation. "Project staff" serve specialized technical roles in housing development, rental operations and management, economic development, education, health, services to the elderly, child care, and employment. While assistance from government, business, church, and university officials contribute in major ways and compensate for gaps in capacity, they do not substitute for stable internal staff, which JVL has been able to maintain for years.

Commitment helps overcome obstacles and produce results. Jeff-Vander-Lou is unlike many neighborhood groups that succumb to a pattern of frustration, passivity, or withdrawal in the face of obstacles, lack of funding, or delayed achievement of stated aims (Gans, 1962; Wilson, 1963). Although they had no government funding and encountered obstacles to their original plans, JVL resolutely moved ahead by seeking voluntary donations and private funds to undertake the project that gave them their start and drew new investment into the neighborhood.

JVL was composed of people rooted in or committed to the neighborhood. Some were homeowners with a strong stake in their property, other were "refugees" who had been displaced before and refused to move again, while yet others were poor people who had no other place to go. Together they evinced a "community-regarding" ethos based on an enlarged view of the community and a sense of obligation to it (Wilson, 1963). They were able to overcome early disappointments, to expand their time perspective, and to participate in an organization that represented their interests, built confidence, and eventually produced results.

Crises and protests can be used to awaken a community and create an organization. JVL originated in reaction to crises that produced protests and confrontations. These events raised local awareness, provided a sense of collective identity, identified issues around which to organize, and provided a vehicle to develop organization and leadership. Protest was the neighborhood's first weapon, and it gave the neighborhood its first victories.

In time, neighborhood leaders decided that it would be a strategic mistake to organize only around crises and protests without creating an independent agenda of their own. This decision helped JVL enter a new period of activism in which they were able to broaden their issues, formulate new goals and plans, and diversify their program. JVL does, however, continue to use protest as a tactic in their general strategy. Specifically, JVL targets city officials for periodic actions to demand improvements in services; such political action also shows strength, exercises the troops, expands the organizational base, and builds support for further organizational development (Lancourt, 1979).

"Out of the house come everything." This favorite saying of Macler Shepard contrasts with the usual meaning of "housing" as a material product, a form of shelter that covers or protects. Shepard and neighborhood leaders appreciate the value of housing as a product, but they see it more as a vehicle for social change. For example, Opportunity House was designed to provide for the temporary relocation of families whose homes were being rehabilitated, but also to serve "as a classroom for teaching families living habits more appropriate to decent, modern housing" (Jeff-Vander-Lou, 1967). Each resident family stayed about ten weeks to complete an intensive education program in homemaking and home maintenance, family health and child care, family finances, consumer education, family planning, and community development. Shepard believes that, with decent housing, families can become politically aware, well educated, properly nourished, morally sound, and active in the community. JVL expects those who reside in its housing and receive services to return payment by attending meetings, providing support, and working for the neighborhood.

Neighborhood leaders also use housing as a community organizing tool. Essential to successful organizing is the ability to choose issues that express broad social concerns, appeal to particular constituencies, provide tactical handles and multiple phases, and produce concrete results (Booth, 1977). Neighborhood leaders have found housing to be such an issue, and their successful use of this issue has built an organization able to point to housing products as tangible evidence of organizational success.

"There's something on the menu for everyone." This, another favorite saying of Macler Shepard, is a core planning idea of JVL. It is the idea that once people share a vision of the future and commit themselves to planning for it, they can recognize or create opportunities for implementation. This is planning as a form of entrepreneurship and as an act of commitment and faith.

Neighborhood leaders formulated a broad strategy for local revitalization and then expressed this in the form of written proposals and plans. This was the first such statement of strategy, in the words of those who lived there and knew it best. It was a proclamation that the neighborhood had taken account of itself and knew where it wanted to go, even if it had little idea of how to get there and how long it might take. The plan was not cosmopolitan but local; not comprehensive but focused on priority areas; not long-range but concerned with immediate needs and projects; not a series of colored maps and designs describing an ideal future but a statement of real problems, objectives, and action programs; not a formal document searching for local support but a community-based strategy searching for outside resources. The process of moving forward was highly incremental and required resourcefulness and the ability to seize opportunities and to generate one project from another. Macler Shepard was able to "go out" for resources to help complete the plan, which itself evolved as new opportunities were recognized or created. This is "opportunity planning," in which local participation serves as the basis to mobilize resources for change.

Funding support for neighborhood planning can come from a variety of sources. Neighborhood leaders began their first project using voluntary donations and private resources. It was community crises, commitment, and leadership, not outside funding support, that gave them their start. Private business leaders recognized their initiative and provided funds to hire staff, expand projects, and build the organization. Churches also gave support by providing loans, skilled personnel, and volunteers for construction. In time, neighborhood leaders developed their track record and received outside government funding, which allowed JVL to expand and diversify the program. Over time JVL has benefited heavily from major private and public resources from outside the neighborhood. Today neighborhood leaders are turning to local development through commercial revitalization of the neighborhood business district. They view this as a way not only to reduce reliance on outside funding but also to stimulate reinvestment and to increase community control. Their combined resources comprise no more than a fraction of what is available to outside economic interests whose previous actions have influenced the neighborhood, but these resources have made it possible to build a neighborhood organization and to achieve real change.

Conclusion

Formed in response to community crises, Jeff-Vander-Lou has grown into a neighborhood organization with an impressive track record. Working in an area that many had considered beyond revitalization, JVL has built and rehabilitated housing, generated capital development, operated social services, attracted new industry and jobs, and formulated plans to boost the local economy. They have increased awareness of neighborhood problems, developed leadership, and produced results.

Has JVL saved the neighborhood? Despite JVL's accomplishments, the surrounding area continues to decline. The heaviest population losses in the city still occur in the north side, and those who stay are disproportionately elderly, young unemployed, and poor. Housing remains badly overcrowded, poorly maintained, or abandoned. While no longer "teeming slums," the area is still badly deteriorated. The tangible JVL accomplishments—the new neighborhood housing, shoe factory, child care program, communications center, and plans for future economic development—contrast sharply with the surrounding area.

This contrast amplifies the magnitude of the JVL accomplishment. Most citizens in low-income neighborhoods still face a pattern in which outside interests dominate planning decisions, private institutions disinvest in favor of more advantaged locations, and public agencies reduce municipal services (Ahlbrandt and Brophy, 1975; Cassidy, 1980; Clay, 1979; Goetze, 1976; National Commission on Neighborhoods, 1979). In the absence of intervention, the result is a downgrading cycle in which potentially viable neighborhoods decline into deteriorated infrastructure, withdrawal of population and institutions, and abandonment. Those who remain may suffer a crisis of confidence and symptoms of alienation. In the face of outside decisions and neighborhood decline, many citizens feel impotent and reduce their participation in the community. There are cases of low-income citizens who have sought neighborhood participation and planning with fervor, of citizens who have moved back to the city, and of neighborhood groups that have organized around planning agencies and issues, but these are not typical in the field.

The JVL case adds to the evidence that neighborhood groups can achieve good housing on their own initiative. It shows that local citizens can take control of their surroundings and order them intelligently without outside interests telling them what they need, that they can handle problems at the local level without the harmful effects of federal intervention, and that they can improve their community when they determine plans and programs for themselves. This does not suggest that JVL has operated without outside assistance. On the contrary, JVL has sought and benefited from major outside private and public resources. But neighborhood leaders have been crucial both in initiating proposals and in taking responsibility for programs. No federal agency can take credit for creating the programs described in this study.

Self-help today is receiving a big boost as national policy. President Reagan and his domestic advisers seek to "restore confidence by returning power to the people." They promise less money for federal programs and advocate self-help as alternatives to government intervention. They suggest an urban policy that emphasizes local development zones, neighborhood development demonstrations, and private community involvement. Because JVL represents an exceptional case of individuals who helped themselves to improve their neighborhood, it may be tempting to use it as a national model of self-help.

But there are serious dangers when self-help is translated into national policy. First, self-help is premised on the ideology that individual neighborhoods have the ability to "pull themselves up by their bootstraps." But what value is such ideology for those without boots? The accomplishments of neighborhoods like JVL are all to be valued. But they are a dream or a cruel joke for those without resources, commitment, and leadership. Many, perhaps most, low-income neighborhoods require resources and initiatives from public programs. Government has a special responsibility to help neighborhoods that are unable to help themselves. Officials should not be permitted to retreat from official action and social responsibility in the name of self-help.

Second, self-help should not be used to divert attention from the context in which neighborhood planning operates. The shift in responsibility to the local area places the burden on the neighborhood to modify its response rather than on society to modify the conditions that create the problems. By singling out of the neighborhood, society is implicitly stating that the neighborhood somehow causes its social and economic problems. This is bad social science and inept social policy. Local problems result from a decision process and institutional context that operate largely outside a given neighborhood; the consequences and policy problems flow from the nature of the process. To alter the consequences, it is first necessary to alter the process. At its worst, self-help as national policy runs the danger of ignoring national obligations and of blaming the victim instead.

This is not intended to deny the importance of self-help as a means to neighborhood revitalization. Nor is it intended to discourage neighborhood organizations like JVL from forming, helping themselves, and working to change the whole social picture. JVL is an exceptional case of self-help that could be initiated elsewhere. But self-help, when it becomes an ideology wed to national policy, may also serve as a retreat from social responsibility and official action. And even the most accomplished neighborhood organization may be unable to save urban areas without public intervention in the larger context in which planning operates.

Notes

1. This chapter is based on work supported by the Graduate College Research Board of the University of Illinois at Urbana-Champaign. It draws on data from site visits, interviews, and neighborhood materials. Neighborhood organization leaders were contacted to enlist their cooperation, provide preliminary materials, and arrange site visits to obtain detailed information and conduct interviews with selected individuals. Neighborhood leaders were assured an opportunity to review drafts for accuracy prior to publication and asked to recommend and contact informed neighborhood sources. Interviews were conducted with organizational staff, board members, community residents, city officials, and others. More than 30 nonstandardized interviews were conducted, using an interview schedule designed to guide questions related to research. Chapter drafts were prepared and forwarded to neighborhood leaders for comment and verification of accuracy prior to publication. The views reported are solely those of the author, not Jeff-Vander-Lou or the University of Illinois. Among those who commented on earlier versions of this paper are Mary Comerio, Paul Davidoff, Jack Kirkland, Carl Patton, Jerome Pratter, Nelson Rosenbaum, and James Sporleder. Judith Lieberman assisted with research and contributed to initial drafts.

2. The JVL name derives from three principal neighborhood streets: Jefferson Avenue, Vandeventer Avenue, and St. Louis Avenue. The declared JVL boundaries are Jefferson on the east, Sarah on the west, Olive on the south, and Natural Bridge on the north.

References

Ahlbrandt, R. S., and P. C. Brophy. 1975. *Neighborhood revitalization*. Lexington, Mass.: Lexington Books.
Arnstein, S. 1969. A ladder of citizen participation. *Journal of the American*

Institute of Planners 35 (July):216–24.

Arrowhead Foundation. 1968. *Progress report*. St. Louis.

Bell, W., and M. T. Boat. 1957. Urban neighborhoods and informal social relations. *American Journal of Sociology* 62 (Jan.):391–95.

Berndt, H. E. 1977. *New rulers in the ghetto: The community development corporation and urban poverty*. Westport, Conn.: Greenwood Press.

Booth, H. 1977. *Direct action organizing*. Chicago: Midwest Academy.

Boyer, B. D. 1973. *Cities destroyed for cash: The FHA scandal at HUD*. Chicago: Follett.

Boyte, H. 1980. *The backyard revolution: Understanding the new citizen movement*. Philadelphia: Temple University Press.

Carnoy, M., and D. Shearer. 1980. *Economic democracy: The challenge of the 1980s*. White Plains, N.Y.: M. E. Sharpe.

Cassidy, R. 1980. *Livable cities: A grass-roots guide to rebuilding urban America*. New York: Holt Rinehart and Winston.

Center for Community Change and National Urban League. 1971. *The national survey of housing abandonment*. Washington, D.C.

Checkoway, B. 1981. The politics of public hearings. *Journal of Applied Behavioral Science* 17 (Oct.-Nov.-Dec.):566–82.

Checkoway, B., and J. Van Til. 1978. What do we know about citizen participation? A selective review of research. In S. Langton, ed., *Citizen participation in America*. Lexington, Mass.: D. C. Heath.

Cooper, K. 1979. Black leadership: A conceptual definition. *Proud* 10:23–26.

Curry, G. E. 1973. Stature for a plain black man. *St. Louis Post-Dispatch*, 6 July, p. 4D.

Downie, L. 1974. *Mortgage on America: The real cost of real estate speculation*. New York: Praeger.

Firey, W. 1945. Sentiment and symbolism as ecological variables. *American Sociological Review* 10 (Apr.):140–48.

Fischer, C. S. 1976. *The urban experience*. New York: Harcourt Brace Jovanovich.

Folkman, D. V., ed. 1978. *Urban community development: Case studies in neighborhood survival*. Madison: University of Wisconsin.

Gans, H. J. 1962. *The urban villagers: Group and class in the life of Italian-Americans*. New York: Free Press.

Goering, J. M. 1979. The national neighborhood movement: A preliminary analysis and critique. *Journal of the American Planning Association* 45 (Oct.):506–14.

Goetze, R. 1976. *Building neighborhood confidence: A humanistic strategy for urban housing*. Cambridge, Mass.: Ballinger.

Groves, E. 1971. Jeff-Vander-Lou: People power changes inner St. Louis. *Christian Living*, Sept., pp. 26–31.

Hartman, C. 1947. *Yerba Buena: Land grab and community resistance in San Francisco*. San Francisco: Glide Publications.

Hawley, A. H. 1950. *Human ecology*. New York: Ronald Press.

Holsendolph, E. 1976. Neighborhood turning to self help. *New York Times*, 6 July, p. 26.

Hoyt, H. 1939. *The structure and growth of residential neighborhoods.* Washington, D.C.: U.S. Government Printing Office.

Human Development Corporation of Metropolitan St. Louis. 1968. *Neighborhood handbook for Human Development Corporation and Model Cities Yeatman subcity.* St. Louis.

Hunter, A. 1974. *Symbolic communities: The persistence and change of Chicago's local communities.* Chicago: University of Chicago Press.

Jackson, W. 1972. Macler G. Shepard, president: Jeff-Vander-Lou Corporation. *Devil's Advocate*, Apr.-May, p. 5.

Jeff-Vander-Lou, Inc. 1967. *Application for demonstration grant.* St. Louis: Jeff-Vander-Lou for U.S. Department of Housing and Urban Development.

——. 1966. *By-laws of Jeff-Vander-Lou, Inc.,* St. Louis.

——. 1977. *Communications center proposal.* St. Louis.

Kinerk, A. M., et al. 1980. *Commercial revitalization: A strategy for Jeff-Vander-Lou Corporation.* St. Louis: Washington University, School of Architecture and Urban Design.

Kirkland, J. A. N.d. *An economic development consortium . . . to revitalize rehabilitate, and restore the Dr. Martin L. King, Jr. Ave., shopping mall.* St. Louis: Washington University, School of Social Work.

Lancourt, J. E. 1979. *Confront or concede: The Alinsky citizen action organizations.* Lexington, Mass.: Lexington Books.

Lee, C. 1978. A neighborhood that refused to die. *Proud* 8:4–10.

Leites, N., and C. Wolf. 1970. *Rebellion and authority.* Chicago: Markham.

Leven, C. L., et al. 1976. *Neighborhood change: Lessons in the dynamics of urban decay.* New York: Praeger.

Leven, C. L., and J. L. Weidenbaum. 1972. *Urban decay in St. Louis.* St. Louis: Washington University, Institute for Urban and Regional Studies.

Liebow, E. 1967. *Tally's corner: A study of Negro streetcorner men.* Boston: Little, Brown.

Maier, F. 1981. St. Louis. *Newsweek* 97 (4 May):35.

Marciniak, E. 1977. *Reviving an inner city community: The drama of urban change in Chicago's East Humboldt Park.* Chicago: Loyola University, Department of Political Science.

Marshall, K. K. 1972. Spotts Apartments: Proof of one woman's work and philosophy. *St. Louis Globe-Democrat*, 23 Oct., p. 17.

Mayer, N., and J. Blake. 1980. *Keys to the growth of neighborhood development organizations.* Washington, D.C.: Urban Institute.

McCarthy, J., and M. Zald. 1973. *The trend of social movements in America: Professionalization and resource mobilization.* Morristown, N.J.: General Learning Corp.

McGrath, E. 1981. St. Louis sings the blues. *Time* 117 (4 May):30.

Meehan, E. 1972. *Public housing policy: Convention versus reality.* New Brunswick, N.J.: Rutgers University Press.

Meier, R. 1975. *Findings of a survey of businesses on Martin Luther King Drive.* St. Louis: Washington University, School of Social Work.

Mendelson, R. E., and M. A. Quinn, eds. 1976. *The politics of housing in older urban areas.* New York: Praeger.

Miers, G. 1972. *Aritha.* St. Louis: Washington University, School of Architecture and Urban Design.

Moore, W. 1969. *The vertical ghetto: Everyday life in an urban project.* New York: Random House.

National Commission on Neighborhoods. 1979. *People, rebuilding neighborhoods.* Washington, D.C.: U.S. Government Printing Office.

National Training and Information Center. 1976. *The American nightmare.* Chicago.

Newman, O. 1972. *Defensible space: Crime prevention through urban design.* New York: Macmillan.

Ochsner and Associates. 1977. *Market study: Martin Luther King business district, St. Louis, Missouri.* Kansas City: Ochsner and Associates with Martin Luther King Business District Association and Jeff-Vander-Lou Corporation for the St. Louis Model City Agency.

Park, R. E., E. W. Burgess, and R. MacKenzie. 1925. *The city.* Chicago: University of Chicago Press.

Pratter, J. 1975. Corporations, cities, and planners: Brown Shoe Company in Jeff-Vander-Lou. Paper presented to the annual conference of the American Institute of Planners, San Antonio.

Pruitt-Igoe Neighborhood Corporation. 1966. *A dream deferred.* St. Louis.

Rainwater, L. 1970. *Behind ghetto walls: Black life in a federal slum.* Chicago: Aldine.

Riesenberger, B. 1977. St. Louis called 'unique' in urban rehabilitation. *St. Louis Post-Dispatch,* 8 Nov., p. 5.

Rohe, W. M., and L. B. Gates. 1981. Neighborhood planning: Promise and product. *Urban and Social Change Review* 14 (Winter):26–32.

St. Louis Community Development Agency. 1976. *Greater Tandy neighborhood plan.* St. Louis.

——. 1981. Yeatman JVL. *Environmental Review Record* 2:279–80.

Sawyer, K. 1981. St. Louis: A modern ghost town. *St. Louis Globe Democrat,* 13 Mar., p. A1.

Schmandt, H. J., G. D. Wendel, and A. E. Tomey. 1979. *The impact of federal aid on the city of St. Louis.* St. Louis: St. Louis University, Center for Urban Programs.

Schoenburg, S. P., and P. L. Rosenbaum. 1980. *Neighborhoods that work: Sources for the viability of the inner city.* New Brunswick, N.J.: Rutgers University Press.

Schweitzer, A. L. 1977. You don't get something for nothing. *St. Louis Globe Democrat,* 5 Dec., p. 17A.

Shevky, E., and M. Williams. 1949. *The social areas of Los Angeles.* Berkeley: University of California Press.

Short, W. G. *Publicity manual*. St. Louis: Training Center for Services.

Smith, F. 1978. Jeff-Vander-Lou, Inc. Testimony presented to the National Commission on Neighborhoods. St. Louis: Jeff-Vander-Lou.

Snipes, K. 1978. Jeff-Vander-Lou. In *People, building neighborhoods*. Washington, D.C.: National Commission on Neighborhoods.

Sporleder, J. H. 1972. *Housing monopoly*. St. Louis: Washington University, School of Social Work.

———. 1971. A place to live...limited options. *Proud* 2 (Apr.):16–20.

Starrels, E. 1975. *Pruitt-Igoe and Jeff-Vander-Lou rehabilitation*. St. Louis: Washington University, School of Architecture and Urban Design.

Stone, C. N. 1976. *Economic growth and neighborhood discontent: System bias in the urban renewal program of Atlanta*. Chapel Hill: University of North Carolina Press.

Stromberg, J. S. 1967. *A comparison of Pruitt-Igoe residents and their non-public housing neighbors*. St. Louis: Washington University, Social Science Institute.

Suttles, G. 1972. *The social construction of communities*. Chicago: University of Chicago Press.

———. 1968. *The social order of the slum*. Chicago: University of Chicago Press.

U.S. Office of Consumer Affairs. 1980. *People power: What communities are doing to counter inflation*. Washington, D.C.: U.S. Government Printing Office.

Urban Systems Research and Engineering, Inc. 1980. *Neighborhood planning primer*. Washington, D.C.: U.S. Department of Housing and Urban Development.

Washington Consulting Group. 1974. Jeff-Vander-Lou, Inc. In *Uplife: What people themselves can do*. Salt Lake City: Olympus Co.

Watson, M. 1977. Jeff-Vander-Lou against all odds. *Focus Midwest* 12 (Oct.):18–22.

Werth, J. T., and D. Bryant. 1979. *A guide to neighborhood planning*. Washington, D.C.: American Planning Association.

Wilson, J.Q. 1963. Planning and politics: Citizen participation in urban renewal. *Journal of the American Institute of Planners* 29 (Nov.):242–49.

Zald, M. N., and M. A. Berger. 1978. Social movements in organizations: Coup d'etat, insurgency and mass movements. *American Journal of Sociology* 83 (Jan.):823–61.

13

Chicago in the 1980s: Community, Politics, and Governance after Daley

MILTON RAKOVE

Any analysis of Chicago's major current problems and future prospects must begin with a realistic evaluation of the three entities that combine to form the totality of the city's body politic: the cultural, social, and economic community of Chicago; the political system of the city; and the governmental apparatus of the city, the county, and the other local government units that make up the composite governmental system of the Chicago metropolitan area. The city's present status and contemporary problems are rooted in the character, relationships, and dynamics of the triad, and its future prospects are inextricably bound up with both short- and long-term changes in these three entities. Furthermore, if the purpose of this inquiry is not only to describe and evaluate the city's current status, but also to suggest public policies to deal with current problems, then this purpose is best served by offering a clear analysis of the community, the political process, and the governmental system of Chicago.[1]

Community

It is, of course, a cliche, to say that the character of Chicago's community structure has changed significantly. But it is with this truism that our inquiry must begin. How has the Chicago community, as a social, cultural, and economic entity, changed over the past several decades?

Culturally, the city has moved from an ethnic community to a racial community. Chicago became a great city as a consequence of the enormous ethnic migrations from central, eastern, and southern Europe between about 1870 and 1920, when the city's population literally exploded, growing from approximately 100,000 to over 3 million people. At this time Chicago became a city of clearly defined, ethnically segregated, and parochially structured neighborhoods. It was not a sophisticated, homogeneous, cultural city but, rather, a highly decentralized collection of neighborhoods, peopled by a citizenry that was working-class socially, ethnic culturally, heavily Catholic religiously, and conservative politically (Kantowicz, 1975).

The great cultural change that has occurred in Chicago since World War II has been the black and Hispanic immigration to the city and a white working-class and middle-class outmigration from the city (Allswang, 1971; Drake and Cayton, 1944; Gosnell, 1935). These two migrations have changed both the makeup of the population and the character of the neighborhoods. There are practically no ethnic neighborhoods left in Chicago today. Instead Chicago has become a city of great racial areas—black, brown, and white. Most of the south side and much of the west side are black, large areas of the near southwest and near northwest sides are Hispanic, and the far southwest and northwest sides contain a heavy concentration of those white ethnics left in the city. The ethnic populations are no longer primarily ethnic but are culturally white before they are ethnic. In other words, race has replaced ethnicity as the dominant cultural factor in Chicago, and great racial areas have replaced small, close-knit ethnic neighborhoods as the basic community structure of the city. Those who talk about neighborhoods in Chicago are describing a past community pattern that barely exists in the present and probably has little future.

Another significant change that is occurring in Chicago is a substantial decline in the city's population (Skogan, 1976). The city continued to grow between 1920 and 1950, when the population peaked at 3,600,000, but Chicago has lost about 600,000 people since 1950. Even more significant is the fact that the population decline has gathered momentum in each decade. From 1950 to 1960 the city lost about 70,000 people, from 1960 to 1970 about 180,000 people, and from 1970 to 1980 about 360,000 people.

Coincident with that population decline has been an accompanying economic pattern that includes a substantial loss of manufacturing jobs to the suburbs and the sunbelt states and an increasing percentage of people working—but not producing anything—in low-paying Chicago service industries. The city's economic decline and the shift in its economic base mean that those who migrate to Chicago are coming to a city that no longer provides the same level of economic opportunity that the ethnic immigrants who came before found. The ethnics came to a growing city, with wide-open economic doors. The new immigrants, the blacks and Hispanics, have been moving to a declining city that offers fewer and less desirable economic opportunities. And, by settling in the central city, where they can afford to live, they separate themselves from the better job opportunities in the northwest and southwest suburbs, where they cannot afford to live.

The situation in which the more recent black and Hispanic immigrants to Chicago find themselves is exacerbated by two other factors. First, unlike the ethnics from central, eastern, and southern Europe, who came from a cultural, social, and economic background that inculcated in them both a work ethic and a savings ethic, the newer immigrants came from different kinds of backgrounds. The blacks came from a southern environment in which there was no work for them, in which they suffered exploitation and discrimination, and in which there was little hope or possibility for them to improve their situations by saving and accumulating money and property. The Mexicans and Puerto Ricans, too, came from countries where there was no work and no hope of changing their status in society. Given these realities, it has not been easy for those immigrants to sever their social and cultural ties with the past and break into the social and economic structure of a city like Chicago, especially since the economic doors are not open as they were for the ethnic immigrants.

Second, even if black or Hispanic immigrants accumulate some money and attempt to alter their social and cultural situations by moving to better neighborhoods, they are inhibited by racial discriminatory practices that make it difficult for them to move to the newer, better neighborhoods on the fringes of the city. And, unlike the ethnics, who created new neighborhoods in the vacant land areas of Chicago, the blacks and Hispanics have no such choices because there is little desirable vacant land on which they can create their own neighborhoods. The best they can hope for is to occupy older property vacated by migrating ethnics who are fleeing the black and Hispanic movement into the city, or to opt for some distant suburban development where prices might still be reasonable. This latter move would, of course, isolate them from the mass of people of their own race and culture.

A more recent development is beginning to affect the social and cultural character of Chicago as a community; this is the recent migration to the city of a new group of immigrants—Koreans, Japanese, Chinese, Filipinos, Indians, Pakistanis, Arabs, Cubans, and a substantial number of Greeks. Many among this new wave of immigrants are people with fairly good educational and professional backgrounds. They are different in many ways from the first wave of white ethnics, and from the more recent black, Mexican, and Puerto Rican migrants, better educated on the whole than all those groups were, highly motivated economically and socially, and at least as close-knit culturally as the original ethnic groups. This new wave clearly constitutes a major resource for the city and may become an influential segment of the population that will affect the city's future evolution and development significantly.

To sum up, Chicago as a community is changing. It is experiencing something of an economic decline; its population is diminishing, and changing, both racially and ethnically; the opportunities it offers are more limited than in the past; and its ethnic neighborhoods have been replaced by racial areas, so that race has replaced ethnicity as the dominant cultural factor in the city. But Chicago is still economically viable, culturally stimulating and adaptable, and socially mobile (Gove and Masotti, 1982).

Politics

Chicago's politics for much of the past half-century has been dominated by two major factors—the control of the city's political and governmental systems by the entrenched Democratic machine, and the prevalence of ethnic politics as the basis for the political practices of that machine.

Chicago's Democratic political machine, like most other big city machines, was built on a quid pro quo relationship among ethnic immigrants who came to the city during its period of explosive growth, politicians who sought political and governmental power, and private economic interest groups who pursued economic and financial power. The ethnic immigrants needed help to gain entrance and adapt to the urban environment, the politicians needed votes to gain and hold political power and public office, and the economic interest groups needed a viable labor force, good city services, and a cooperative, if not subservient, local government to provide them a decent economic environment and maximum profits.

The survival of Chicago's Democratic machine long after the other big city machines disappeared is a testament to the efficacy of that relationship. The Chicago machine has been more than a political organization. It was—and still is—a political/governmental/private interest-group coalition, whose constituent elements cooperated with each other in a common interest—the seizure, retention, and control of political and economic power. The ability to grasp and keep power also served the private interests of the politicians, public officials, and economic and financial overlords who were the key movers and shapers of the system.

The internal politics of the machine grew out of the cultural patterns of the city. Machine politics in Chicago was ethnic politics. That meant that ethnic groups in the city shared in the spoils of politics—jobs, money, contact, and influence—in proportion to their contributions to the electoral success of the machine. The Irish dominated both the political machine and the city and county government, but the Poles, Germans, Jews, Bohemians, Italians, and Lithuanians also took part and received recognition, jobs, influence, and status.

The great migration of blacks into Chicago and the exodus of much of the white population to the suburbs changed not only the cultural patterns of the city but also the internal politics of the machine. In Richard J. Daley's early years as Chicago's mayor the power base of the machine shifted from the ethnic areas of the city to the black wards. Black votes elected and re-elected Daley and kept the machine in power. The machine compensated black politicians by taking perquisites away from those ethnic groups who no longer contributed to the machine's electoral needs—Germans, Bohemians, Lithuanians, and Jews—and giving more to the blacks: not as much as the blacks wanted or felt they deserved, but as little as possible and as much as was necessary to keep black politicians quiescent and cooperative (O'Connor, 1975; Rakove, 1975; Royko, 1971).

In the later Daley years the internal politics of the machine began to change again. As the black population grew to become the largest entity in the city's body politic, the machine moved to defuse the threat of a black takeover of the machine and the city government. It shifted its efforts and altered the reward system to benefit the white ethnic wards of the southwest and northwest sides in order to establish a new power base in those areas. The inner city black ward organizations deteriorated in quality, voter registrations dropped significantly, and voter turnout on behalf of the machine's candidates fell precipitously. At the same time voter registration and turnout in the white ethnic wards on the southwest and northwest sides increased substantially. Chicago politics entered a new period of declining black influence and resurgent white dominance over the machine.

Within the black community a major political rift has appeared. The poor black areas of the city have generally remained faithful to the machine and its leaders, voting substantially, although in reduced numbers, for machine candidates in elections and following the dictates of the black and white machine politicians in their areas. But the middle-class black areas of the city have become centers of resistance to the traditional pattern of a delivered black vote. Middle-class black groups are increasingly critical of the old-style black machine politicians, and they are potential loci for a revolt against the machine and its policies. In other words, the black community is becoming ever more fragmented politically along economic and class lines, with poor blacks and the black machine politicians who represent that constituency on one side, and middle-class blacks who are emerging as independent of and hostile to the machine on the other side. This second group is organizing to force black political leaders to subordinate their machine ties to the interests and aspirations of the middle-class black community.

The great migration of Hispanics into Chicago is another major cultural factor that must be considered in evaluating Chicago's political present and future (Belenchia, 1982). The black migration is over, but the Hispanic migration, particularly the Mexican movement, is likely to continue for some years. The political impact of that migration is just beginning to be felt, for although the Mexicans have become a major social force in the city, they are not yet a political one. This, however, is almost certain to change in the near future as they settle in, become citizens, register, and vote. What political impact will the Hispanic migration have on the political machine and on the city's politics?

There are those who lump Hispanics and blacks together as minorities who are likely to coalesce politically and seize political and governmental power in Chicago from the white ethnics who control the machine and the city government. It is, however, much more probable that the white ethnics will form a coalition with the Hispanics, seduce their political leaders, make concessions to the interests and aspirations of this rapidly growing population, and use the aid of the Hispanics to fend off the middle-class black leadership's emerging thrust for power. The cultural, social, and economic underpinnings of this potential political alliance are already becoming clear. Hispanics identify culturally, religiously, and racially not with blacks but with white ethnics. Economically, Hispanics presently compete with blacks, not with white ethnics, for jobs and opportunities. In the schools Hispanic interest in bilingual education is irrelevant to blacks, and competition between Hispanics and blacks for control of school policies and funds is a growing fact of life. Given these realities, a future alliance of white ethnics and Hispanics is probably the next step in the evolution of Chicago's ethnic and racial politics.

That possibility has not materialized as yet because the Hispanics, like the poor blacks in the city who have been steadily dropping out of the political process, do not vote in any significant numbers. The illegal immigrants cannot vote, and many Hispanics who can vote do not do so because they have language problems, are unfamiliar with the system, are unwilling to commit themselves to permanent residency, or are fundamentally suspicious of the governmental process.

The black voter dropout and the Hispanic unwillingness to register and vote have left Chicago with a large and steadily growing percentage of its population divorced from the political process and unable to influence politics as the ethnic immigrants did. The city is in a situation in which much of its population has become irrelevant politically and, consequently, governmentally. As a result, whites hold political and governmental power in Chicago far in excess of their percentage of the city's population. It is not a healthy situation.

The machine's domination of the city's politics is also undergoing a metamorphosis. That change, which became evident after the death of Mayor Richard J. Daley, actually began in the late Daley years. These years were marked by a weakening of the monolithic control Daley and the machine had over the city's political and governmental systems, but Daley was so entrenched that he and the machine fended off any serious challenge. Daley and the machine lost some battles—to Dan Walker, Richard Ogilvie, Bernard Carey, and two state supreme court primary nomination contests—but they were still able to win the war.

The weakening of the machine's hold on the city's electorate manifested itself in the central core of the machine's usual strength in the 1975 mayoral primary, when Daley, in his last run for office, garnered only about 60 percent of the Democratic vote. His three opponents—William Singer, Richard Newhouse, and Edward Hanrahan—together received 40 percent of the Democratic primary vote. Singer has since argued that he beat the machine in the primary but that Daley's personal appeal and following, not the machine, ensured Daley's victory. In the 1977 Democratic mayoral primary two years later, Michael Bilandic, the machine's candidate for nomination, won only 50 percent of the primary vote, while Hanrahan, Roman Pucinski, and Harold Washington split the other 50 percent. It was clear that a new day was dawning in the internal politics of the machine, and that new day came when Jane Byrne defeated the machine's Bilandic in the 1979 Democratic mayoral primary. Byrne's victory showed that an antimachine coalition of dissident white ethnics, angry blacks, lake-front liberals, and cross-over Republicans, although unstructured and not formally organized, could defeat the machine in its key effort, the mayoral primary.

The machine's defeat reflected the concatenation of three forces on the contemporary Chicago political scene: the machine's growing inability to pacify both the white ethnics and the blacks at the same time; the gradual erosion of the machine's basic strength in the city's neighborhoods, caused by the deterioration of the machine's organizations in many wards; and the significantly increased power of the media, especially television, to influence the voters and the electoral process of the city.

Those three trends are still continuing and are probably accelerating since Byrne came to power in Chicago. In her years in office Mayor Byrne lost the support of the middle-class black community, much of the white ethnic constituency, and most of the liberals. The caliber of most of the machine's ward organization has continued to deteriorate. And the 6 o'clock and 10 o'clock television news has replaced precinct workers and newspapers as the voter's major source of information about the city's political goings on. Television now colors and influences voter thinking about the effectiveness of Chicago's leaders and their ability to deal with the city's problems. Senator Edward Kennedy's defeat in Chicago in the 1980 presidential primary and State's Attorney Richard M. Daley's double victory over the machine in both the primary and general elections testify to the realities of the new Chicago politics.

This development has deprived the city of one of its most stable elements, the political machine, an ongoing, conservative, entrenched, and efficient organization that provided Chicago with the major components of a successfully functioning system. The machine gave stability, continuity, responsible power, and a mechanism that reflected, responded to, and dealt with the prejudices, conflicts, and problems of the city's body politic. The consequences of its decline are significant although, as yet, difficult to fathom and impossible to predict.

Governance

Like the city's cultural, social, and economic community and its political system, Chicago's governmental system is in the throes of change. The linkage between the three major entities of Chicago's body politic—the community, the political system, and the governmental process—continues to affect all three. The changes in the structure of the community and the dynamics of the political system are reflected in the contemporary formulation and execution of public policies by the city government.

As is typical in the evolution of political and governmental systems, there are some things that are new in Chicago's contemporary governmental process, but there is also much that is old. Chicago might be said to be experiencing the Hegelian dialectic of a historical process, in which a force creates a new opposing force, which then merges with the old to become a status quo. As Edmund Burke once wrote, "Society is ... a partnership not only between those who are living, but between

those who are living, those are dead, and those who are to be born"
(1790, pp. 143–44).

Burke's dictum holds true in Chicago government today. The past is
still with us, even while the present has come upon us. And the future
will inevitably be affected by both past and present. Richard J. Daley is
dead, but his memory, pervasive image, and legacy linger on. The shape
and character of Chicago's governmental system are hard to foresee.
However, the present operation and effectiveness of the city government
can be described and evaluated. This analysis can best be done by
looking separately at the three governmental organs that control and
affect the formulation and execution of public policy—the city council,
the bureaucracy, and the office of the mayor—and then by examining the
composite governmental whole.

Chicago's contemporary city council, following Hegel's dialectic and
Burke's dictum, is a meld of past practices and present changes. Given
the mix of those two ingredients, its future prospects as an effective
legislative body are not good. The council reflects both the racial fragmentation of the community and the deterioration of the political
machine. Those two underlying forces dominate legislative clashes in
the city council, within the continuing general rubric of mayoral control of the council.

To understand the contemporary council, one must understand its
past half-century history. Before Mayor Daley took office, the council
was controlled by the political machine through the influence of a group
of powerful Democratic party ward committeemen who also served as
aldermen. Those committeemen/aldermen made up the budget, allocated governmental funds, passed out patronage jobs, and controlled
public policies. In other words, Chicago's city council was subordinate
to the dictates of the political machine as expressed by the most powerful
committeemen/aldermen.

Daley changed all that by taking control of the budget and thus of the
perquisites of politics—jobs, money, and influence (Rakove, 1982).
Daley, not the ward committeemen, dominated the council after 1955.
The council became not a legislative body but merely a ratifying
assembly, approving whatever Mayor Daley proposed. The once powerful committeemen/aldermen became eunuchs who represented no
longer their wards but rather the public will of the city as it was interpreted by Daley.

The council is being forced to reflect and respond to the pressures of
the deepening racial fragmentation of the city. In addition, the aldermen
have been cast adrift by the deterioration of the ward organizations in
their neighborhoods and the increased impotence of the position of

ward committeemen, for most aldermen are still ward committeemen themselves or are chosen and controlled by their ward committeemen. During Byrne's term, the black aldermen had to balance the racial interests of their constituents against their obligations as minions of the political machine as its interests were formulated by Mayor Byrne. Similarly, the white aldermen had to balance the wishes of their constituencies against their need to live with the mayor. A few aldermen, in deference to the concept of the council as a supposed legislative body, tried to maintain some semblance of independence. All of them were prisoners of several new realities: Jane Byrne was not Richard J. Daley; the system remained the same as in the Daley years, but the game was not being played as well; and the aldermen's roles and obligations were greatly complicated by the changing racial situation in the community and the deterioration of the political machine. In other words, the council as a body was behaving as it did when Daley was alive and directing its proceedings, but it played a subordinate role to a weakened political machine. The aldermen's roles and loyalties had been further fragmented and bifurcated by their need to represent their racial constituencies in the city's body politic. It became too much for many of them, so they existed from session to session, doing little, voting faithfully, and hoping to survive their time of troubles.

This condition of ennui has been exacerbated by another development within the city's body politic that has thrown the aldermen's role as legislative representatives out of kilter—the fact that Chicago is no longer a city of ethnic neighborhoods but has become a city of racial areas. The old ward system was closely tied to ethnic neighborhoods, and representation in both the political and governmental system, that is, in the Democratic party's central committee and the city council, was generally worked out on that basis. But in a city made up of great racial areas it is much more difficult for aldermen and committeemen from wards to keep in touch with the desires and aspirations of their constituencies. In other words, the political organization (the machine) and the system of governmental representation (the city council) have become increasingly separated from and irrelevant to the community they are supposed to represent.

Given all of these forces and conditions, plus the fact that legislative bodies like Chicago's council are, by definition, ineffective and inefficient, it is too much to hope that the city council will become a relevant, representative, and effective legislative body in the foreseeable future. One has to look elsewhere in the governmental system of Chicago for that possibility.

What of the city bureaucracy as a functioning governmental organ that can maintain and further the quality of life for Chicago's citizenry? Here, too, one must go back to the past in order to understand the present and anticipate the future. Again Daley's tenure is significant, especially in the crucial role he played in creating an effective bureaucracy during his more than 20 years of rule in Chicago.

Before Daley the city bureaucracy, like the city council, was subservient to the political machine and its most powerful ward committeemen. Daley's major contribution to effective government in Chicago was to strengthen the bureaucracy at the expense of the ward committeemen, thus altering the balance of power between those two elements in favor of the appointed public officials who governed the city. Daley recruited, appointed, and supervised a cadre of professionals to direct the major city departments. These officials were responsible to him, not to the council or the ward committeemen. Daley formulated public policies, the council ratified them, and his administrators (who were beholden not to the politicians but to him) carried them out.

Daley was a superb administrator as well as a great politician. He understood finances, taxes, and revenue. He also had an intuitive, life-long grasp of bureaucratic procedures. And he knew that governments survive or fall not on how well they deal with great issues but on how well they service the basic needs of the citizenry. His successor, Mayor Michael Bilandic, who also understood that principle, maintained Daley's basic policies until he was brought down by the collapse of the city's public services during the great snowstorm in the winter of 1979.

Mayor Jane Byrne shook Daley's bureaucracy to its very foundations. She replaced every major administrator except one from the Daley era, probably because she trusted no one from the past. In her first years in office she thus brought down the Daley system in Chicago without creating one of her own. The expulsion of the Daley administrators and the subsequent revolving doors in the major city departments created instability at the top of the bureaucracy and a passion for anonymity and survival at the lower levels.

But, despite her break with the past, Byrne still had deep and instinctive ties to the old system. She changed the players but not the game. As a part of the political machine, and as a long-time city hall bureaucrat herself, she relied on the machine's traditional practices for public policies and its philosophic foundations for guidance. She knew that the collapse of public services had brought Bilandic down, so she staked her program for the city on good public services. And Byrne stabilized the city bureaucracy to some extent, after a shaky and erratic start. She pursued traditional patronage practices, rewarded supporters, punished opponents, and made her peace with most of the powerful ward committeemen.

Byrne's mayoralty was also marked by the formalization of a power shift that began in the Daley years, was continued and strengthened during Bilandic's mayoral term, and was enhanced after Byrne took office—the evolution of a powerful mayor, in fact if not in legal status.

Legally, Chicago has a modified weak mayor/strong council form of government, since the council has the legal power to do almost anything, including stripping the mayor of authority and seizing control of the budget, which is the core of real city government power. But, as has been pointed out in this essay, Daley strengthened his power as mayor, both formally by getting control of budget planning and execution, and informally by using his power as chairman of the Cook County Democratic Central Committee to take control of the city council and of public policies. In these ways Daley became a powerful mayor.

Concentration of power in the mayor's office continued and advanced during Mayor Bilandic's two-year term. The Democratic machine, the party organization, became decentralized and weakened under its new chairman, George Dunne, when control of city patronage passed after Daley's death to Bilandic and his deputy, Tom Donovan, who were neither ward committeemen nor members of the political organization's ruling body, the county central committee. The decentralization of power in the political organization fragmented the machine. But under Bilandic's and Donovan's control, the bureaucracy in the city government remained highly centralized and grew in power. This powerful bureaucracy strengthened the mayor, Bilandic, at the expense of the politicians, that is, the ward committeemen, and at the expense of the party's governing body, the county central committee and its chairman, George Dunne.

That power shift and mayoral strengthening was further formalized and accepted under Mayor Byrne, who recognized the new strength in the mayoralty and moved quickly to stake out control of patronage and perquisites while retaining domination of the city council. The party organization was even further weakened under Byrne. Chicago had a powerful mayor, a weak party chairman, a passive city council, a potentially strong bureaucracy, and a coterie of relatively ineffective ward committeemen.

But Byrne also became a prisoner of many forces and cleavages in the Chicago community and its political and governmental systems. The deepening racial gap between the growing middle-class black constituency, which is demanding more political and governmental power, and the entrenched white ethnic leadership and its supporters, who are unwilling to surrender control to the blacks, cost her some support in both groups. She was unable to pacify and satisfy the more vocal and intransigent elements in the two constituencies. As for Chicago's liberals, Byrne's unwillingness to move forward rapidly on a broad front to resolve the city's deep social problems alienated most of them.

To compensate for her declining support from the coalition that elected her, Byrne moved to strengthen her ties to other elements in the city's body politic. In doing so, she sought supporters for her program and allies for her re-election effort in 1983. She tried to solidify her bonds to the traditional machine constituency in Chicago, the ward committeemen and precinct workers, to re-establish the connections to the business, labor, and media interests, to reach out to the poor black voters, and to blunt the developing hostility of the northwest- and southwest-side white ethnics. For the politicians, Byrne promised patronage, influence, status, and economic rewards. For the businessmen, she offered a projected building boom in the Loop and its environs, sound fiscal practices, and concessions to their interests as bankers, real estate developers, and entrepreneurs who seek profits in Chicago. For the unions, after a series of confrontations with teachers, firemen, and CTA workers in Byrne's first years, there was a quieter period of collective bargaining and of continued influence for the old-time leadership. For the broadcast and print media, Byrne provided a plethora of news, happenings, and personal exposure that helped guarantee an expanding audience for their news shows and daily publications. For the poor blacks, there were still political jobs and services and dramatic appeals like the temporary mayoral residence in a public housing unit. For the ethnics, Byrne displayed resistance to school busing and integration programs and facilitated their representation on and control of the school board. And for everybody, there was a continuing stream of Chicago chauvinism, parades, festivals, neighborhood events, and an expanded Chicagofest.

But deep, underlying problems remained. Mayor Byrne did not create those problems, nor did her predecessors, mayors Daley and Bilandic. They were caused by the great changes in the American national, social, economic, and political community, which have unleashed forces that local city governments in this country can seldom control or influence. Local governments have been powerless to halt or interfere with the great post–World War II migrations of poor blacks and Hispanics into the cities and of the white middle classes to the suburbs. Nor have they been able to deal with the social and economic problems these migrations have engendered in their communities. In addition, the population decline of the cities and the growth of the suburbs have weakened the political influence of cities on national and state politics and on governmental policies.

Those trends have been gathering momentum for years in Chicago. Mayor Richard J. Daley could not block those forces or solve the social problems of Chicago. But he did maintain a fairly tight hold on his city, postponed the impending deterioration, shifted the financial burdens of Chicago to county, state, national, and other local governments, and kept the city's problems under control. He did not heal Chicago's social ills of illiteracy, poverty, racial tension, inadequate health care, and neighborhood decline. It may nevertheless be true, given the realities of the root causes of the city's decline, of its inherent inability to deal adquately with those enormous forces, and of Daley's own philosophical, social, and political limitations, that he did as much, and probably more, than any mayor could have done during his tenure in office.

Those social problems are still with us—unsolved, underfinanced, and increasing in intensity as the city continues to decline and the trends and forces set in motion by the events of the past three decades continue to affect it. The white exodus to the suburbs continues. The hoped-for return of the expatriates has not materialized. The city's economic decline in contrast to the suburbs and the sunbelt states shows no sign of reversal. Chicago's loss of population means reduced political power and diminished influence on state and national governments. The racial bifurcation of the city's population inhibits the creation of a political consensus in the city's body politic, which would be the necessary prelude to successful governmental action. The city's political machine is in a state of drift and deterioration. And the governmental apparatus of Chicago, reflecting the divisions of the community and the lethargy of the political system, is marking time, unsure of what to do and where to go next. In such a milieu the adoption of public policies designed to deal with the city's burgeoning social problems would seem to be difficult at best.

Even so, there is no rational alternative to moving rapidly in that direction. The Daley years, which were characterized by control of the community and the political and governmental processes of the city while leaving the root causes of Chicago's social problems untouched, are over. The Bilandic interregnum was a continuation of the Daley years and the Daley policies. And the Byrne term of office saw the initial destruction of the Daley system followed by an attempt to return to that system. Byrne stressed good public services, fiscal responsibility, and physical rejuvenation of the Loop and its environs at the governmental level while she continued Daley's practices of patronage, interest-group pacification, and machine politics at the political level.

Those policies no longer work in Chicago. The Daley years are over, and the Daley policies cannot solve the problems of a city and a body politic in which the social and cultural communal fabric is disrupted by increasing racial tensions, the economic life of the city deteriorates, and the political system is inert. What is needed instead is a realistic appraisal of the problems, an understanding of the contemporary dynamics of the community, a restructuring of the political system to make it reflect and represent the contemporary body politic, and a redirection of governmental processes toward improved schools, better race relations, good health care, and neighborhood revitalization.

During the War of 1812, when the British redcoats were attacking New Orleans and the American cannoneers were firing over the heads of the advancing British soldiers, Andrew Jackson was supposed to have ordered his artillerymen, "Elevate them guns a little lower!" Perhaps that is what we need to do in Chicago: not to spike the guns of public policy, or to fire them randomly at the same old targets, but to "elevate them a little lower" in order to reduce, and perhaps even wipe out, the social problems of the city—to make it, if no longer a great city, at least a decent place in which to live, work, raise families, and retire.

Note

1. An earlier version of this paper was delivered to the City Club of Chicago, Sept. 1981. As this version was going to press, Milton Rakove died. We did not wish to alter Rakove's thoughts by revising the chapter to reflect changes in Chicago between the time he completed this paper and publication. The reader will note, however, that Rakove's observations still hold even after the election of Mayor Harold Washington. The machine has not been rebuilt, the city council remains divided on critical issues, and race rather than ethnicity operates as a dominant force.—Eds.

References

Allswang, J. M. 1971. *A house for all peoples.* Lexington: University of Kentucky Press.

Belenchia, J. 1982. Latinos and Chicago politics. In S. K. Gove and L. H. Masotti, eds., *After Daley: Chicago politics in transition.* Urbana: University of Illinois Press, pp. 118–45.

Burke, E. 1790. *Reflections on the revolution in France*. London: J. Dodsley.

Drake, St. C., and H. Cayton. 1944. *Black metropolis*. New York: Harcourt Brace.

Gosnell, H. F. 1935. *Negro politicians: The rise of Negro politics in Chicago*. Chicago: University of Chicago Press.

Gove, S. K., and L. H. Masotti, eds. 1982. *After Daley: Chicago politics in transition*. Urbana: University of Illinois Press.

Kantowicz, E. R. 1975. *Polish-American politics in Chicago 1888–1940*. Chicago: University of Chicago Press.

O'Connor, L. 1975. *Clout*. New York: Avon.

Rakove, M. 1975. *Don't make no waves, don't back no losers*. Bloomington: University of Indiana Press.

———. 1982. *Jane Byrne and the new Chicago politics*. In S. K. Gove and L. H. Masotti, eds., *After Daley: Chicago politics in transition*. Urbana: University of Illinois Press, pp. 217–36.

Royko, M. 1971. *Boss*. New York: Signet.

Skogan, W. G. 1976. *Chicago since 1840: A time series analysis*. Urbana: University of Illinois, Institute of Government and Public Affairs.

14

Metropolitan Government and Planning: Lessons in Shared Power

ROBERT C. EINSWEILER

The Twin Cities of St. Paul and Minneapolis, like many midwestern metropolitan areas, have undergone significant population changes in recent years. These include an increase in total population, a significant shift in migration both to and from the region, and a wave of internal population movement from the center of this metropolitan area to its periphery.

During the decade of the 1940s population in the Twin Cities region increased by 185,000. Regionwide population growth peaked during the 1960s, with an increase of 349,000 persons, and slowed in the 1970s, with a regionwide increase of only 111,000 persons. These gross totals were affected by a net migration into the region of 108,000 persons in the 1960s as the rural-to-urban population shift peaked, and by a net outmigration of 41,000 persons as a new pattern of exurban settlement began in the 1970s. The population change within the region is reflected in population figures for the central cities. Although Minneapolis and St. Paul together increased by 53,000 persons during the 1940s, in the next three decades they experienced increasing losses of 37,000, 52,000, and then 103,000.

These population redistribution patterns posed challenges for Twin Cities planners. Their primary task was to cope with this wavelike change by dealing with both the sharp population increases on the advancing edge of the expanding region and the sharp population decreases that spread from the region's center.

The geographical growth of the Twin Cities expanded the federal definition of the metropolitan area from four counties in 1940, to five counties for the 1950 and 1960 censuses, to seven counties in 1972, and to ten counties for the 1980 census. The population growth spread across an increasingly fine grain of suburban jurisdictions. The number of contiguous incorporated municipalities grew from 22 in 1950, to 76 in 1960, and to 103 in 1970.

The Metropolitan Council[1] of the Twin Cities was formed in 1967 to respond to this metropolitan growth. Established as a means to guide development in the region, the council, in one of its first efforts, blocked the building of a major airport on an environmentally sensitive site. It also prevented construction of a heavy rail transit system. Subsequently the council worked with both special districts to expand the air and ground transit systems in ways that would create a minimal disruption to the region's unique environment. In other spheres the council and its subordinate sewer board organized the region's fragmented sanitary sewer systems into one management entity and extended service to areas scheduled for development. In cooperation with the counties and central cities, the council expanded the regional park and trail system, and it joined local governments to establish a nationally recognized program of subsidized housing in both the suburbs and the central cities. Later accomplishments included a regional program in land use planning, farmland preservation, and regional capital investment, all backed up by legislation. These accomplishments are only a partial list of the council's work.

This chapter builds on earlier analyses of the Metropolitan Council by discussing the "lessons" of this successful case. It argues that four key organizing concepts distinguished this regional government from others, that these concepts proved beneficial, and that they could be applied elsewhere. It also shows that any innovative approach to planning and development requires regular review and evaluation to keep it from reverting to traditional patterns.

Rapid urban expansion in the Twin Cities region created problems that required physical service solutions. The Metropolitan Council was invented to provide such solutions, but its guiding principles could be applied to a broad range of urban problem solving. The four key concepts of the Metropolitan Council eventually embodied in legislation were: (1) a strong, interactive relation to the state legislature; (2) the separation of policy from operation; (3) the direct relating of planning to decision making; and (4) representation by population-equal districts, not by local government, on the policy board.

This chapter is written by a participant-observer who worked for the Metropolitan Planning Commission during its last eight years and for the Metropolitan Council during its first four years. He has been engaged since then as a private consultant in council evaluations. The author is an acknowledged pro-metropolitan planner who initially had doubts about the concepts described in this chapter.

Relation to the Legislature

Minnesota has both one of the higher percentages of local governments and one of the lower ratios of special districts per capita in the nation (Baldinger, 1971). This pattern of governance reflects a strong belief that government should remain close to the people. However, the post–World War II building boom created water pollution, sewage disposal, transit, and open-space problems that exceeded the capacities of small local governments. Furthermore, the multiplicity of local jurisdictions necessitated complex contractual arrangements in order to provide facilities that extended beyond individual borders.

Historically, the Minnesota legislature has been responsive to local and metropolitan area needs, a responsiveness that may stem in part from the state's small legislative districts (Harrigan and Johnson, 1978; Kolderie, 1973). For example, there are almost twice as many legislators as councilmen in Minneapolis, and almost eight times as many legislators as county board members in Hennepin County. Moreover, legislative responsiveness is necessary, because use of the referendum is severely restricted.

Until the mid-1950s the typical legislative solution to a metropolitan problem was the creation of a special metropolitan district governed by representatives from the two central cities. The first one, the Minneapolis–St. Paul Sanitary District (MSSD), came into being in 1933. In the 1950s MSSD extended services by contract to suburbs. As the years passed, the legal complexities of subordinate contracts through first-, second-, and third-tier suburbs became so intricate that this approach to service grew increasingly difficult. Furthermore, the extension of city services to suburbs that competed against each other economically raised political problems. The absence of suburban representation on the Minneapolis–St. Paul Sanitary District also became an issue (Einsweiler, 1976). A political outcry arose when the Metropolitan Airport Commission (MAC), which also lacked suburban representation, located airports in the suburbs. As the legislature wrestled with metropolitan area problems, it found that the special district solution would not work, and it lacked the staff expertise to devise new solutions. Thus the legislature gave more attention to the Metropolitan Council concept.

The community also sensed a need for a problem-solving authority that had the ability to coordinate and control independent metropolitan districts. Clayton LeFevere expressed one view when he said at a public meeting: "Whatever structure of government is finally agreed upon . . . that structure will be like a vessel into which certain metropolitan or regional problems are poured, one at a time. It will not be possible to decide in advance whether we're going to feed one, two, or three or a dozen problems into this organization. Government structure is always a growing and changing thing" (Twin Cities Metropolitan Planning Commission, 1966, p. 1). Verne Johnson, then executive director of the Citizens League, expressed a complementary viewpoint: "The Legislature must do one of two things. By constitutional amendment or some other way it must become the policy and budget agency for all of the various single-purpose special districts. Or it must allow the Metropolitan Area to organize itself . . ." (Twin Cities Metropolitan Planning Commission, 1966, p. 1).

During the 1967 legislative session the metropolitan area supporters pushed their view, while a powerful group in the Senate pursued a different approach. Both agreed on the principle that such an agency should be "non-home rule . . . exercising only those powers and responsibilities specifically granted by the legislature" (Baldinger, 1971, p. 95). The two sides disagreed about the extent of authority that should be vested in such an agency. The community wanted devolved decision-making authority to execute solutions for legislatively specified problems. The conservative senators envisioned a state administrative agency that would be a research arm of the Senate or state legislature and that would advise on specific individual solutions for legislative action.

There was a precedent for the Senate view. The Twin Cities Metropolitan Planning Commission (TCMPC), created in 1957, was established to address metropolitan problems (Minnesota Laws, 1957, c. 468). Initially the commission adopted a local point of view, but the legislature soon changed this by requiring biennial reports on activities, finances, and proposed work programs (Minnesota Laws, 1963, c. 866; 1965, c. 501). For the 1965 session the TCMPC prepared a report on necessary legislative actions for metropolitan problems. In the fall of 1966 the TCMPC prepared position papers on each item of legislation needed to implement the metropolitan plan or solve a current critical problem, and during the 1967 legislative session the TCMPC staff prepared anonymous overnight critiques of all metropolitan bills as requested by chairs of the House and Senate metropolitan committees. A former chairman of the TCMPC was an advisor to the leader of the powerful conservative Senate group during this 1967 session. By 1967, then, the TCMPC was responding to local problems by advising both the local governments and the legislature.

The 1967 legislature passed a Metropolitan Council bill that essentially embodied the state research agency concept. The taxing authority of TCMPC was also incorporated into the Metropolitan Council bill because 1967 was a year when appropriations would be difficult to pass. The incorporation led to an opinion by the attorney general declaring the new Metropolitan Council to be a unique agency between state and local governments and possessing attributes of each (Head and Hartfeldt, 1967).

Subsequent legislation, most notably in 1969 and 1974, has given the Metropolitan Council the three capabilities most widely sought by both sides. The first is the capacity to evolve, to change form and structure in response to changing regional needs and demands. The second is the devolved authority to coordinate special districts: sewers, airports, transit, and open space (Gleeson, 1976; Harrigan and Johnson, 1978; Knudson, 1976; Naftalin and Brandl, 1980). (This substantial achievement was less than the elected, operating metropolitan-scale local government many of the most ardent council supporters desired.) The third is the power to function as an advisor to the legislature. The influence of the council's proposals is demonstrated by the legislation—over a dozen major bills—passed to implement them (Harrigan and Johnson, 1978; Naftalin and Brandl, 1980).

Separation of Policy and Operation

A common assertion in public administration is that policy is the realm of the elected official, and operation or administration is the realm of staff. Although this view is generally discounted as too simplistic, a version of it was incorporated into the design of the metropolitan agency. At the time the agency was being formed, one of the key actors in the Citizens League had just participated in an evaluation of the Minneapolis school board, and he had been struck by how the board continually bogged down in day-to-day contract problems. He noted that the preoccupation with such routine administrative matters left the school board with little time for the major policy issues that confronted this central city school system during a crisis period marked by population decline, increasing segregation, and an aging faculty. Because of this experience, he proposed to separate metropolitan policy setting from operation by vesting each in a separate, but related, agency (Baldinger, 1971; Harrigan and Johnson, 1978).

There were additional reasons for this division. Another league participant had been struck with Alfred P. Sloan's description of a similar problem in his days as head of General Motors, where he had introduced a policy-administration separation (Baldinger, 1971; Harrigan and Johnson, 1978). Furthermore, several pressing problems required policy decisions on such matters as where facilities should be located, how services should be priced, and who should pay for them. Existing operating agencies—state, metropolitan, district, or local government—could implement, but their views were either functionally or geographically too narrow. An agency with a broader view and a capacity to make binding policy was needed.

An initial test of the separation concept came in late 1968 and early 1969 when the council drafted legislation for the first proposed subordinate board, the Metropolitan Sewer Board (MSB). The proposed law would reserve policy authority to the council and allocate operating authority to the board. But because the policy function would have no meaning without the authority to make it stick, council supporters in 1966–67 had come to see control of finance as the means both to enforce policy and to tie policy to operation. This emphasis on financing closely resembled Sloan's General Motors view.

The council staff, however, viewed programming as the most important link. Without it, they saw no way to control the location of sewer extensions and, in turn, the pattern of development. They also realized that in urban development little is more political than the programming of capital facilities (American Planning Association, 1980). Elected officials and operating agencies compete for program control, and because a program is a scheduled allocation of projects, it is the document in which political promises are either fulfilled or renounced.

In the spring of 1970 the first policy plan on sewers was completed. However, only the Sewer Board had access to data to prepare a capital program, and the topic was especially sensitive because the Sewer Board was in the midst of buying out the existing regional sewer system facilities owned by local governments. In this setting the council chairman asked the Sewer Board to prepare the policy program.

The Sewer Board met with local governments and moved aggressively to meet their needs. Because acquisition was still incomplete, it was impossible to know how much the total system would cost and what the cost of operation would be. Thus there was no basis for calculating bills to local governments for service, and so price did not restrain local government requests for new facilities. The list of proposed projects grew long. If approved, it would open new areas for development. The plan had strong local support. Although the board and the council fought with each other over how large the program should be, the council eventually approved the board's larger, more expensive program, with certain limited exceptions and conditions, including a requirement for a five-year program (Kolderie, 1973). Today the region still has some areas with excess sewer capacity.

The lines of power remained fuzzy. In 1974 the Metropolitan Reorganization Act collected, augmented, and codified all prior laws as *Metropolitan Government* (Minnesota Statutes Annotated, c. 473). Even here, however, the programming issue was not fully clarified. The council was directed to establish general parameters of timing, cost, and location. The Sewer Commission (formerly Board) was charged with preparing details on these items and also on methods of financing, impacts, and noncapital alternatives (MSA secs. 473.146 and 473.161). However, the Metropolitan Council program element for sewers usually lists actual projects rather than limiting itself to general parameters. To link policy and operation, programming must be a shared power, but as this history illustrates, an adequate process of sharing that power has yet to be developed.

In spite of these difficulties, the concept of the separation of policy and operation has been continuously supported and put into effect. In 1966 the region was governed by a group of agencies as peers; no agency exercised control over another. In 1967 the Metropolitan Council, by virtue of its power to veto plans or actions contrary to council policy, was elevated above the special district. In 1969 the new subordinate boards were created—the Metropolitan Sewer Board and the Metropolitan Open Space Board—to which the council could give positive policy direction. Then in 1974 two existing districts came under similar positive direction—the Metropolitan Transit Commission and the Metropolitan Airports Commission—and the council also became a regional housing authority. With the Land Planning Act of 1976, local governments also came under council direction for development related to regional systems. In the same year major private sector developments were coordinated under the Metropolitan Significance Act.

Relation of Planning to Decision Making

Metropolitan Planning Commission members represented all types of government—central cities, suburbs, counties, townships, school districts, and special metropolitan districts—in a ratio analogous to today's weighted-representation councils of government. The TCMPC members were advisors rather than decision makers, planners rather than politicians. Yet they and the TCMPC staff, influenced by the works of Chapin (1963), Fagin (1959), and Mitchell (1961), saw the need for an approach that related planning to decisions. Both Chapin and Fagin were in fact consultants to the program. A Citizens League report reveals that this approach achieved some measure of success:

> The program dealt not so much in specific proposals about *what*, that is what roads or transit lines or commercial centers or parks were to be built, as in proposals for *the way in which the decisions were to be made* about the location of these major facilities. The thrust of the effort was to understand the process of development and to bring the key elements of the process under public control. This was part of a conscious decision to concentrate on implementation rather than newer, more sophisticated research techniques. (Citizens League, 1968, p. 20)

The effort was hampered in several ways, however. Agreements with federal funding agencies required use of mathematical models and a rational, goal-oriented planning process. Lack of experience on the part of staff, combined with the absence of recorded experience with this newer planning approach, caused slippage in schedules and occasional changes of direction (Boyce, 1970). As the schedules extended, the TCMPC and staff were diverted from work on specific water, sewer, and transit issues. This period of confusion culminated in the resignation of the chairman of the commission in 1966 and a challenge to the agency to become more relevant to the public agenda.

July 1966 witnessed a significant change. The executive director resigned to take a position in the East. A number of commission seats turned over, with elected mayors and county commissioners replacing former citizens, engineers, and others. The commission shifted from quarterly to monthly meetings and appointed task forces to write position papers upon which the necessary legislation for the plan's implementation would be based.

At that time the plan format emphasized policies and programs. Policies were often general, because they went through sieves of technical committees, a citizens' advisory committee, an elected officials' review committee, and committees of the commission itself. Many of these general policies still survive. On the other hand, the program component proved to be the "Achilles heel" of the staff, because too few staff members had the necessary experience to draft meaningful implementing programs.

With the creation of the Metropolitan Council in 1967, a new approach began. The council was mandated to prepare a plan. Although the Twin Cities Metropolitan Planning Commission plan had been only advisory, the council plan had legal standing. This legal status was not sought by the original council supporters, but it evolved because the Senate needed a way for the council to control independent districts that were not administratively answerable to the council. The organization was not to be a general government; it could not therefore be given ordinance authority. A binding plan was substituted (Baldinger, 1971).

Another shift was equally significant but less visible. The prime task of the TCMPC had been the creation of a comprehensive plan. The council made the advising of the legislature on major metropolitan problems that required attention during the next biennium its primary task. The shift was from plan making to decision making, from a long-term to a short-term horizon, and from a comprehensive to a functional approach.

The 1969 legislative session was a great success for the council. The legislature enacted the majority of its programs—sewers, open space, solid waste, highway, zoo creation, airport noise zones—including a tax-sharing provision. In addition, a new plan format, the Development Guide, was adopted. This guide was intended as a reference document for those, including council members themselves, who needed it to make decisions. It would also be used to give policy direction to the newly created Sewer Board and Open Space Board and as a basis to veto plan proposals of independent metropolitan districts. Because policy statements in the guide could potentially be used in legal actions, they resembled in form the statements of regulatory agencies.

The Development Guide was unique in many respects. Its format contained problems, policies, system plans, programs, procedures for referral or review, and a data appendix. All of this was prefaced by a policy index that employed headings identifying possible actions contemplated by a user of the guide, a device that enabled users to identify easily those portions of policy relevant to their needs.

While this format is still visible in some chapters, changes have occurred. The problem focus is diminishing and a goal orientation is increasing. Federal guidelines rather than council formats are beginning to dominate, most notably in the chapter on health. Chapters have increased greatly in length, often growing fourfold. The index has become a table of contents rather than a guide for users. These shifts have combined to make the Development Guide today a relatively standard planning document rather than the unique local policy statement it once was.

Representation

The Metropolitan Planning Commission represented local governments, but when tough political choices had to be made against local opposition, the commission voted not to intervene. For example, the commission stayed out of an argument involving the location of a coal-fired power plant on the scenic St. Croix River. The plant would bring needed taxes to an area with a low tax base, but would be located in a natural area. Supporters of the Metropolitan Council used this history of passivity as an argument for metropolitan representation based on the one man/one vote principle. Today each council member district comprises two Senate districts and four House districts, and it is apportioned with the legislative districts. Because its representatives are independent of local municipal jurisdiction, the council has been able to make difficult policy choices (Knudson, 1976; Naftalin and Brandl, 1980), including the prevention of airport construction on an environmentally sensitive site, the blocking of a rail transit system, the denial of open-space funds to a wealthy community that had rejected low-income housing, and the designing of an acceptable sewer system and a solid waste system.

Most original supporters favored—and still favor—the election of council members. The Senate, however, preferred appointment by the governor, and this method has been employed since 1967. Observers have argued that the council would be more responsive to local needs if it were elected (Knudson, 1976; Naftalin and Brandl, 1980). On the other hand, because the council must speak through a legally binding plan that is adopted after lengthy hearings, it could never achieve the responsive behavior of a normal legislative body. It may well be that with a very large body of policy in place, change would be slow even if members were elected (Einsweiler, 1977).

Lessons from the First 14 Years

Experience shows that the four key aspects of the council concept— relation to the legislature, separation of policy from operation, relation of planning to decision making, and representation—have proven effective and are valued. It is not any one element by itself, but the sum of the four as they reinforce each other, that has made the Metropolitan Council successful.

The separation of policy from operation has enabled the council to focus on policy, and this focus has reinforced the utility of the council to the legislature. In turn, the legislature has increased its enactment of metropolitan problem solutions, a process that had virtually stopped from 1961 to 1967 when the area faced intractable sewer problems. Because the plan is the repository of development policy that guides the activities of state, metropolitan, and local agencies, planning has become central to short-term decision making. This linking of planning and decision making is facilitated by representation based on population rather than by local governments. Some problems in the system concepts remain, however, and are discussed below.

The strong tie to the legislature has been beneficial in several ways. It set up a workable structure from the outset. Different solutions could be designed to fit each problem, and issues could be treated at the appropriate time. Because of confidence and trust built through continuing performance, the council evolved into a stronger organization than originally envisioned. In the Twin Cities, as elsewhere, the need is not for elevated local authority but for devolved state authority. However, such authority, when it is based on local joint-powers agreements or other interlocal arrangements, is not effective. The council's work would have been impossible without legislative support. In fact, the creation of a mutually beneficial interactive process between the council and the legislature was perhaps more important than the creation of the council itself.

The separation of policy from operation has achieved the intended effect of focusing Metropolitan Council effort on policy. However, because the split is an unnatural separation and has no obvious demarcation, constant vigilance is necessary to retain the policy thrust. The Metropolitan Council has moved with time from an emphasis on policy formulation to include policy administration (referrals), program administration (particularly human services), and operating agency status (housing).

The initial council functions were regional physical service systems and, in general, these continue to be treated in accord with the original model. But the council now also performs work in human services. This is significant because such work is not mandated, although it is enabled in certain instances by state statute. Most of the human services activity derives from federal legislation and includes such administrative functions as the allocation of funds, regulation, and housing construction, although some policy-setting functions remain. In this work the council is more an implementer of federal policy than an initiator of metropolitan policy. Under the original model that pertained to regional capital investments, the administrative function would have been delegated.

Recent critics of the council's thrust and direction (Metropolitan Council, 1981) have suggested that the council delegate some of its operating and administrative functions and take up a new policy agenda as it did in 1967. At that time the issues revolved around public facilities to support development. Today the policy voids are concerned with energy and its costs, the loss of social service support, fiscal stringency, and ways to plan and manage in a setting where these problems reinforce each other. Critics argue that the council should free itself from its operating functions so that it can deal effectively with these policy issues.

The relation of planning to decision making has worked well in some cases, for example, with sewers in 1967–68 and the development framework in 1972–75. The legal status of the plan has been a two-edged sword. It has forced the use of planning or thoughtful strategy development and has generated continuity and predictability in decision making. On the other hand, when planning stopped and administration began, the council moved into the realm of regulation. To be effective, planning must be a continuing exercise of integration and synthesis among affected interests, not a one-on-one interpretation of rules (Benveniste, 1981). The plan format itself—whether the document is a policy statement, a map, or text referring to complementary action—can influence the decision process. This impact has not been studied well, and the lack of information in this area is more noticeable when a number of jurisdictions share power.

The experience has also shown that policy documents formed out of intense political bargaining, e.g., sewers, development framework, and housing, have been more widely respected and used than ones that reflect staff, intellectual, or ideological views, e.g., social framework and protection of open space. This finding is consistent with the views of Lindblom (1977) and Wildavsky (1979) and runs counter to the classical rational planning notion firmly established in the field since the reform movement and well delineated in more recent terms by Ozbekhan (1973).

All of these hard-learned lessons could have been anticipated. Those who espoused the separation of binding policy from operation simply did not know that such a split was the general formula for a regulatory agency. The structural form was reinforced when the plan was given legal status. A policy body does not, however, have to behave like a regulatory agency. The pace-setting, policy-initiating institution could be designed as originally conceived.

Metropolitan representation led to metropolitan politics, an essential precondition to decision making (Knudson, 1976). The planning activity before the council was instituted produced suggestions rather than decisions. More of an intellectual than a political exercise, this planning was a necessary precedent to thoughtful decision making but had no real clout. Metropolitan representation freed the council members from voting their local jurisdiction's views. When combined with devolved authority in policy making, representation led to effective political action.

Conclusion

The Metropolitan Council is working. Its strongest supporters do not consider it to be perfect, but even its detractors admit that it has made useful contributions. The council was created to deal with the difficulties of a high-growth area, in particular to guide regional infrastructure development. The need for such guidance still exists in other parts of the country. Although population is no longer growing rapidly and in many regions is declining, migration still continues and creates problems. The waves of peak population for metropolitan communities ripple ever outward, and service demands change with them. New services are needed on the fringe; rebuilding is needed in the inner areas. Population trends in the Twin Cities area reflect nationwide phenomena.

The Metropolitan Council concept is far broader and more useful than the Twin Cities application may suggest. The council concept represents a sharing of power with the legislature, with local governments, and with metropolitan districts. For the local governments it facilitates the design of solutions that transcend their local geography. For example, each local government can build sewers, but it cannot force its neighbors to connect into a regional network. The council's subordinate sewer agency has been able to build the regional components of the system.

The council concept has enabled authority to be exercised, although serious difficulties remain. The legislature has the authority to write bills and enact policy, but it lacks an organizational means to hold the extensive meetings and hearings necessary to reach local consensuses, and it lacks the wide-ranging technical staff to assist in workable policy formulation. The Congress, even with its vast staff, has a similar problem. Consequently, it has devolved that level of policy development to functional agencies, but the results are often disastrous when programs conflict or when multiagency solutions are necessary. A parallel exists with special districts. These districts, like federal agencies, often lack technical, legal, or political capacity to pursue policies inconsistent with functional charters or tradition. The key principle, then, is to fill this policy gap in a way that releases and facilitates the exercise of authority by state and local bodies, and this principle would apply to all metropolitan regions with fragmented governmental jurisdictions.

The metropolitan governance concept includes other state, metropolitan, and local actors. It represents not concentrated authority, but coordinated, dispersed authority. The Metropolitan Council provides a setting in which the diverse elements of regional governance can be glued together. However, because of a lack of a central financial mechanism to effect policy that cannot be implemented with funding that is limited to functional areas, this potential has not been fully realized. Even without this funding, however, more coordinated programs are moving forward.

The separation of policy from operation also means that the functional operating authority of state and local governments and metropolitan authorities is not infringed upon. Rather, the policy framework is altered to become a framework that legitimizes action. This legitimation derives from law but is strengthened by legislative action to create new authorities and through appropriations.

Metropolitan policy toward development of regional infrastructure was lacking across the country from the 1950s through the 1970s. Current policy problems include related issues such as human services, fiscal stress, and the sharing of implementation with public and private groups. Both the earlier difficulties, and some of the remaining energy problems, require physical system solutions. Many current unsolved issues are contingent on internal jurisdictional decision-making capability. But the policy void is similar. Local governments and the state legislature have latent authority they do not know how to exercise. There is much room for creative and cooperative policy development.

It was almost by accident that planning was tied to decision making in the first step toward the Metropolitan Council concept. The linkage has been honed with the passing years. However, most of the concepts of traditional planning have been based in the executive branch and oriented to the preparation of long-range plans. The emerging practice, as in the Metropolitan Council, of policy analysis and design rather than the designing of plans for the long-range future is a move in the right direction. The linkage of planning and decision making should be tightened. Planning involves the design of institutions as well as programs. Perhaps more important, it involves designing the process, forums, and problem frame in which interests will converge to forge solutions, and all of this must be executed in a setting of shared power. At the present time the field of metropolitan planning lacks proven guidelines for either this form of power sharing or the appropriate planning to accompany it. The charge to metropolitan areas is not to prepare comprehensive plans but to solve problems in a comprehensive context. Although the difference may seem semantic, it is not.[2] Less attention should be focused on guessing what the future ought to look like and more effort should be put into designing policies and actions to move a metropolitan area toward a general concept of the future.

The Metropolitan Council's move into regulatory actions may be a concern to some observers. This growing pattern of regulatory behavior has been caused in part by the structural form of governance chosen but also because the council for the most part reacts to the problems and proposals of others instead of forming its own. The council itself has acknowledged this pattern as a problem. However, a strong public interest group, like the Citizen League, and periodic legislative oversight, could help avoid the regulatory behavior of the Metropolitan Council. When this chapter went to press, a joint committee of the Minnesota House and Senate was evaluating the concept.

The shift from policy to administration that has occurred in the area of human services appears to be the consequence of three factors: (1) the legislation did not address human services; (2) the policy-operation split was not well understood and was not kept constantly in mind as these activities began; and (3) the "picket-fence" structure of federal functional programs that ties together bureaucrats at federal, state, and local levels was not fully understood by third-generation council members. Without council understanding and guidance in this matter, the bureaucrats created what they wanted. The current national transformation in the handling of human services provides an opportunity in the Twin Cities and in other metropolitan regions to break the "pickets" and engage in planning that cuts across functional as well as geographic areas.

The first three concepts of the Metropolitan Council—a strong relationship to the legislature, a separation of policy from operation, and a firm connection between planning and decision making—can be applied to all urban regions, if the concepts are well understood and if there is an acknowledged lack of policy in a region. The fourth concept—representation—was a key ingredient for success in the Twin Cities but it developed under special circumstances. It was brought about by the policy failures of independent districts run by central cities and the proven ineffectiveness of a council-of-governments type of agency, the Metropolitan Planning Commission. These institutions were drawn together in a new structure that attempted to give equal voice to all people and made it possible for effective metropolitan political action to occur. Furthermore, the council filled a gap. In the early years it exercised leadership in filling that gap so effectively that greater authority was conferred on it. Had the governance structure been designed differently, it probably would not have been accepted and it may not have succeeded so well. Although the Twin Cities metropolitan area structure will not apply everywhere, the four key concepts certainly should.

In these times of governmental reshaping and financial stress, there are policy gaps to be filled in all parts of the United States. An effectively designed institution like the Metropolitan Council could ease the passage of other metropolitan areas through this time of transition.

Notes

1. The Metropolitan Council consists of 16 members from population-equal districts and a chairman, all appointed by the governor. The Metropolitan Council jurisdiction encompasses 7 of the SMSA's 10 counties, 140 cities, 49 townships, 49 school districts, 6 metropolitan agencies, and 2 other special districts and agencies. The region encompasses 3,000 square miles, of which 1,300 square miles are agricultural. It has 950 lakes. The seven-county area population is about 2 million. St. Paul has a population of 270,000; Minneapolis has a population of 370,000. The seven-county region comprises less than 4 percent of the area of the state and includes just over 50 percent of the state population. The largest city—Minneapolis—contains less than 20 percent of the regional population. While Minneapolis and St. Paul abut, the two downtowns are 10 miles apart. As of 1980 the Twin Cities were the 14th largest SMSA. Of the 25 largest SMSAs in 1980, the Twin Cities ranked 12th in family income, 23rd in percent of low-income families, and 23rd in number of violent crimes (Bowman et al., 1981; Boyer and Savageau, 1981).

2. Research is currently underway by John Bryson and Robert Einsweiler on these issues using Metropolitan Council data.

References

American Planning Association. 1980. *Allocating capital funds: Some new approaches for local governments.* Chicago.

Baldinger, S. 1971. *Planning and governing the metropolis: The Twin Cities experience.* New York: Praeger.

Benveniste, G. 1981. *Regulation and planning.* San Francisco: Boyde and Fraser.

Bowman, T. F., G. A. Giuliani, and M. R. Mingé. 1981. *Finding your best place to live in America.* West Babylon, N.Y.: Red Lion Books.

Boyce, D. E., N. D. Day, and C. McDonald. 1970. *Metropolitan plan making.* Philadelphia: Regional Science Research Institute.

Boyer, R., and D. Savageau. 1981. *Places rated almanac: Your guide to finding the best places to live in America.* Chicago: Rand McNally.

Chapin, F. S., Jr. 1963. Taking stock of techniques for shaping urban growth. *Journal of the American Institute of Planners* 29 (May):76–87.

Citizens League. 1968. *Metropolitan policy and metropolitan development.* Minneapolis.

Einsweiler, R. C. 1976. Organizational history of environmental management in the Twin Cities metropolitan area. In *Case study of the Metropolitan Council as an environmental management organization.* Minneapolis: University of Minnesota, School of Public Affairs.

———. 1977. Thoughts about an elected vs. appointed Metropolitan Council. *Perspectives,* vol. 2. St. Paul: Metropolitan Council.

Fagin, H. 1959. Organizing and carrying out planning activities within urban government. *Journal of the American Institute of Planners* 25 (Aug.):109–14.

Gleeson, M. E. 1976. Selected analysis of the Metropolitan Council as an environmental management organization. In *Case study of the Metropolitan Council as an environmental management organization.* Minneapolis: University of Minnesota, School of Public Affairs.

Harrigan, J. J., and W. C. Johnson. 1978. *Governing the Twin Cities region: The Metropolitan Council in comparative perspective.* Minneapolis; University of Minnesota Press.

Head, D. M., and W. H. Hartfeldt. 1967. Letter to James Hetland, Jr., chairman of Metropolitan Council, 6 Oct.

Knudson, E. 1976. *Regional politics in the Twin Cities: A report of the politics and planning of urban growth policy.* St. Paul: Metropolitan Council.

Kolderie, T. 1973. Governance in the Twin Cities area of Minnesota. In *Regional governance: Promise and performance.* Washington, D.C.: Advisory Commission on Intergovernmental Relations.

Lindblom, C. 1977. *Politics and markets.* New York: Basic Books.

Metropolitan Council. 1981. Notes on budget meetings with academics and business executives, 8 and 9 July (Facsimile).

Mitchell, R. S. 1961. The new frontier in metropolitan planning. *Journal of the American Institute of Planners* 27 (Aug.):169–75.

Naftalin, A., and J. Brandl. 1980. *The Twin Cities regional strategy.* St. Paul: Metropolitan Council.

Ozbekban, H. 1973. The emerging methodology of planning. *Fields* 10 (Winter):63–80.

Twin Cities Metropolitan Planning Commission. 1966. Abridged transcript of MPC staff-commission meeting on "Suggested changes in the structure of governance in the metropolitan area," 12 Jan.

Wildavsky, A. 1979. *Speaking truth to power.* Boston: Little, Brown.

15

Policy Problems and Prospects for Change in the Metropolitan Midwest

BARRY CHECKOWAY and CARL V. PATTON

A Midwest newspaper reports that a new phrase has entered the lexicon in Texas: "Black Tag People." Texans use it to describe recent migrants from Michigan, whose cars bear black license plates with white lettering, and who increasingly are seen on the freeways around major cities in Texas. They include unemployed people who, once arrived, may find themselves not in new jobs but instead in pawnshops or soup kitchens, unemployment lines or welfare offices, church relief centers or emergency shelters. Black Tag People are not the only migrants to Texas— many others find better jobs and living conditions than those left behind—but they indicate policy problems nonetheless.

Elsewhere in the same newspaper an analyst predicts that while the South and West will continue to grow, the Midwest will decline. He predicts that many industries will move to the sunbelt because unions are less developed, labor is cheaper, and energy costs are lower there. He also predicts that while sunbelt growth will create new demands and problems in cities in the sunbelt, these will not discourage people from leaving the Midwest. The newspaper also reports the story of a resident who went to Texas to search for work and was encouraged by the prospects. He returned home, packed his station wagon, and drove to Houston. However, he found few jobs for those without skills. He knocked on doors, submitted applications, became discouraged, and finally returned to the Midwest.

Midwest media regularly report the human dimensions of change in the region. They report that growth rates will drop and problems will increase in the sunbelt, and they publicize plants that stay open and jobs that remain in the Midwest. But they cannot camouflage the recent pattern of decline in the Midwest or the image that prospects are brighter in the South and West.

This book analyzes what growing numbers of people are coming to realize: that the metropolitan Midwest is experiencing changes which are causing problems in land use, housing, neighborhood development, social and human services, transportation, and other areas. The authors substantiate that population in the region is growing more slowly than in the nation as a whole, and that cities and metropolitan areas are declining relative to those in the South and West. Curtis Roseman analyzes the changing population of the region overall and the redistribution of population from central cities and metropolitan areas to suburban and nonmetropolitan areas. Arthur Getis examines population patterns in the Chicago metropolitan area and finds that, despite increased energy costs, movement to the suburbs continues. They caution against painting too gloomy a picture of the Midwest, for although some large urban areas have declined, other smaller places have grown, and as John Jakle shows, rich and varied images of Midwestern cities remain. Nonetheless, population change and decline continue to characterize the region.

The authors also analyze factors that contribute to change, including shifts in national economic activity, government policies, and consumer preferences. Economic activity in the region has declined, in part as a result of deceleration in national growth and of shifts in demand from industry to other productive activities. Manufacturing is moving from the region's cities to other areas, shifts in the national economy have lowered the demand for goods produced in the region, sluggish employment growth has displaced workers from the labor force, and job losses in manufacturing have been substantial in cities and metropolitan areas. Nonmanufacturing jobs have not grown fast enough to employ those searching for work, and the job growth that is taking place is occurring in the suburbs and nonmetropolitan areas. Differences in growth rates among regions have been dramatic, with sunbelt gains especially evident in population and economic activity.

Alfred Watkins in this volume attributes the economic decline of the Midwest to disinvestment decisions of large corporations and disparities between national and regional growth rates, which cause competitive disadvantages in manufacturing, retailing, and wholesaling for the region. Others attribute change to government policies, as the Midwest receives a relatively low proportion of federal program funds and sends more money to Washington than it receives in return. There is debate over the usefulness of this "balance of payments" concept, but it appears that federal favoritism toward the South and West contributes to change. Yet others attribute change to shifting preferences of consumers, who may perceive the sunbelt as a better location in which to live and work.

The promotional image of the sunbelt as an escape from decline, an arena for opportunities, and an attractive new environment is difficult to dispel. Whatever the explanation, Midwest cities have been losing their traditional strength and have been failing to attract new population and industry. Plant closings and job decline are daily symptoms seen across the region. There are exceptions to the pattern of decline, but the Midwest will likely continue to grow more slowly than the nation as a whole.

Change has caused problems for those who remain in the metropolitan Midwest. In this volume Robert Mendelson and Michael Quinn analyze St. Louis as a case where change has worsened housing conditions and intensified racial segregation. Barry Checkoway describes an area in St. Louis where disinvestment has resulted in population loss, substandard housing, physical deterioration, and a tangle of pathologies. David Berry and Stephanie Wilson discuss barriers to employment that they argue are deeply woven into the fabric of the economy. Norman Krumholz and Janice Cogger analyze barriers to mobility that confront people in Cleveland and many cities throughout the region. Carl Patton shows that declining population, municipal budgets, and federal aid have contributed to capital infrastructure deterioration in many cities. Milton Rakove examines Chicago as a case where economic decline and community change have produced a political system increasingly incapable of dealing with economic and social problems.

Citizens and planners are wrestling with these changes. At the national level Mendelson and Quinn note that some federal programs intended to ameliorate housing problems have exacerbated conditions or evoked resistance. Roger Montgomery concludes that while federal housing programs are needed, their chances for achieving objectives are slim in a society with a de facto commitment to maintain poverty and racism. Heywood Sanders analyzes the impact of the federal community development block grant program and shows that community development has taken a variety of meanings with no sustained concern for the poorest neighborhoods. Berry and Wilson assess federal employment programs and conclude that these have had little influence on structural barriers to employment, that industrial decline may increase barriers in the future, and that outmigration of workers may further increase the concentration of hard-core unemployed in midwestern cities.

At the citywide level Patton examines local efforts to address capital infrastructure deterioration and concludes that while some cities have developed capacity for capital improvement planning and programming, most cities are unorganized and even organized ones lack resources, staff support, and citizen demand. Krumholz and Cogger describe efforts to widen the range of transportation choices for the "transit-dependent" of Cleveland. While they were able to strengthen services and expand access to the handicapped and elderly, they were seriously challenged by county commissioners, suburban politicians, and downtown business interests. Robert Einsweiler describes formation of the Metropolitan Council to increase planning and coordination in the Minneapolis–St. Paul area. Citizens and planners were able to overcome some of the obstacles to areawide planning, but fragmentation continues to characterize local governmental units in metropolitan areas throughout the region.

At the grass-roots level Barry Checkoway analyzes the case of Jeff-Vander-Lou, a community organization in St. Louis. Working in a neighborhood that many had considered beyond revitalization, JVL has developed a strong track record with impressive results in housing, community development, and social services. But Checkoway warns that the promise of local initiative may fail on a larger scale. Neighborhood problems result from decisions largely outside the neighborhood, and local initiative as national policy runs the risk of diverting attention from national responsibility to address problems. These problems, in the final analysis, are not local.

The authors surely share the conclusion that prospects in the Midwest are tied to those for the nation. Regional decline is a national problem, and efforts to solve regional problems must be viewed in that larger context. It would be bad scholarship and inept public policy to treat the Midwest as if it were separable from the nation as a whole.

The focus of this book is on the metropolitan Midwest, but the authors raise issues of broader significance in urban and regional policy and planning. Past policy and planning have operated in a context of growth and development. Agricultural, manufacturing, and other economic activities have resulted in long-term growth and steady increases in population, production, and income. Economic interests viewed the region as an advantageous investment location and the heartland of the nation. Planners applied skills and developed programs to forecast employment and population growth, locate new transportation and land uses, and estimate space requirements for business and residential developments. Citizens had faith that the economic system would result in better jobs and income, housing and living conditions, individual prosperity and gain. If some exceptional planners questioned the reactive nature of their work, or if some citizens benefited more than others, the image of growth prevailed nonetheless.

Today policy and planning are changing in the Midwest. Manufacturing, industrial, and other business interests often consider sites across the nation, view the Midwest as an unattractive economic environment, and locate outside the region. Planners no longer expect to advance growth in cities of the region but, instead, struggle in the face of decline and austerity. No wonder citizens themselves turn away from conditions in the region and toward the "sunbelt ideal."

The authors of this volume signal new directions in policy and planning. Several authors describe federal programs intended to solve employment, housing, and community development programs. Patton analyzes efforts of municipal officials to devise planning and programming procedures to address capital facility problems. Krumholz and Cogger analyze their work to challenge the establishment and advocate the needs of groups that lack access to transportation services. Checkoway analyzes citizens who organize themselves, build and renovate housing, operate a range of social services, attract new industry and jobs, and formulate plans for commercial development. Einsweiler describes formation of a council for participation, planning, and coordination at the metropolitan-regional level. None of these authors individually formulates a new paradigm for practice, but together they contribute to an image of what planning may become in the years ahead.

This book does not question that the metropolitan Midwest is experiencing change and decline, or that this is causing problems for those who remain, or that people are turning away from the region toward other locations offering opportunities that historically have characterized the Midwest. However, this book does question those who view the decline of the Midwest as inevitable, or who take the present as an indication of the future, or who fail to specify the narrow range of choices available to those who decide to locate outside the region. The evidence that individuals and institutions decide to live, work, or transact business outside the Midwest is not proof that they would choose to do so if different alternatives were available in the region. This book also questions those who consider decline as a given fact rather than as a problem to be worked on, or who ignore efforts by citizens and planners to address conditions and stem decline. One consequence of change has been an awareness of problems in the metropolitan Midwest, but another has been an effort to wrestle with conditions and create the future.

The authors of this volume recognize the need to apply knowledge and skills to urban and regional policy problems and planning. They know that initiatives are needed to develop capacity in the years ahead, and they write as if it were possible.

About the Contributors

BARRY CHECKOWAY is associate professor of social work at the University of Michigan. He has taught at the University of Pennsylvania, the University of California at Berkeley, and the University of Illinois at Urbana-Champaign. His work on community organization and planning, citizen participation, and urban social policy has been published in national and international journals. He has been active in local citizen organizations and served on the boards of directors of major statewide, regional, and national consumer organizations.

CARL V. PATTON is professor of urban planning and dean of the School of Architecture and Urban Planning at the University of Wisconsin-Milwaukee. He previously was professor and head of the department of Urban and Regional Planning at the University of Illinois at Urbana-Champaign, directed the department's Bureau of Urban and Regional Planning Research, and has engaged in private planning practice. His research interests include urban capital investment planning and budgeting, policy analysis, rural transportation, and retirement and career change policy. His publications include chapters, articles, and reports on planning issues, and *Academia in Transition: Mid Career Change or Early Retirement.*

DAVID BERRY is a geographer at Abt Associates in Cambridge, Mass. He previously served as a research associate at the Regional Science Research Institute in Philadelphia, and taught at the University of Illinois at Urbana-Champaign. He has published widely on regional economics, employment discrimination, land use, and conflicts between agriculture and urbanization.

JANICE COGGER is a city planner with the Cleveland City Planning Commission, where she has been concerned with equity and access issues in transportation, community development, and municipal services. She has worked actively with neighborhood groups to expand their participation in the planning decisions that affect them. She has co-authored articles on planning issues with Norman Krumholz in the *Journal of the American Planning Association* and other journals.

ROBERT C. EINSWEILER is professor and director of the urban planning program in the Hubert H. Humphrey Institute at the University of Minnesota. He has served as president of the American Planning Association and in a variety of roles as a planning practitioner. He was active in the formation and development of the Minneapolis-St. Paul Metropolitan Council. Among his publications is *The Design of State, Regional and Local Development Management Systems.*

ARTHUR GETIS is professor of geography at the University of Illinois at Urbana-Champaign. He has conducted research on urban and population spatial patterning issues, including journey-to-work problems and the spatial distribution of urban services. Among his publications are *Geography* and *Models of Spatial Processes: An Approach to the Study of Point, Line and Area Patterns.*

JOHN A. JAKLE is professor of geography at the University of Illinois at Urbana-Champaign. His research interests include historical geography, urban social geography, and historic preservation planning. He has done extensive research on the midwestern landscape, particularly on people's images of the places where they live and visit. Among his publications are *The American Small Town: Twentieth Century Place Images, Images of the Ohio Valley: A Historical Geography of Travel, 1740 to 1860,* and *Human Spatial Behavior: A Social Geography.*

NORMAN KRUMHOLZ is adjunct professor of urban affairs and director of the Cleveland Center for Neighborhood Development at Cleveland State University's College of Urban Affairs. He previously directed the Cleveland City Planning Commission, where he developed the *Cleveland Policy Planning Report,* and served on the National Commission on Neighborhoods. He is author of several works on housing, transportation, and other planning issues.

ROBERT E. MENDELSON is professor of earth science, geography, and planning, and research associate in the Center for Urban and Environmental Research and Services at Southern Illinois University at Edwardsville. He previously was self-employed in housing investment and rehabilitation in St. Louis and served as chief planner for the Model Cities program in East St. Louis, Ill. His housing and urban redevelopment research is reported in *Community Harmony: The Reuse of Ordinary Structures* and *The Politics of Urban Planning: The East St. Louis Experience.* He also co-edited *The Politics of Housing in Older Urban Areas.*

ROGER MONTGOMERY is professor of urban design and city and regional planning and director of the environmental studies program at the University of California at Berkeley. He previously directed the Urban Renewal Design Center at Washington University in St. Louis, and has conducted research on the physical design and social, political, and economic context of housing. Among his publications is *Housing in America: Problems and Perspectives.*

MICHAEL A. QUINN is associate professor of government and public affairs and of urban affairs and policy analysis, and research associate in the Center for Urban and Environmental Research and Services at Southern Illinois University at

Edwardsville. He has written on urban housing and public policy for *Journal of the American Real Estate and Urban Economics Association, Housing and Society,* and *Urban Affairs Quarterly.* He co-edited *The Politics of Housing in Older Urban Areas.*

MILTON RAKOVE was professor of political science at the University of Illinois at Chicago Circle. He served as a political consultant and speechwriter, as a precinct captain in the 49th Ward regular Democratic organization in Chicago, and as a candidate for the Cook County Board of Commissioners. His publications include *We Don't Want Nobody Nobody Sent: An Oral History of the Daley Years* and *Don't Make No Waves, Don't Back No Losers—An Insider's Analysis of the Daley Machine.*

CURTIS C. ROSEMAN is professor of geography at the University of Illinois at Urbana-Champaign. His research interests include geographical issues of population and migration. Among his publications are *Changing Migration Patterns within the United States* and *Population Redistribution in the Midwest,* the proceedings of a major conference he organized on population dynamics in the region.

HEYWOOD T. SANDERS is assistant professor of urban studies at Trinity University in San Antonio, Tex. He previously taught and served on the staff of the Institute of Government and Public Affairs and in the Department of Political Science at the University of Illinois at Urbana-Champaign, as program analyst in the Office of Community Planning and Development at the U.S. Department of Housing and Urban Development, and as guest scholar at the Brookings Institution conducting research on the politics of urban infrastructure.

ALFRED J. WATKINS is an economist on the staff of the U.S. House of Representatives. He previously taught government at the University of Texas at Austin, Columbia University, Cornell University, and Queens College of the City University of New York. He is also a journalist who writes widely on reindustrialization and urban regional economic issues, including *The Rise of the Sunbelt Cities* (co-edited with David Perry) and *The Practice of Urban Economics.*

STEPHANIE WILSON is manager of the international research group at Abt Associates in Cambridge, Mass. Her recent work includes an analysis of the availability of minorities and women for employment under affirmative action programs, and an evaluation of a service delivery system to provide guaranteed work or training as an alternative to income transfers. Her research on economic development and employment issues has been published in the *American Economic Review* and other journals.